The Easiest Way in Housekeeping and Cooking

Adapted to Domestic Use or Study in Classes

Helen Campbell

Contents

THE EASIEST WAY IN HOUSEKEEPING AND COOKING

ADAPTED TO DOMESTIC USE OR

STUDY IN CLASSES

BY

Helen Campbell

PREFACE TO REVISED EDITION.

The little book now revised and sent out with some slight additions, remains substantially the same as when first issued in 1880. In the midst of always increasing cookery-books, it has had a firm constituency of friends, especially in the South, where its necessity was first made plain. To enlarge it in any marked degree would violate the original plan, for which the critic will please read the pages headed "Introductory," where he or she will find full explanation of the growth and purpose of the book. Whoever desires more receipts and more elaborate forms of preparation must look for their sources in the bibliography at the end, since their introduction in these pages would practically nullify the title, proved true by years of testing at the hands of inexperienced housekeepers, whose warm words have long been very pleasant to the author of "The Easiest Way."

NEW YORK, June, 1893.

Introductory.

That room or toleration for another "cook-book" can exist in the public mind, will be denied at once, with all the vigor to be expected from a people overrun with cook-books, and only anxious to relegate the majority of them to their proper place as trunk-linings and kindling-material. The minority, admirable in plan and execution, and elaborate enough to serve all republican purposes, are surely sufficient for all the needs that have been or may be. With Mrs. Cornelius and Miss Parloa,

Marion Harland and Mrs. Whitney, and innumerable other trustworthy authorities, for all every-day purposes, and Mrs. Henderson for such festivity as we may at times desire to make, another word is not only superfluous but absurd; in fact, an outrage on common sense, not for one instant to be justified.

Such was my own attitude and such my language hardly a year ago; yet that short space of time has shown me, that, whether the public admit the claim, or no, one more cook-book MUST BE. And this is why:--

A year of somewhat exceptional experience--that involved in building up several cooking-schools in a new locality, demanding the most thorough and minute system to assure their success and permanence--showed the inadequacies of any existing hand-books, and the necessities to be met in making a new one. Thus the present book has a twofold character, and represents, not only the ordinary receipt or cook book, usable in any part of the country and covering all ordinary household needs, but covers the questions naturally arising in every lesson given, and ending in statements of the most necessary points in household science. There are large books designed to cover this ground, and excellent of their kind, but so cumbrous in form and execution as to daunt the average reader.

Miss Corson's "Cooking-School Text-Book" commended itself for its admirable plainness and fullness of detail, but was almost at once found impracticable as a system for my purposes; her dishes usually requiring the choicest that the best city market could afford, and taking for granted also a taste for French flavorings not yet common outside of our large cities, and to no great extent within them. To utilize to the best advantage the food-resources of whatever spot one might be in, to give information on a hundred points suggested by each lesson, yet having no place in the ordinary cook-book, in short, *to teach household science as well as cooking*, became my year's work; and it is that year's work which is incorporated in these pages. Beginning with Raleigh, N.C., and lessons given in a large school there, it included also a seven-months' course at the Deaf and Dumb Institute, and regular classes for ladies. Straight through, in those classes, it became my business to say, "This is no infallible system, warranted to give the whole art of cooking in twelve lessons. All I can do for you is to lay down clearly certain fixed principles; to show you how to economize thoroughly, yet get a better result than by the expenditure of perhaps much more material. Before our course ends, you will have had performed before you every essential operation in cooking, and will know, so far as I can make you know, prices, qualities, constituents, and physiological effects of every type of food. Beyond this, the work lies in your own hands."

Armed with manuals,--American, English, French,--bent upon systematizing the subject, yet finding none entirely adequate, gradually, and in spite of all effort to the contrary, I found that my teaching rested more and more on my own personal experience as a housekeeper, both at the South and at the North. The mass of material in many books was found confusing and paralyzing, choice seeming impossible when a dozen methods were given. And for the large proportion of receipts, directions were so vague that only a trained housekeeper could be certain of the order of combination, or results when combined. So from the crowd of authorities was gradually eliminated a foundation for work; and on that foundation has risen a structure designed to serve two ends.

For the young housekeeper, beginning with little or no knowledge, but eager to do and know the right thing, not alone for kitchen but for the home as a whole, the list of topics touched upon in Part I. became essential. That much of the knowledge compressed there should have been gained at home, is at once admitted: but, unfortunately, few homes give it; and the aim has been to cover the ground concisely yet clearly and attractively. As to Part II., it does not profess to be the whole art of cooking, but merely the line of receipts most needed in the average family, North or South. Each receipt has been tested personally by the writer, often many times; and each one is given so minutely that failure is well-nigh impossible, if the directions are intelligently followed. A few distinctively Southern dishes are included, but the ground covered has drawn from all sources; the series of excellent and elaborate manuals by well-known authors having contributed here and there, but the majority of rules being, as before said, the result of years of personal experiment, or drawn from old family receipt-books.

To facilitate the work of the teacher, however, a scheme of lessons is given at the end, covering all that can well be taught in the ordinary school year: each lesson is given with page references to the receipts employed, while a shorter and more compact course is outlined for the use of classes for ladies. A list of topics is also given for school use; it having been found to add greatly to the interest of the course to write each week the story of some ingredient in the lesson for the day, while a set of questions, to be used at periodical intervals, fixes details, and insures a certain knowledge of what progress has been made. The course covers the chemistry and physiology of food, as well as an outline of household science in general, and may serve as a text-book wherever such study is introduced. It is hoped that this presentation of the subject will lessen the labor necessary in this new field, though no text-book can fully take the place of personal enthusiastic work.

That training is imperatively demanded for rich and poor alike, is now unquestioned; but the mere taking a course of cooking-lessons alone does not meet the need in full. The present book aims to fill a place hitherto unoccupied; and precisely the line of work indicated there has been found the only practical method in a year's successful organization of schools at various points. Whether used at home with growing girls, in cooking-clubs, in schools, or in private classes, it is hoped that the system outlined and the authorities referred to will stimulate interest, and open up a new field of work to many who have doubted if the food question had any interest beyond the day's need, and who have failed to see that nothing ministering to the best life and thought of this wonderful human body could ever by any chance be rightfully called "common or unclean." We are but on the threshold of the new science. If these pages make the way even a little plainer, the author will have accomplished her full purpose, and will know that in spite of appearances there is "room for one more."

HELEN CAMPBELL.

THE EASIEST WAY.

CHAPTER I.
THE HOUSE: SITUATION AND ARRANGEMENT.

From the beginning it must be understood that what is written here applies chiefly to country homes. The general principles laid down are applicable with equal force to town or city life; but as a people we dwell mostly in the country, and, even in villages or small towns, each house is likely to have its own portion of land about it, and to look toward all points of the compass, instead of being limited to two, as in city blocks. Of the comparative advantages or disadvantages of city or country life, there is no need to speak here. Our business is simply to give such details as may apply to both, but chiefly to the owners of moderate incomes, or salaried people, whose expenditure must always be somewhat limited. With the exterior of such homes, women at present have very little to do; and the interior also is thus far much in the hands of architects, who decide for general prettiness of effect, rather than for the most convenient arrangement of space. The young bride, planning a home, is resolved upon a bay-window, as large a parlor as possible, and an effective spare-room; but, having in most cases no personal knowledge of work, does not consider whether kitchen and dining-room are conveniently planned, or not, and whether the arrangement of pantries and closets is such that both rooms must be crossed a hundred times a day, when a little foresight might have reduced the number certainly by one-half, perhaps more.

Inconvenience can, in most cases, be remedied; but unhealthfulness or unwholesomeness of location, very seldom: and therefore, in the beginning, I write that ignorance is small excuse for error, and that every one able to read at all, or use common-sense about any detail of life, is able to form a judgment of what is healthful or unhealthful. If no books are at hand, consult the best physician near, and have his verdict as to the character of the spot in which more or less of your life in this world will be spent, and which has the power to affect not only your mental and bodily health, but that of your children. Because your fathers and mothers have been neglectful of these considerations, is no reason why you should continue in ignorance; and the first duty in making a home is to consider earnestly and intelligently certain points.

Four essentials are to be thought of in the choice of any home; and their neglect, and the ignorance which is the foundation of this neglect, are the secret of not only the chronic ill-health supposed to be a necessity of the American organization, but of many of the epidemics and mysterious diseases classed under the head of "visitations of Providence."

These essentials are: a wholesome situation, good ventilation, good drainage, and a dry cellar. Rich or poor, high or low, if one of these be disregarded, the result will tell, either on your own health or on that of your family. Whether palace or hut, brown-stone front or simple wooden cottage, the law is the same. As a rule, the ordinary town or village is built upon low land, because it is easier to obtain a water-supply from wells and springs. In such a case, even where the climate itself may be tolerably healthy, the drainage from the hills at hand, or the nearness of swamps and marshes produced by the same cause, makes a dry cellar an impossibility; and this shut-in and poisonous moisture makes malaria inevitable. The dwellers on low lands are the pill and patent-medicine takers; and no civilized country swallows the amount of tonics and bitters consumed by our own.

If possible, let the house be on a hill, or at least a rise of ground, to secure the thorough draining-away of all sewage and waste water. Even in a swampy and malarious country, such a location will insure all the health possible in such a region, if the other conditions mentioned are faithfully attended to.

Let the living-rooms and bedrooms, as far as may be, have full sunshine during a part of each day; and reserve the north side of the house for store-rooms, refrigerator, and the rooms seldom occupied. Do not allow trees to stand so near as to shut out air or sunlight; but see that, while near enough for beauty and for shade, they do not constantly shed moisture, and make twilight in your rooms even at mid-day. Sunshine is the enemy of disease, which thrives in darkness and shadow. Consumption or scrofulous disease is almost inevitable in the house shut in by trees, whose blinds are tightly closed lest some ray of sunshine fade the carpets; and over and over again it has been proved that the first conditions of health are, abundant supply of pure air, and free admission of sunlight to every nook and cranny. Even with imperfect or improper food, these two allies are strong enough to carry the day for health; and, when the three work in harmony, the best life is at once assured.

If the house must be on the lowlands, seek a sandy or gravelly soil; and avoid those built over clay beds, or even where clay bottom is found under the sand or loam. In the last case, if drainage is understood, pipes may be so arranged as to secure against any standing water; but, unless this is done, the clammy moisture on walls, and the chill in every closed room, are sufficient indication that the conditions for disease are ripe or ripening. The only course in such case, after seeking proper drainage, is, first, abundant sunlight, and, second, open fires, which will act not only as drying agents, but as ventilators and purifiers. Aim to have at least one open fire in the house. It is not an extravagance, but an essential, and economy may better come in at some other place.

Having settled these points as far as possible,--the question of water-supply and ventilation being left to another chapter,--it is to be remembered that the house is not merely a place to be made pleasant for one's friends. They form only a small portion of the daily life; and the first consideration should be: Is it so planned that the necessary and inevitable work of the day can be accomplished with the least expenditure of force? North and South, the kitchen is often the least-considered room of the house; and, so long as the necessary meals are served up, the difficulties that may have hedged about such serving are never counted. At the South it is doubly so, and necessarily; old conditions having made much consideration of convenience for servants an unthought-of thing. With a throng of unemployed women and children, the question could only be, how to secure some small portion of work for each one; and in such case, the greater the inconveniences, the more chance for such employment. Water could well be half a mile distant, when a dozen little darkies had nothing to do but form a running line between house and spring; and so with wood and kindling and all household necessities.

To-day, with the old service done away with once for all, and with a set of new conditions governing every form of work, the Southern woman faces difficulties to which her Northern or Western sister is an utter stranger; faces them often with a patience and dignity beyond all praise, but still with a hopelessness of better things, the necessary fruit of ignorance. Old things are passed away, and the new order is yet too unfamiliar for rules to have formulated and settled in any routine of action. While there is, at the North, more intuitive and inherited sense of how things should be done, there is on many points an almost equal ignorance, more especially among the cultivated classes, who, more than at any period of woman's history, are at the mercy of their servants. Every science is learned but domestic science. The schools ignore it; and, indeed, in the rush toward an early graduation, there is small room for it.

"She can learn at home," say the mothers. "She will take to it when her time comes, just as a duck takes to water," add the fathers; and the matter is thus dismissed as settled.

In the mean time the "she" referred to--the average daughter of average parents in both city and country--neither "learns at home," nor "takes to it naturally," save in exceptional cases; and the reason for this is found in the love, which, like much of the love given, is really only a higher form of selfishness. The busy mother of a family, who has fought her own way to fairly successful administration, longs to spare her daughters the petty cares, the anxious planning, that have helped to eat out her own youth; and so the young girl enters married life with a vague sense of the dinners that must be, and a general belief that somehow or other they come of themselves. And so with all household labor. That to perform it successfully and skillfully, demands not only training, but the best powers one can bring to bear upon its accomplishment, seldom enters the mind; and the student, who has ended her course of chemistry or physiology enthusiastically, never dreams of applying either to every-day life.

This may seem a digression; and yet, in the very outset, it is necessary to place this work upon the right footing, and to impress with all possible earnestness the fact, that Household Science holds every other science in tribute, and that only that home which starts with this admission and builds upon the best foundation the best that thought can furnish, has any right to the name of "home." The swarms of drunkards, of idiots, of insane, of deaf and dumb, owe their existence to an ignorance of the laws of right living, which is simply criminal, and for which we must be judged; and no word can be too earnest, which opens the young girl's eyes to the fact that in her hands lie not alone her own or her husband's future, but the future of the nation. It is hard to see beyond one's own circle; but if light is sought for, and there is steady resolve and patient effort to do the best for one's individual self, and those nearest one, it will be found that the shadow passes, and that progress is an appreciable thing.

Begin in your own home. Study to make it not only beautiful, but perfectly appointed. If your own hands must do the work, learn every method of economizing time and strength. If you have servants, whether one or more, let the same laws rule. It is not easy, I admit; no good thing is: but there is infinite reward for every effort. Let no failure discourage, but let each one be only a fresh round in the ladder all must climb who would do worthy work; and be sure that the end will reward all pain, all self-sacrifice, and make you truly the mistresses of the home for which every woman naturally and rightfully hopes, but which is never truly hers till every shade of detail in its administration has been mastered.

The house, then, is the first element of home to be considered and studied; and we have settled certain points as to location and arrangement. This is no hand-book of plans for houses, that ground being thoroughly covered in various books,--the titles of two or three of which are given in a list of reference-books at the end. But, whether you build or buy, see to it that your kitchens and working-rooms are well lighted, well aired, and of good size, and that in the arrangement of the kitchen especially, the utmost convenience becomes the chief end. Let sink, pantries, stove or range, and working-space for all operations in cooking, be close at hand. The difference between a pantry at the opposite end of the room, and one opening close to the sink, for instance, may seem a small matter; but when it comes to walking across the room with every dish that is washed, the steps soon count up as miles, and in making even a loaf of bread, the time and strength expended in gathering materials together would go far toward the thorough kneading, which, when added to the previous exertion, makes the whole operation, which might have been only a pleasure, a burden and an annoyance.

Let, then, stove, fuel, water, work-table, and pantries be at the same end of the kitchen, and within a few steps of one another, and it will be found that while the general labor of each day must always be the same, the time required for its accomplishment will be far less, under these favorable conditions. The successful workman,--the type-setter, the cabinet-maker, or carpenter,--whose art lies in the rapid combination of materials, arranges his materials and tools so as to be used with the fewest possible movements; and the difference between a skilled and unskilled workman is not so much the rate of speed in movement, as in the ability to make each motion tell. The kitchen is the housekeeper's workshop; and, in the chapter on *House-work*, some further details as to methods and arrangements will be given.

CHAPTER II.
THE HOUSE: VENTILATION.

Having settled the four requisites in any home, and suggested the points to be made in regard to the first one,--that of wholesome situation,-- *Ventilation* is next in order. Theoretically, each one of us who has studied either natural philosophy or physiology will state at once, with more or less glibness, the facts as to the atmosphere, its qualities, and the amount of air needed by each individual; practically nullifying such statement by going to bed in a room with closed windows and doors, or sitting calmly in church or public hall, breathing over and over again the air ejected from the lungs all about,--practice as cleanly and wholesome as partaking of food chewed over and over by an indiscriminate crowd.

Now, as to find the Reason Why of all statements and operations is our first consideration, the familiar ground must be traversed again, and the properties and constituents of air find place here. It is an old story, and, like other old stories accepted by the multitude, has become almost of no effect; passive acceptance mentally, absolute rejection physically, seeming to be the portion of much of the gospel of health. "Cleanliness is next to godliness," is almost an axiom. I am disposed to amend it, and assert that cleanliness *is* godliness, or a form of godliness. At any rate, the man or woman who demands cleanliness without and within, this cleanliness meaning pure air, pure water, pure food, must of necessity have a stronger body and therefore a clearer mind (both being nearer what God meant for body and mind) than the one who has cared little for law, and so lived oblivious to the consequences of breaking it.

Ventilation, seemingly the simplest and easiest of things to be accomplished, has thus far apparently defied architects and engineers. Congress has spent a million

in trying to give fresh air to the Senate and Representative Chambers, and will probably spend another before that is accomplished. In capitols, churches, and public
halls of every sort, the same story holds. Women faint, men in courts of justice fall
in apoplectic fits, or become victims of new and mysterious diseases, simply from
the want of pure air. A constant slow murder goes on in nurseries and schoolrooms;
and white-faced, nerveless children grow into white-faced and nerveless men and
women, as the price of this violated law.

What is this air, seemingly so hard to secure, so hard to hold as part of our daily
life, without which we can not live, and which we yet contentedly poison nine
times out of ten?

Oxygen, nitrogen, carbonic acid, and watery vapor; the last two being a small
portion of the bulk, oxygen and nitrogen making up four-fifths. Small as the proportion of oxygen seems, an increase of but one-fifth more would be destruction.
It is the life-giver, but undiluted would be the life-destroyer; and the three-fifths
of nitrogen act as its diluent. No other element possesses the same power. Fires and
light-giving combustion could not exist an instant without oxygen. Its office seems
that of universal destruction. By its action decay begins in meat or vegetables and
fruits; and it is for this reason, that, to preserve them, all oxygen must be driven
out by bringing them to the boiling point, and sealing them up in jars to which no
air can find entrance. With only undiluted oxygen to breathe, the tissues would
dry and shrivel, fuel burn with a fury none could withstand, and every operation
of nature be conducted with such energy as soon to exhaust and destroy all power.
But "a mixture of the fiery oxygen and inert nitrogen gives us the golden mean. The
oxygen now quietly burns the fuel in our stoves, and keeps us warm; combines with
the oil in our lamps, and gives us light; corrodes our bodies, and gives us strength;
cleanses the air, and keeps it fresh and invigorating; sweetens foul water, and makes
it wholesome; works all around us and within us a constant miracle, yet with such
delicacy and quietness, we never perceive or think of it, until we see it with the eye
of science."

Food and air are the two means by which bodies live. In the full-grown man,
whose weight will average about one hundred and fifty-four pounds, one hundred
and eleven pounds is oxygen drawn from the air we breathe. Only when food has
been dissolved in the stomach, absorbed at last into the blood, and by means of cir-

culation brought into contact with the oxygen of the air taken into our lungs, can it begin to really feed and nourish the body; so that the lungs may, after all, be regarded as the true stomach, the other being not much more than the food-receptacle.

Take these lungs, made up within of branching tubes, these in turn formed by myriads of air-cells, and each air-cell owning its network of minute cells called *capillaries*. To every air-cell is given a blood-vessel bringing blood from the heart, which finds its way through every capillary till it reaches another blood-vessel that carries it back to the heart. It leaves the heart charged with carbonic acid and watery vapor. It returns, if pure air has met it in the lung, with all corruption destroyed, a dancing particle of life. But to be life, and not slow death, thirty-three hogsheads of air must pass daily into the lungs, and twenty-eight pounds of blood journey from heart to lungs and back again three times in each hour. It rests wholly with ourselves, whether this wonderful tide, ebbing and flowing with every breath, shall exchange its poisonous and clogging carbonic acid and watery vapor for life-giving oxygen, or retain it to weigh down and debilitate every nerve in the body.

With every thought and feeling some actual particles of brain and nerve are dissolved, and sent floating on this crimson current. With every motion of a muscle, whether great or small, with every process that can take place in the body, this ceaseless change of particles is going on. Wherever oxygen finds admission, its union with carbon to form carbonic acid, or with hydrogen to form water, produces heat. The waste of the body is literally burned up by the oxygen; and it is this burning which means the warmth of a living body, its absence giving the stony cold of the dead. "Who shall deliver me from the body of this death?" may well be the literal question for each day of our lives; and "pure air" alone can secure genuine life. Breathing bad air reduces all the processes of the body, lessens vitality; and thus, one in poor health will suffer more from bad air than those who have become thoroughly accustomed to it. If weakened vitality were the only result, it would not be so serious a matter; but scrofula is soon fixed upon such constitutions, beginning with its milder form as in consumption, but ending in the absolute rottenness of bone and tissue. The invalid may live in the healthiest climate, pass hours each day in the open air, and yet undo or neutralize much of the good of this by sleeping in an unventilated room at night. Diseased joints, horrible affections of the eye or ear or skin, are inevitable. The greatest living authorities on lung-diseases pronounce deficient ventilation the chief cause of consumption, and more fatal *than all other causes put together*; and, even where food and clothing are both unwholesome, free air has been found able to counteract their effect.

In the country the balance ordained in nature has its compensating power. The poisonous carbonic acid thrown off by lungs and body is absorbed by vegetation whose food it is, and which in every waving leaf or blade of grass returns to us the oxygen we demand. Shut in a close room all day, or even in a tolerably ventilated one, there may be no sense of closeness; but go to the open air for a moment, and, if the nose has not been hopelessly ruined by want of education, it will tell unerringly the degree of oxygen wanting and required.

It is ordinarily supposed that carbonic-acid gas, being heavier, sinks to the bottom of the room, and that thus trundle-beds, for instance, are especially unwholesome. This would be so, were the gas pure. As a matter of fact, however, being warmed in the body, and thus made lighter, it rises into the common air, so that usually more will be found at the top than at the bottom of a room. This gas is, however, not the sole cause of disease. From both lungs and skin, matter is constantly thrown off, and floats in the form of germs in all impure air. To a person who by long confinement to close rooms has become so sensitive that any sudden current of air gives a cold, ventilation seems an impossibility and a cruelty; and the problem becomes: How to admit pure air throughout the house, and yet avoid currents and draughts. "Night-air" is even more dreaded than the confined air of rooms; yet, as the only air to be had at night must come under this head, it is safer to breathe that than to settle upon carbonic acid as lung-food for a third, at least, of the twenty-four hours. As fires feed on oxygen, it follows that every lamp, every gas-jet, every furnace, are so many appetites satisfying themselves upon our store of food, and that, if they are burning about us, a double amount of oxygen must be furnished.

The only mode of ventilation that will work always and without fail is that of a warm-air flue, the upward heated air-current of which draws off the foul gases from the room: this, supplemented by an opening on the opposite side of the room for the admission of pure air, will accomplish the desired end. An open fire-place will secure this, provided the flue is kept warm by heat from the kitchen fire, or some other during seasons when the fire-place is not used. But perhaps the simplest way is to have ample openings (from eight to twelve inches square) at the top and bottom of each room, opening into the chimney-flue: then, even if a stove is used, the flue can be kept heated by the extension of the stove-pipe some distance up within the chimney, and the ascending current of hot air will draw the foul air from the room into the flue. This, as before stated, must be completed by a fresh-air opening into the room on another side: if no other can be had, the top of the window may be lowered a little. The stove-pipe *extension* within the chimney would better be of cast-iron, as more durable than the sheet-iron. When no fire is used in the sleeping-rooms, the chimney-flue must be heated by pipes from the kitchen or other fires; and, with the provision for *fresh* air never forgotten, this simple device will invariably secure pure and well-oxygenated air for breathing. "Fussy and expensive," may be the comment; but the expense is less than the average yearly doctor's bill, and the fussiness nothing that your own hands must engage in. Only let heads take it in, and see to it that no neglect is allowed. In a southern climate doors and windows are of necessity open more constantly; but at night they are closed from the fear referred to, that night-air holds some subtle poison. It is merely colder, and perhaps moister, than day-air; and an extra bed-covering neutralizes this danger. Once accustomed to sleeping with open windows, you will find that taking cold is impossible.

If custom, or great delicacy of organization, makes unusual sensitiveness to cold, have a board the precise width of the window, and five or six inches high. Then raise the lower sash, putting this under it; and an upward current of air will be created, which will in great part purify the room.

Beyond every thing, watch that no causes producing foul air are allowed to exist for a moment. A vase of neglected flowers will poison the air of a whole room. In the area or cellar, a decaying head of cabbage, a basket of refuse vegetables, a forgotten barrel of pork or beef brine, a neglected garbage pail or box, are all premiums upon disease. Let air and sunlight search every corner of the house. Insist upon as nearly spotless *cleanliness* as may be, and the second prime necessity of the home is secure.

When, as it is written, man was formed from the dust of the earth, the Lord God "breathed into his nostrils the breath of life; and man became a *living soul*."

Shut off that breath of life, or poison it as it is daily poisoned, and not only body, but soul, dies. The child, fresh from its long day out of doors, goes to bed quiet, content, and happy. It wakes up a little demon, bristling with crossness, and determined not to "be good." The breath of life carefully shut out, death has begun its work, and you are responsible. And the same criminal blunder causes not only the child's suffering, but also the weakness which makes many a delicate woman complain that it "takes till noon to get her strength up."

Open the windows. Take the portion to which you were born, and life will grow easier.

CHAPTER III.
DRAINAGE AND WATER-SUPPLY.

Air and sunshine having been assured for all parts of the house in daily use, the next question must be an unfailing and full supply of pure water. "Dig a well, or build near a spring," say the builders; and the well is dug, or the spring tapped, under the general supposition that water is clean and pure, simply because it is water, while the surroundings of either spring or well are unnoticed. Drainage is so comparatively new a question, that only the most enlightened portions of the country consider its bearings; and the large majority of people all over the land not only do not know the interests involved in it, but would resent as a personal slight any hint that their own water-supply might be affected by deficient drainage.

Pure water is simply oxygen and hydrogen, eight-ninths being oxygen and but one-ninth hydrogen; the latter gas, if pure, having, like oxygen, neither taste nor smell. Rain-water is the purest type; and, if collected in open vessels as it falls, is necessarily free from any possible taint (except at the very first of a rain, when it washes down considerable floating impurity from the atmosphere, especially in cities). This mode being for obvious reasons impracticable, cisterns are made, and rain conducted to them through pipes leading from the roof. The water has thus taken up all the dust, soot, and other impurities found upon the roof, and, unless filtered, can not be considered desirable drink. The best cistern will include a filter of some sort, and this is accomplished in two ways. Either the cistern is divided into two parts, the water being received on one side, and allowed to slowly filter through a wall of porous brick, regarded by many as an amply sufficient means of purification; or a more elaborate form is used, the division in such case being into upper and under compartments, the upper one containing the usual filter of iron, charcoal, sponge, and gravel or sand. If this water has a free current of air passing over it, it will acquire more sparkle and character; but as a rule it is flat and unpleasant in flavor, being entirely destitute of the earthy salts and the carbonic-acid gas to be found in the best river or spring water.

Distilled water comes next in purity, and is, in fact, identical in character with rain-water; the latter being merely steam, condensed into rain in the great alembic of the sky. But both have the curious property of taking up and dissolving *lead* wherever they find it; and it is for this reason that lead pipes as leaders from or to cisterns should *never* be allowed, unless lined with some other metal.

The most refreshing as well as most wholesome water is river or spring water, perfectly filtered so that no possible impurity can remain. It is then soft and clear; has sufficient air and carbonic acid to make it refreshing, and enough earthy salts to prevent its taking up lead, and so becoming poisonous. River-water for daily use of course requires a system of pipes, and in small places is practically unavailable; so that wells are likely, in such case, to be the chief source of supply. Such water will of course be spring-water, with the characteristics of the soil through which it rises. If the well be shallow, and fed by surface springs, all impurities of the soil will be found in it; and thus to *dig deep* becomes essential, for many reasons. Dr. Parker of England, in some papers on practical hygiene, gives a clear and easily understood statement of some causes affecting the purity of well-water.

"A well drains an extent of ground around it, in the shape of an inverted cone, which is in proportion to its own depth and the looseness of the soil. In very loose soils a well of sixty or eighty feet will drain a large area, perhaps as much as two hundred feet in diameter, or even more; but the exact amount is not, as far as I know, precisely determined.

"Certain trades pour their refuse water into rivers, gas-works; slaughter-houses; tripe-houses; size, horn, and isinglass manufactories; wash-houses, starch-works, and calico-printers, and many others. In houses it is astonishing how many instances occur of the water of butts, cisterns, and tanks, getting contaminated by leaking of pipes and other causes, such as the passage of sewer-gas through overflow-pipes, &c.

"As there is now no doubt that typhoid-fever, cholera, and dysentery may be caused by water rendered impure by the evacuations passed in those diseases, and as simple diarrhoea seems also to be largely caused by animal organic [matter in] suspension or solution, it is evident how necessary it is to be quick-sighted in regard to the possible impurity of water from incidental causes of this kind. Therefore all tanks and cisterns should be inspected regularly, and any accidental source of impurity must be looked out for. Wells should be covered; a good coping put round to prevent substances being washed down; the distances from cess-pools and dung-heaps should be carefully noted; no sewer should be allowed to pass near a well. The same precautions should be taken with springs. In the case of rivers, we must consider if contamination can result from the discharge of fecal matters, trade refuse, &c."

Now, suppose all such precautions have been disregarded. Suppose, as is most usual, that the well is dug near the kitchen-door,--probably between kitchen and barn; the drain, if there is a drain from the kitchen, pouring out the dirty water of wash-day and all other days, which sinks through the ground, and acts as feeder to the waiting well. Suppose the manure-pile in the barnyard also sends down its supply, and the privies contribute theirs. The water may be unchanged in color or odor: yet none the less you are drinking a foul and horrible poison; slow in action, it is true, but making you ready for diphtheria and typhoid-fever, and consumption, and other nameless ills. It is so easy to doubt or set aside all this, that I give one case as illustration and warning of all the evils enumerated above.

The State Board of Health for Massachusetts has long busied itself with researches on all these points, and the case mentioned is in one of their reports. The house described is one in Hadley, built by a clergyman. "It was provided with an open well and sink-drain, with its deposit-box in close proximity thereto, affording facility to discharge its gases in the well as the most convenient place. The cellar was used, as country cellars commonly are, for the storage of provisions of every kind, and the windows were never opened. The only escape for the soil-moisture and ground-air, except that which was absorbed by the drinking-water, was through the crevices of the floors into the rooms above. After a few months' residence in the house, the clergyman's wife died of fever. He soon married again; and the second wife also died of fever, within a year from the time of marriage. His children were sick. He occupied the house about two years. The wife of his successor was soon taken ill, and barely escaped with her life. A physician then took the house. He married, and his wife soon after died of fever. Another physician took the house, and within a few months came near dying of erysipelas. He deserved it. The house, meanwhile, received no treatment; the doctors, according to their usual wont, even in their own families, were satisfied to deal with the consequences, and leave the causes to do their worst.

"Next after the doctors, a school-teacher took the house, and made a few changes, for convenience apparently, for substantially it remained the same; for he, too, escaped as by the skin of his teeth. Finally, after the foreclosure of many lives, the sickness and fatality of the property became so marked, that it became unsalable. When at last sold, every sort of prediction was made as to the risk of occupancy; but, by a thorough attention to sanitary conditions, no such risks have been encountered."

These deaths were suicides,--ignorant ones, it is true, not one stopping to think what causes lay at the bottom of such "mysterious dispensations." But, just as surely as corn gives a crop from the seed sown, so surely typhoid fever and diphtheria follow bad drainage or the drinking of impure water.

Boiling such water destroys the germs of disease; but neither boiled water nor boiled germs are pleasant drinking.

If means are too narrow to admit of the expense attendant upon making a drain long enough and tight enough to carry off all refuse water to a safe distance from the house, then adopt another plan. Remember that to throw dirty water on the ground near a well, is as deliberate poisoning as if you threw arsenic in the well itself. Have a large tub or barrel standing on a wheelbarrow or small hand-cart; and into this pour every drop of dirty water, wheeling it away to orchard or garden, where it will enrich the soil, which will transform it, and return it to you, not in disease, but in fruit and vegetables. Also see that the well has a roof, and, if possible, a lattice-work about it, that all leaves and flying dirt may be prevented from falling into it. You do not want your water to be a solution or tincture of dead leaves, dead frogs and insects, or stray mice or kittens; and this it must be, now and again, if not covered sufficiently to exclude such chances, *though not the air*, which must be given free access to it.

As to hard and soft water, the latter is always most desirable, as soft water extracts the flavor of tea and coffee far better than hard, and is also better for all cooking and washing purposes. Hard water results from a superabundance of lime; and this lime "cakes" on the bottom of tea-kettles, curdles soap, and clings to every thing boiled in it, from clothes to meat and vegetables (which last are always more tender if cooked in soft water; though, if it be too soft, they are apt to boil to a porridge).

Washing-soda or borax will soften hard water, and make it better for all household purposes; but rain-water, even if not desired for drinking, will be found better than any softened by artificial means.

If, as in many towns, the supply of drinking-water for many families comes from the town pump or pumps, the same principles must be attended to. A well in Golden Square, London, was noted for its especially bright and sparkling water, so much so that people sent from long distances to secure it. The cholera broke out; and all who drank from the well became its victims, though the square seemed a healthy location. Analysis showed it to be not only alive with a species of fungus growing in it, but also weighted with dead organic matter from a neighboring churchyard. Every tissue in the living bodies which had absorbed this water was inflamed, and ready to yield to the first epidemic; and cholera was the natural outcome of such conditions. Knowledge should guard against any such chances. See to it that no open cesspool poisons either air or water about your home. Sunk at a proper distance from the house, and connected with it by a drain so tightly put together that none of the contents can escape, the cesspool, which may be an elaborate, brick-lined cistern, or merely an old hogshead thoroughly tarred within and without, and sunk in the ground, becomes one of the most important adjuncts of a good garden. If, in addition to this, a pile of all the decaying vegetable matter--leaves, weeds, &c.--is made, all dead cats, hens, or puppies finding burial there; and the whole closely covered with earth to absorb, as fresh earth has the power to do, all foul gases and vapors; and if at intervals the pile is wet through with liquid from the cesspool, the richest form of fertilizer is secured, and one of the great agricultural duties of man fulfilled,--that of "returning to the soil, as fertilizers, all the salts produced by the combustion of food in the human body."

Where the water-supply is brought into the house from a common reservoir, much the same rules hold good. We can not of course control the character of the general supply, but we can see to it that our own water and waste pipes are in the most perfect condition; that traps and all the best methods of preventing the escape of sewer-gas into our houses are provided; that stationary or "set" basins have the plug always in them; and that every water-closet is provided with a ventilating pipe sufficiently high and long to insure the full escape of all gases from the house. Simple disinfectants used from time to time--chloride of lime and carbolic acid--will be found useful, and the most absolute cleanliness is at all times the first essential.

With air and water at their best, the home has a reasonable chance of escaping many of the sorrows brought by disease or uncertain health; and, the power to work to the best advantage being secured, we may now pass to the forms that work must take.

CHAPTER IV.
THE DAY'S WORK.

It is safe to say that no class of women in the civilized world is subjected to such incessant trials of temper, and such temptation to be fretful, as the American housekeeper. The reasons for this state of things are legion; and, if in the beginning we take ground from which the whole field may be clearly surveyed, we may be able to secure a better understanding of what housekeeping means, and to guard against some of the dangers accompanying it.

The first difficulty lies in taking for granted that successful housekeeping is as much an instinct as that which leads the young bird to nest-building, and that no specific training is required. The man who undertakes a business, passes always through some form of apprenticeship, and must know every detail involved in the management; but to the large proportion of women, housekeeping is a combination of accidental forces from whose working it is hoped breakfasts and dinners and suppers will be evolved at regular periods, other necessities finding place where they can. The new home, prettily furnished, seems a lovely toy, and is surrounded by a halo, which, as facts assert themselves, quickly fades away. Moth and rust and dust invade the most secret recesses. Breakage and general disaster attend the progress of Bridget or Chloe. The kitchen seems the headquarters of extraordinary smells, and the stove an abyss in its consumption of coal or wood. Food is wasted by bad cooking, or ignorance as to needed amounts, or methods of using left-over portions; and, as bills pile up, a hopeless discouragement often settles upon both wife and husband, and reproaches and bitterness and alienation are guests in the home, to which they need never have come had a little knowledge barred them out.

In the beginning, then, be sure of one thing,--that all the wisdom you have or can acquire, all the patience and tact and self-denial you can make yours by the most diligent effort, will be needed every day and every hour of the day. Details are in themselves wearying, and to most men their relation to housekeeping is unaccountable. The day's work of a systematic housekeeper would confound the best-trained man of business. In the woman's hand is the key to home-happiness, but it is folly to assert that all lies with her. Let it be felt from the beginning that her station is a difficult one, that her duties are important, and that judgment and skill must guide their performance; let boys be taught the honor that lies in such duties,--and there will be fewer heedless and unappreciative husbands. On the other hand, let the woman remember that the good general does not waste words on hindrances, or leave his weak spots open to observation, but, learning from every failure or defeat, goes on steadily to victory. To fret will never mend a matter; and "Study to be quiet" in thought, word, and action, is the first law of successful housekeeping. Never under-estimate the difficulties to be met, for this is as much an evil as over-apprehension. The best-arranged plans may be overturned at a moment's notice. In a mixed family, habits and pursuits differ so widely that the housekeeper must hold herself in readiness to find her most cherished schemes set aside. Absolute adherence to a system is only profitable so far as the greatest comfort and well-being of the family are affected; and, dear as a fixed routine may be to the housekeeper's mind, it may often well be sacrificed to the general pleasure or comfort. A quiet, controlled mind, a soft voice, no matter what the provocation to raise it may be, is "an excellent thing in woman." And the certainty that, hard as such control may be, it holds the promise of the best and fullest life here and hereafter, is a motive strong enough, one would think, to insure its adoption. Progress may be slow, but the reward for every step forward is certain.

We have already found that each day has its fixed routine, and are ready now to take up the order of work, which will be the same in degree whether one servant is kept, or many, or none. The latter state of things will often happen in the present uncertain character of household service. Old family servants are becoming more and more rare; and, unless the new generation is wisely trained, we run the risk of being even more at their mercy in the future than in the past.

First, then, on rising in the morning, see that a full current of air can pass through every sleeping-room; remove all clothes from the beds, and allow them to air at least an hour. Only in this way can we be sure that the impurities, thrown off from even the cleanest body by the pores during the night, are carried off. A neat housekeeper is often tempted to make beds, or have them made, almost at once; but no practice can be more unwholesome.

While beds and bedrooms are airing, breakfast is to be made ready, the table set, and kitchen and dining-room put in order. The kitchen-fire must first be built. If a gas or oil stove can be used, the operations are all simpler. If not, it is always best to have dumped the grate the night before if coal is used, and to have laid the fire ready for lighting. In the morning brush off all ashes, and wipe or blacken the stove. Strong, thick gloves, and a neat box for brushes, blacking, &c., will make this a much less disagreeable operation than it sounds. Rinse out the tea-kettle, fill it with fresh water, and put over to boil. Then remove the ashes, and, if coal is used, sift them, as cinders can be burned a large part of the time where only a moderate fire is desired.

The table can be set, and the dining or sitting room swept, or merely brushed up and dusted, in the intervals of getting breakfast. To have every thing clean, hot, and not only well prepared but ready on time, is the first law, not only for breakfast, but for every other meal.

After breakfast comes the dish-washing, dreaded by all beginners, but needlessly so. With a full supply of all conveniences,--plenty of soap and sapolio, which is far better and cleaner to use than either sand or ashes; with clean, soft towels for glass and silver; a mop, the use of which not only saves the hands but enables you to have hotter water; and a full supply of coarser towels for the heavier dishes,--the work can go on swiftly. Let the dish-pan be half full of hot soap and water. *Wash glass first*, paying no attention to the old saying that "hot water rots glass." Be careful never to put glass into hot water, bottom first, as the sudden expansion may crack it. Slip it in edgeways, and the finest and most delicate cut-glass will be safe. *Wash silver next.* Hot suds, and instant wiping on dry soft cloths, will retain the brightness of silver, which treated in this way requires much less polishing, and therefore lasts longer. If any pieces require rubbing, use a little whiting made into a paste, and put on wet. Let it dry, and then polish with a chamois-skin. Once a month will be sufficient for rubbing silver, if it is properly washed. *China comes next*--all plates having been carefully scraped, and all cups rinsed out. To fill the pan with unscraped and unrinsed dishes, and pour half-warm water over the whole, is a method too often adopted; and the results are found in sticky dishes and lustreless silver. Put all china, silver, and glass in their places as soon as washed. Then take any tin or iron pans, wash, wipe with a dry towel, and put near the fire to dry thoroughly. A knitting-needle or skewer may be kept to dig out corners unreachable by dishcloth or towel, and if perfectly dried they will remain free from rust.

The cooking-dishes, saucepans, &c., come next in order; and here the wire dish-cloth will be found useful, as it does not scratch, yet answers every purpose of a knife. Every pot, kettle, and saucepan must be put into the pan of hot water. If very greasy, it is well to allow them to stand partly full of water in which a few drops of ammonia have been put. The *outside must be washed* as carefully as the inside. Till this is done, there will always be complaint of the unpleasantness of handling cooking-utensils. Properly done, they are as clean as the china or glass.

Plated knives save much work. If steel ones are used, they must be polished after every meal. In washing them, see that the handles are never allowed to touch the water. Ivory discolors and cracks if wet. Bristol-brick finely powdered is the best polisher, and, mixed with a little water, can be applied with a large cork. A regular knife-board, or a small board on which you can nail three strips of wood in box form, will give you the best mode of keeping brick and cork in place. After rubbing, wash clean, and wipe dry.

The dish-towels are the next consideration. A set should be used but a week, and must be washed and rinsed each day if you would not have the flavor of dried-in dish-water left on your dishes. Dry them, if possible, in the open air: if not, have a rack, and stand them near the fire. On washing-days, let those that have been used a week have a thorough boiling. The close, sour smell that all housekeepers have noticed about dish-towels comes from want of boiling and drying in fresh air, and is unpardonable and unnecessary.

Keep hot water constantly in your kettles or water-pots, by always remembering to fill with cold when you take out hot. Put away every article carefully in its place.

If tables are stained, and require any scrubbing, remember that to wash or scrub wood you must follow the grain, as rubbing across it rubs the dirt in instead of taking it off.

The same rule applies to floors. A clean, coarse cloth, hot suds, and a good scrubbing-brush, will simplify the operation. Wash off the table; then dip the brush in the suds, and scour with the grain of the wood. Finally wash off all soapy water, and wipe dry. To save strength, the table on which dishes are washed may be covered with kitchen oilcloth, which will merely require washing and wiping; with an occasional scrubbing for the table below.

The table must be cleaned as soon as the dishes are washed, because if dishes stand upon tables the fragments of food have time to harden, and the washing is made doubly hard.

Leaving the kitchen in order, the bedrooms will come next. Turn the mattresses daily, and make the bed smoothly and carefully. Put the under sheet with the wrong side next the bed, and the upper one with the marked end always at the top, to avoid the part where the feet lie, from being reversed and so reaching the face. The sheets should be large enough to tuck in thoroughly, three yards long by two and a half wide being none too large for a double bed. Pillows should be beaten and then smoothed with the hand, and the aim be to have an even, unwrinkled surface. As to the use of shams, whether sheet or pillow, it is a matter of taste; but in all cases, covered or uncovered, let the bed-linen be daintily clean.

Empty all slops, and with hot water wash out all the bowls, pitchers, &c., using separate cloths for these purposes, and never toilet towels. Dust the room, arrange every thing in place, and, if in summer, close the blinds, and darken till evening, that it may be as cool as possible.

Sweeping days for bedrooms need come but once a week, but all rooms used by many people require daily sweeping; halls, passages, and dining and sitting rooms coming under this head. Careful dusting daily will often do away with the need of frequent sweeping, which wears out carpets unnecessarily. A carpet-sweeper is a real economy, both in time and strength; but, if not obtainable, a light broom carefully handled, not with a long stroke which sends clouds of dust over every thing, but with a short quick one, which only experience can give, is next best. For a thorough sweeping, remove as many articles from the room as possible, dusting each one thoroughly, and cover the larger ones which must remain with old sheets or large squares of common unbleached cotton cloth, kept for this purpose. If the furniture is rep or woolen of any description, dust about each button, that no moth may find lodgment, and then cover closely. A feather duster, long or short, as usually applied, is the enemy of cleanliness. Its only legitimate use is for the tops of pictures or books and ornaments; and such dusting should be done *before* the room is swept, as well as afterward, the first one removing the heaviest coating, which would otherwise be distributed over the room. For piano, and furniture of delicate woods generally, old silk handkerchiefs make the best dusters. For all ordinary purposes, squares of old cambric, hemmed, and washed when necessary, will be found best. Insist upon their being kept for this purpose, and forbid the use of toilet towels, always a temptation to the average servant. Remember that in dusting, the process should be a *wiping*; not a flirting of the cloth, which simply sends the dust up into the air to settle down again about where it was before.

If moldings and wash-boards or wainscotings are wiped off with a damp cloth, one fruitful source of dust will be avoided. For all intricate work like the legs of pianos, carved backs of furniture, &c., a pair of small bellows will be found most efficient. Brooms, dust-pan, and brushes long and short, whisk-broom, feather and other dusters, should have one fixed place, and be returned to it after every using. If oil-cloth is on halls or passages, it should be washed weekly with warm milk and water, a quart of skim-milk to a pail of water being sufficient. Never use soap or scrubbing-brush, as they destroy both color and texture.

All brass or silver-plated work about fire-place, doorknobs, or bath-room faucets, should be cleaned once a week and before sweeping. For silver, rub first with powdered whiting moistened with a little alcohol or hot water. Let it dry on, and then polish with a dry chamois-skin. If there is any intricate work, use a small toothbrush. Whiting, silver-soap, cloths, chamois, and brushes should all be kept in a box together. In another may be the rotten-stone necessary for cleaning brass, a small bottle of oil, and some woolen cloths. Old merino or flannel under-wear makes excellent rubbing-cloths. Mix the rotten-stone with enough oil to make a paste; rub on with one cloth, and polish with another. Thick gloves can be worn, and all staining of the hands avoided.

The bedrooms and the necessary daily sweeping finished, a look into cellar and store-rooms is next in order,--in the former, to see that no decaying vegetable matter is allowed to accumulate; in the latter, that bread-jar or boxes are dry and sweet, and all stores in good condition.

Where there are servants, it should be understood that the mistress makes this daily progress. Fifteen minutes or half an hour will often cover the time consumed; but it should be a fixed duty never omitted. A look into the refrigerator or meat-safe to note what is left and suggest the best use for it; a glance at towels and dish-cloths to see that all are clean and sweet, and another under all sinks and into each pantry,--will prevent the accumulation of bones and stray bits of food and dirty rags, the paradise of the cockroach, and delight of mice and rats. A servant, if honest, will soon welcome such investigation, and respect her mistress the more for insisting upon it, and, if not, may better find other quarters. One strong temptation to dishonesty is removed where such inspection is certain, and the weekly bills will be less than in the house where matters are left to take care of themselves.

The preparation of dinner if at or near the middle of the day, and the dish-washing which follows, end the heaviest portion of the day's work; and the same order must be followed. Only an outline can be given; each family demanding variations in detail, and each head of a family in time building up her own system. Remember, however, that, if but one servant is kept, she can not do every thing, and that your own brain must constantly supplement her deficiencies, until training and long practice have made your methods familiar. Even then she is likely at any moment to leave, and the battle to begin over again; and the only safeguard in time of such disaster is personal knowledge as to simplest methods of doing the work, and inexhaustible patience in training the next applicant, finding comfort in the thought, that, if your own home has lost, that of some one else is by so much the gainer.

CHAPTER V.
FIRES, LIGHTS, AND THINGS TO WORK WITH.

The popular idea of a fire to cook by seems to be, a red-hot top, the cover of every pot and saucepan dancing over the bubbling, heaving contents, and coal packed in even with the covers. Try to convince a servant that the lid need not hop to assure boiling, nor the fire rise above the fire-box, and there is a profound skepticism, which, even if not expressed, finds vent in the same amount of fuel and the same general course of action as before the remonstrance.

The modern stove has brought simplicity of working, and yet the highest point of convenience, nearly to perfection. With full faith that the fuel of the future will be gas, its use is as yet, for many reasons, very limited; the cost of gas in our smaller cities and towns preventing its adoption by any but the wealthy, who are really in least need of it. With the best gas-stoves, a large part of the disagreeable in cooking is done away. No flying ashes, no cinders, no uneven heat, affected by every change of wind, but a steady flame, regulated to any desired point, and, when used, requiring only a turn of the hand to end the operation.

Ranges set in a solid brick-work are considered the best form of cooking-apparatus; but there are some serious objections to their use, the first being the large amount of fuel required, and then the intense heat thrown out. Even with water in the house, they are not a necessity. A water-back, fully as effectual as the range water-back, can be set in any good stove, and connected with a boiler, large or small, according to the size of the stove; and for such stove, if properly managed, only about half the amount of coal will be needed.

Fix thoroughly in your minds the directions for making and keeping a fire; for, by doing so, one of the heaviest expenses in housekeeping can be lessened fully half.

First, then, remove the covers, and gather all ashes and cinders from the inside top of the stove, into the grate. Now put on the covers; shut the doors; close all the draughts, and dump the contents of the grate into the pan below. In some stoves there is an under-grate, to which a handle is attached; and, this grate being shaken, the ashes pass through to the ash-pan, and the cinders remain in the grate. In that case, they can simply be shoveled out into the extra coal-hod, all pieces of clinker picked out, and a little water sprinkled on them. If all must be dumped together, a regular ash-sifter will be required, placed over a barrel which receives the ashes, while the cinders remain, and are to be treated as described.

Into the grate put shavings or paper, or the fat pine known as lightwood. If the latter be used, paper is unnecessary. Lay on some small sticks of wood, *crossing them* so that there may be a draught through them; add then one or two sticks of hard wood, and set the shavings or paper on fire, seeing that every draught is open. As soon as the wood is well on fire, cover with about six inches of coal, the smaller, or nut-coal, being always best for stove use. When the coal is burning brightly, shut up all the dampers save the slide in front of the grate, and you will have a fire which will last, without poking or touching in any way, four hours. Even if a little more heat is needed for ovens, and you open the draughts, this rule still holds good.

Never, for any reason, allow the coal to come above the edge of the fire-box or lining. If you do, ashes and cinders will fall into the oven-flues, and they will soon be choked up, and require cleaning. Another reason also lies in the fact that the stove-covers resting on red-hot coals soon burn out, and must be renewed; whereas, by carefully avoiding such chance, a stove may be used many years without crack or failure of any sort.

If fresh heat is required for baking or any purpose after the first four hours, let the fire burn low, then take off the covers, and with the poker *from the bottom* rake out all the ashes thoroughly. Then put in two or three sticks of wood, fill as before with fresh coal, and the fire is good for another four hours or more. If only a light fire be required after dinner for getting tea, rake only slightly; then, fill with *cinders*, and close all the dampers. Half an hour before using the stove, open them, and the fire will rekindle enough for any ordinary purpose. As there is great difference in the "drawing" of chimneys, the exact time required for making a fire can not be given.

In using wood, the same principles apply; but of course the fire must be fed much oftener. Grate-fires, as well as those in the ordinary stove, are to be made in much the same way. In a grate, a blower is fastened on until the coal is burning well; but, if the fire is undisturbed after its renewal, it should burn from six to eight hours without further attention. Then rake out the ashes, add coal, put on the blower a few minutes, and then proceed as before. If an exceedingly slow fire is desired, cover the top with cinders, or with ashes moistened with water. In making a grate or stove fire, keep a coarse cloth to lay before it, that ashes may not spoil the carpet; and wipe about the fire-place with a damp, coarse cloth. In putting on coal in a sick-room, where noise would disturb the patient, it is a good plan to put it in small paper bags or in pieces of newspaper, in which it can be laid on silently. A short table of degrees of heat in various forms of fuel is given below; the degree required for baking, &c, finding place when we come to general operations in cooking.

DEGREES OF HEAT FROM FUEL.

Willow charcoal	600 deg.
Fah. Ordinary charcoal	700 deg.
Fah. Hard wood	800 deg. to 900 deg.
Fah. Coal	1000 deg. *Fah.*

Lights are next in order. Gas hardly requires mention, as the care of it is limited to seeing that it is not turned too high, the flame in such case not only vitiating the air of the room with double speed, but leaving a film of smoke upon every thing in it. Kerosene is the oil most largely used for lamps; and the light from either a student-lamp, or the lamp to which a "student-burner" has been applied, is the purest and steadiest now in use. A few simple rules for the care of lamps will prevent, not only danger of explosion, but much breakage of chimneys, smoking, &c.

1. Let the wick always touch the bottom of the lamp, and see that the top is trimmed square and even across, with a pair of scissors kept for the purpose.

2. Remember that a lamp, if burned with only a little oil in it, generates a gas which is liable at any moment to explode. Fill lamps to within half an inch of the top. If filled brimming full, the outside of the lamp will be constantly covered with

the oil, even when unlighted; while as soon as lighted, heat expanding it, it will run over, and grease every thing near it.

3. In lighting a lamp, turn the wick up gradually, that the chimney may heat slowly: otherwise the glass expands too rapidly, and will crack.

4. Keep the wick turned high enough to burn freely. Many persons turn down the wick to save oil, but the room is quickly poisoned by the evil smell from the gas thus formed. If necessary, as in a sick-room, to have little light, put the lamp in the hall or another room, rather than to turn it down.

5. Remember, that, as with the fire, plenty of fresh air is necessary for a free blaze, and that your lamp must be kept as free from dirt as the stove from ashes. In washing the chimneys, use hot suds; and wipe with bits of newspaper, which not only dry the glass better than a cloth, but polish it also.

6. In using either student-lamps, whether German or American, or the beautiful and costly forms known as moderator-lamps, remember, that, to secure a clear flame, the oil which accumulates in the cup below the wick, as well as any surplus which has overflowed from the reservoir, must be *poured out daily*. The neglect of this precaution is the secret of much of the trouble attending the easy getting out of order of expensive lamps, which will cease to be sources of difficulty if this rule be followed carefully.

7. Keep every thing used in such cleaning in a small box; the ordinary starch-box with sliding lid being excellent for this purpose. Extra wicks, lamp-scissors, rags for wiping off oil, can all find place here. See that lamp-rags are burned now and then, and fresh ones taken; as the smell of kerosene is very penetrating, and a room is often made unpleasant by the presence of dirty lamp-rags. If properly cared for, lamps need be no more offensive than gas.

Things to work with.

We have settled that our kitchen shall be neat, cheerful, and sunny, with closets as much as possible near enough together to prevent extra steps being taken. If the servant is sufficiently well-trained to respect the fittings of a well-appointed kitchen, and to take pleasure in keeping them in order, the whole apparatus can be arranged in the kitchen-closets. If, however, there is any doubt on this point, it will be far better to have your own special table, and shelf or so above it, where the utensils required for your own personal use in delicate cooking can be arranged.

In any kitchen not less than two tables are required: one for all rough work,--preparing meat, vegetables, &c, and dishing up meals; the other for general convenience. The first must stand as near the sink and fire as possible; and close to it, on a dresser, which it is well to have just above the table and within reach of the hand, should be all the essentials for convenient work, namely:--

A meat-block or board;

A small meat-saw;

A small cleaver and meat-knife;

Spoons, skewers, vegetable-cutters, and any other small conveniences used at this table, such as potato-slicer, larding and trussing needles, &c.;

A chopping-knife and wooden tray or bowl;

Rolling-pin, and bread and pastry board;

Narrow-bladed, very sharp knife for paring, the French cook-knife being the best ever invented for this purpose.

A deep drawer in the table for holding coarse towels and aprons, balls of twine of two sizes, squares of cloth used in boiling delicate fish or meats, &c., will be found almost essential. Basting-spoons and many small articles can hang on small hooks or nails, and are more easily picked up than if one must feel over a shelf for them. These will be egg-beaters, graters, ladle, &c. The same dresser, or a space over the sink, must hold washing-pans for meat and vegetables, dish-pans, tin measures from a gill up to one quart, saucepans, milk-boiler, &c. Below the sink, the closet for iron-ware can be placed, or, if preferred, be between sink and stove. A list in detail of every article required for a comfortably-fitted-up kitchen is given at the end of the book. House-furnishing stores furnish elaborate and confusing ones. The present list is simply what is needed for the most efficient work. Of course, as you experiment and advance, it may be enlarged; but the simple outfit can be made to produce all the results likely to be needed, and many complicated patent arrangements are hindrances, rather than helps.

The *Iron-ware* closet must hold at least two iron pots, frying-pans large and small, and a Scotch kettle with frying-basket for oysters, fish-balls, &c.,--this kettle being a broad shallow one four or five inches deep. Roasting-pans, commonly called dripping-pans, are best of Russia iron.

Tin-ware must include colander, gravy and jelly strainers, and vegetable-sifter or *puree*-sieve; six tin pie-plates, and from four to six jelly-cake tins with straight edges; and at least one porcelain-lined kettle, holding not less than four quarts, while a three-gallon one for preserving and canning is also desirable;

Muffin rings or pans; "gem-pans;"

Four bread-tins, of best tin (or, better still, Russia iron), the best size for which is ten inches long by four wide and four deep; the loaf baked in such pan requiring less time, and giving a slice of just the right shape and size;

Cake-tins of various shapes as desired, a set of small tins being desirable for little cakes.

A small sifter in basket shape will be found good for cake-making, and a larger one for bread; and spices can be most conveniently kept in a spice-caster, which is a stand holding six or eight small labeled canisters. Near it can also be small tin boxes or glass cans for dried sweet herbs, the salt-box, &c.

The *Crockery* required will be: at least two large mixing-bowls, holding not less than eight or ten quarts, and intended for bread, cake, and many other purposes; a bowl with lip to pour from, and also a smaller-sized one holding about two quarts; half a dozen quart and pint bowls;

Half a dozen one-and two-quart round or oval pudding-dishes or nappies;

Several deep plates for use in putting away cold food;

Blancmange-molds, three sizes;

One large pitcher, also three-pint and quart sizes; Yeast-jar, or, what is better, two or three Mason's glass cans, kept for yeast. This list does not include any crockery for setting a servant's table; that being governed by the number kept, and other considerations. Such dishes should be of heavier ware than your own, as they are likely to receive rougher handling; but there should be a full supply as one means of teaching neatness. *Wooden-ware* is essential in the shape of a nest of boxes for rice, tapioca, &c.; and wooden pails for sugar, Graham-flour, &c.; while you will gradually accumulate many conveniences in the way of jars, stone pots for pickling, demijohns, &c., which give the store-room, at last, the expression dear to all thrifty housekeepers. Scrubbing and water pails, scrubbing and blacking brushes, soap-dishes, sand-box, knife-board, and necessities in cleaning, must all find place, and, having found it, keep it to the end; absolute order and system being the first condition of comfortable housekeeping.

CHAPTER VI.
WASHING-DAY, AND CLEANING IN GENERAL.

Why Monday should be fixed upon as washing-day, is often questioned; but, like many other apparently arbitrary arrangements, its foundation is in common-sense. Tuesday has its advantages also, soon to be mentioned; but to any later period than Tuesday there are serious objections. All clothing is naturally changed on Sunday; and, if washed before dirt has had time to harden in the fiber of the cloth, the operation is much easier. The German custom, happily passing away, of washing only annually or semi-annually, is both disgusting, and destructive to health and clothes; the air of whatever room such accumulations are stored in being poisoned, while the clothes themselves are rubbed to pieces in the endeavor to get out the long-seated dirt.

A weekly wash being the necessity if perfect cleanliness exists, the simplest and best method of thoroughly accomplishing it comes up for question. While few women are obliged to use their own hands in such directions, plenty of needy and unskilled workwomen who can earn a living in no other way being ready to relieve us, it is yet quite as necessary to know every detail, in order that the best work may be required, and that where there is ignorance of methods in such work they may be taught.

The advantages of washing on Tuesday are, that it allows Monday for setting in order after the necessary rest of Sunday, gives opportunity to collect and put in soak all the soiled clothing, and so does away with the objection felt by many good people to performing this operation Sunday night.

To avoid such sin, bed-clothing is often changed on Saturday; but it seems only part of the freshness and sweetness which ought always to make Sunday the white-day of the week, that such change should be made on that morning, while the few minutes required for sorting the clothes, and putting them in water, are quite as legitimate as any needed operation.

If Monday be the day, then, Saturday night may be chosen for filling the tubs, supposing the kitchen to be unfurnished with stationary tubs. Sunday night enough hot water can be added to make the whole just warm--not hot. Now put in one tub all fine things,--collars and cuffs, shirts and fine underwear. Bed-linen may be added, or soaked in a separate tub; but table-linen must of course be kept apart. Last, let the coarsest and most soiled articles have another. Do not add soap, as if there is any stain it is likely to set it. If the water is hard, a little borax may be added. And see that the clothes are pressed down, and well covered with water.

Monday morning, and the earlier the better (the morning sun drying and sweetening clothes better than the later), have the boiler full of clean warm suds. Soft soap may be used, or a bar of hard dissolved in hot water, and used like soft soap. All the water in which the clothes have soaked should be drained off, and the hot suds poured on. Begin with the cleanest articles, which when washed carefully are wrung out, and put in a tub of warm water. Rinse out from this; rub soap on all the parts which are most soiled, these parts being bands and sleeves, and put them in the boiler with cold water enough to cover them. To boil up once will be sufficient for fine clothes. Then take them out into a tub of clean cold water; rinse them in this, and then in a tub of water made very slightly blue with the indigo-bag or liquid indigo. From this water they must be wrung out very dry, and hung out, always out of doors if possible. A wringer is much better than wringing by hand, as the latter is more unequal, and also often twists off buttons. The lines must be perfectly clean. A galvanized-iron wire is best of all; as it never rusts, and needs only to be wiped off each week. If rope is used, never leave it exposed to weather, but bring it in after each washing. A dirty, weather-stained line will often ruin a nice garment. Leave clothes on the line till perfectly dry. If any fruit-stains are on napkins or table-cloths, lay the stained part over a bowl, and pour on boiling water till they disappear. Ink can be taken out if the spot is washed while fresh, in cold water, or milk and water; and a little salt will help in taking out wine-stains. Machine-oil must have a little lard or butter rubbed on the spot, which is then to be washed in warm suds. Never rub soap directly on any stain, as it sets it. For iron-rust, spread the garment in the sun, and cover the spot with salt; then squeeze on lemon-juice enough to wet it. This is much safer and quite as sure as the acids sold for this purpose. In bright sunshine the spot will disappear in a few hours.

Remember that long boiling does not improve clothes. If washed clean, simply scalding is all that is required.

If delicate curtains, either lace or muslin, are to be washed, allow a tablespoonful of powdered borax to two gallons of warm water, and soap enough to make a strong suds. Soak the curtains in this all night. In the morning add more warm water, and press every part between the hands, without rubbing. Put them in fresh suds, and, if the water still looks dark after another washing, take still another. Boil and rinse as in directions given for other clothes. Starch with very thick hot starch, and dry, not by hanging out, and then ironing, but by putting a light common mattress in the sun, and pinning the curtain upon it, stretching carefully as you pin. One mattress holds two, which will dry in an hour or two. If there is no sun, lay a sheet on the floor of an unused room, and pin the curtains down upon it.

In washing flannels, remember that it must be done in a sunny day, that they may dry as rapidly as possible. Put them into hot suds. Do not rub them on a washing-board, as this is one means of fulling and ruining them. Press and rub them in the hands, changing them soon to fresh hot suds. Rinse in a pail of clear hot water; wring very dry; shake, and hang at once in the sun. Flannels thus treated, no matter how delicate, retain their softness and smoothness, and do not shrink.

Starch is the next consideration, and is made in two ways,--either raw or boiled. Boiled starch is made by adding cold water to raw starch in the proportion of one cup of water to three-quarters of a cup of starch, and then pouring on boiling water till it has thickened to a smooth mass, constantly stirring as you pour. A bit of butter is added by many excellent laundresses, the bit not to be larger than a filbert. Any thing starched with boiled starch must be dried and sprinkled before ironing, while with raw starch this is not necessary.

To make raw starch, allow four even tablespoonfuls to a half-pint of cold water. Dip collars, cuffs, and shirt-bosoms, or any thing which must be very stiff, into this starch, being careful to have them dry. When wet, clap them well between the hands, as this distributes the starch evenly among the fibers of the cloth. The same rule must be followed in using boiled starch. Roll the articles in a damp cloth, as this makes them iron more smoothly; and in an hour they will be ready for the iron. In using boiled starch, after the articles have been dried, and then dampened by sprinkling water lightly upon them, either by the hand, or by shaking over them a small whisk-broom which is dipped as needed in water, it is better to let them lie ten or twelve hours.

All clothes require this folding and dampening. Sheets and table-cloths should be held by two persons, shaken and "snapped," and then folded carefully, stretching the edges if necessary.

Colored clothing must be rinsed before starching, and the starch should be thin and cool.

For ironing neatly and well, there will be required, half a dozen flat-irons, steel bottoms preferred; a skirt-board and bosom-board, both covered, first with old blanket or carpet, then with thick strong cotton-cloth, and over this a cover of lighter cloth, sewed on so that it may be removed as often as may be necessary to wash it. If a bag the size of each is made, and they are hung up in this as soon as used, such washing need very seldom be. Having these, many dispense with ironing-sheet and blanket; but it is better to use a table for all large articles, and on this the ironing-sheet can be pinned, or tied by tapes, or strips of cloth, sewed to each corner. A stand on which to set the irons, a paper and coarse cloth to rub them off on, and a bit of yellow wax tied in a cloth, and used to remove any roughness from the iron, are the requirements of the ironing-table.

Once a month, while the irons are still slightly warm, wash them in warm water in which a little lard has been melted. Never let them stand day after day on the stove, and never throw cold water on them, as it makes them very rough.

If the starch clings to the irons, put a little Bristol-brick on a board, and rub them up and down till free. If they are too hot for use, put in a current of air a few moments; and in all cases try them on a piece of paper or cloth before putting them on a garment. If through carelessness or accident an article is scorched, lay it in the hottest sunshine to be found. If the fiber is not burned, this will often take the spot entirely out.

Let the ironed clothes hang in the air for at least twenty-four hours after ironing. Unaired sheets have often brought on fatal sickness. Examine all clothes sent up from the wash. If the laundress is sure this inspection will take place, it is a constant spur to working in the best way, and a word of praise for good points is always a stimulus. Mending should be done as the clothes are looked over, before putting away. Place the sheets from each wash at the bottom of the pile, that the same ones may not be used over and over, but all come in rotation; and the same with table-linen. If the table-cloth in use is folded carefully in the creases, and kept under a heavy piece of plank, it will retain a fresh look till soiled. Special hints as to washing blankets and dress-materials will be given in the latter part of the book.

However carefully and neatly a house may be kept, it requires a special putting in order, known as *House-cleaning*, at least once a year. Spring and fall are both devoted to it in New England; and, if the matter be conducted quietly, there are many advantages in the double cleaning. In a warmer climate, where insect-life is more troublesome and the reign of flies lasts longer, two cleanings are rather a necessity. As generally managed, they are a terror to every one, and above all to gentlemen, who resent it from beginning to end. No wonder, if at the first onslaught all home comfort ends, and regular meals become irregular lunches, and a quiet night's rest something sought but not found.

A few simple rules govern here, and will rob the ordeal of half its terrors.

If coal or wood are to be laid in for the year's supply, let it be done before cleaning begins, as much dust is spread through the house in such work.

Heavy carpets do not require taking up every year; once in two, or even three, being sufficient unless they are in constant use. Take out the tacks, however, each year; fold back the carpet half a yard or so; have the floor washed with a strong suds in which borax has been dissolved,--a tablespoonful to a pail of water; then dust black pepper along the edges, and retack the carpet. By this means moths are kept away; and, as their favorite place is in corners and folds, this laying back enables one to search out and destroy them.

Sapolio is better than sand for scouring paint, and in all cases a little borax in the water makes such work easier.

Closets should be put in order first; all winter clothing packed in trunks, or put in bags made from several thicknesses of newspaper, printers' ink being one of the most effectual protections against moths. Gum-camphor is also excellent; and, if you have no camphor-wood chest or closet, a pound of the gum, sewed into little bags, will last for years. In putting away clothing, blankets, &c., look all over, and brush and shake with the utmost care before folding, in order to get rid of any possible moth-eggs.

If matting is used, wipe it with borax-water, using a cloth wet enough to dampen but *not* wet.

Window-glass thoroughly washed can be dried and polished with old newspapers; or whiting can be used, and rubbed off with a woolen cloth.

Hard-wood furniture, black walnut, or other varieties, requires oiling lightly with boiled linseed oil, and rubbing dry with a woolen cloth; and varnished furniture, mahogany or rosewood, if kept carefully dusted, requires only an occasional rubbing with chamois-skin or thick flannel to retain its polish perfectly. Soap should never be used on varnish of any sort.

Ingrain and other carpets, after shaking, are brightened in color by sprinkling a pound or two of salt over the surface, and sweeping carefully; and it is also useful to occasionally wipe off a carpet with borax-water, using a thick flannel, and taking care not to wet, but only dampen the carpet. Mirrors can be cleaned with whiting. Never scrub oil-pictures: simply wipe with a damp cloth, and, if picture-cord is used, wipe it off to secure against moths.

It is impossible to cover the whole ground of cleaning in this chapter. Experience is the best teacher. Only remember that a household earthquake is not necessary, and that the whole work can be done so gradually, quietly, and systematically, that only the workers

need know much about it. The sense of purity transfused through the air and breathing from every nook and corner should be the only indication that upheaval has existed. The best work is always in silence.

CHAPTER VII.
THE BODY AND ITS COMPOSITION.

The lamp of life" is a very old metaphor for the mysterious principle vitalizing nerve and muscle; but no comparison could be so apt. The full-grown adult takes in each day, through lungs and mouth, about eight and a half pounds of dry food, water, and the air necessary for breathing purposes. Through the pores of the skin, the lungs, kidneys, and lower intestines, there is a corresponding waste; and both supply and waste amount in a year to one and a half tons, or three thousand pounds.

The steadiness and clear shining of the flame of a lamp depend upon quality, as well as amount of the oil supplied, and, too, the texture of the wick; and so all human life and work are equally made or marred by the food which sustains life, as well as the nature of the constitution receiving that food.

Before the nature and quality of food can be considered, we must know the constituents of the body to be fed, and something of the process through which digestion and nutrition are accomplished.

I shall take for granted that you have a fairly plain idea of the stomach and its dependences. Physiologies can always be had, and for minute details they must be referred to. Bear in mind one or two main points: that all food passes from the mouth to the stomach, an irregularly-shaped pouch or bag with an opening into the duodenum, and from thence into the larger intestine. From the mouth to the end of this intestine, the whole may be called the alimentary canal; a tube of varying size and some thirty-six feet in length. The mouth must be considered part of it, as it is in the mouth that digestion actually begins; all starchy foods depending upon the action of the saliva for genuine digestion, saliva having some strange power by which starch is converted into sugar. Swallowed whole, or placed directly in the stomach, such food passes through the body unchanged. Each division of the alimentary canal has its own distinct digestive juice, and I give them in the order in which they occur.

First, The saliva; secreted from the glands of the mouth:--alkaline, glairy, adhesive.

Second, The gastric juice; secreted in the inner or third lining of the stomach,--an acid, and powerful enough to dissolve all the fiber and albumen of flesh food.

Third, The pancreatic juice; secreted by the pancreas, which you know in animals as sweetbreads. This juice has a peculiar influence upon fats, which remain unchanged by saliva and gastric juice; and not until dissolved by pancreatic juice, and made into what chemists call an *emulsion*, can they be absorbed into the system.

Fourth, The bile; which no physiologist as yet thoroughly understands. We know its action, but hardly *why* it acts. It is a necessity, however; for if by disease the supply be cut off, an animal emaciates and soon dies.

Fifth, The intestinal juice; which has some properties like saliva, and is the last product of the digestive forces.

A meal, then, in its passage downward is first diluted and increased in bulk by a watery fluid which prepares all the starchy portion for absorption. Then comes a still more profuse fluid, dissolving all the meaty part. Then the fat is attended to by the stream of pancreatic juice, and at the same time the bile pours upon it, doing its own work in its own mysterious way; and last of all, lest any process should have been imperfect, the long canal sends out a juice having some of the properties of all.

Thus each day's requirements call for

	PINTS.
Of saliva	3-3/4
gastric juice	12
bile	3-3/4
pancreatic juice	1-1/2
intestinal juice	1/2

	21-1/2

Do not fancy this is all wasted or lost. Very far from it: for the whole process seems to be a second circulation, as it were; and, while the blood is moving in its wonderful passage through veins and arteries, another circulation as wonderful, an endless current going its unceasing round so long as life lasts, is also taking place. But without food the first would become impossible; and the quality of food, and its proper digestion, mean good or bad blood as the case may be. We must follow our mouthful of food, and see how this action takes place.

When the different juices have all done their work, the *chyme*, which is food as it passes from the stomach into the duodenum or passage to the lower stomach or bowels, becomes a milky substance called *chyle*, which moves slowly, pushed by numberless muscles along the bowel, which squeeze much of it into little glands at the back of the bowels. These are called the mesenteric glands; and, as each one receives its portion of chyle, a wonderful thing happens. About half of it is changed into small round bodies called corpuscles, and they float with the rest of the milky fluid through delicate pipes which take it to a sort of bag just in front of the spine. To this bag is fastened another pipe or tube--the thoracic duct--which follows the line of the spine; and up this tube the small bodies travel till they come to the neck and a spot where two veins meet. A door in one opens, and the transformation is complete. The small bodies are raw food no more, but blood, traveling fast to where it may be purified, and begin its endless round in the best condition. For, as you know, venous blood is still impure and dirty blood. Before it can be really alive it must pass through the veins to the right side of the heart, flow through into the upper chamber, then through another door or valve into the lower, where it is pumped out into the lungs. If these lungs are, as they should be, full of pure air, each corpuscle is so charged with oxygen, that the last speck of impurity is burned up, and it goes dancing and bounding on its way. That is what health means: perfect food made into perfect blood, and giving that sense of strength and exhilaration that we none of us know half as much about as we should. We get it sometimes on mountain-tops in clear autumn days when the air is like wine; but God meant it to be our daily portion, and this very despised knowledge of cookery is to bring it about. If a lung is imperfect, supplied only with foul air as among the very poor, or diseased as in consumption, food does not nourish, and you now know why. We have found that the purest air and the purest water contain the largest proportion of oxygen; and it is this that vitalizes both food and, through food, the blood.

To nourish this body, then, demands many elements; and to study these has been the joint work of chemists and physiologists, till at last every constituent of the body is known and classified. Many as these constituents are, they are all resolved into the simple elements, oxygen, hydrogen, nitrogen, and carbon, while a little sulphur, a little phosphorus, lime, chlorine, sodium, &c., are added.

FLESH and BLOOD are composed of water, fat, fibrine, albumen, gelatine, and the compounds of lime, phosphorus, soda, potash, magnesia, iron, &c.

BONE contains cartilage, gelatine, fat, and the salts of lime, magnesia, soda, &c., in combination with phosphoric and other acids.

CARTILAGE consists of chondrine, a substance somewhat like gelatine, and contains also the salts of sulphur, lime, soda, potash, phosphorus, magnesia, and iron.

BILE is made up of water, fat, resin, sugar, cholesterine, some fatty acids, and the salts of potash, iron, and soda.

THE BRAIN is made up of water, albumen, fat, phosphoric acid, osmazone, and salts.

THE LIVER unites water, fat, and albumen, with phosphoric and other acids, and lime, iron, soda, and potash.

THE LUNGS are formed of two substances: one like gelatine; another of the nature of caseine and albumen, fibrine, cholesterine, iron, water, soda, and various fatty and organic acids.

How these varied elements are held together, even science with all its deep searchings has never told. No man, by whatsoever combination of elements, has ever made a living plant, much less a living animal. No better comparison has ever been given than that of Youmans, who makes a table of the analogies between the human body and the steam-engine, which I give as it stands.

ANALOGIES OF THE STEAM-ENGINE AND THE LIVING BODY.

The Steam Engine in Action takes:
1. Fuel: coal and wood, both combustible.
2. Water for evaporation.

3. Air for combustion.

And Produces:

4. A steady boiling heat of 212 deg. by quick combustion.

5. Smoke loaded with carbonic acid and watery vapor.

6. Incombustible ashes.

7. Motive force of simple alternate push and pull in the piston, which, acting through wheels, bands, and levers, does work of endless variety.

8. A deficiency of fuel, water, or air, disturbs, then stops the motion.

The Animal Body in Life takes:

1. Food: vegetables and flesh, both combustible.

2. Water for circulation.

3. Air for respiration.

And Produces:

4. A steady animal heat, by slow combustion, of 98 deg..

5. Expired breath loaded with carbonic acid and watery vapor.

6. Incombustible animal refuse.

7. Motive force of simple alternate contraction and relaxation in the muscles, which, acting through joints, tendons, and levers, does work of endless variety.

8. A deficiency of food, drink, or air, first disturbs, then stops the motion and the life.

Carrying out this analogy, you will at once see why a person working hard with either body or mind requires more food than the one who does but little. The food taken into the human body can never be a simple element. We do not feed on plain, undiluted oxygen or nitrogen; and, while the composition of the human body includes really sixteen elements in all, oxygen is the only one used in its natural state. I give first the elements as they exist in a body weighing about one hundred and fifty-four pounds, this being the average weight of a full-grown man; and add a table, compiled from different sources, of the composition of the body as made up from these elements. Dry as such details may seem, they are the only key to a full understanding of the body, and the laws of the body, so far as the food-sup-ply is concerned; though you will quickly find that the day's food means the day's thought and work, well or ill, and that in your hands is put a power mightier than you know,--the power to build up body, and through body the soul, into a strong and beautiful manhood and womanhood.

ELEMENTS OF THE HUMAN BODY.

	Lbs.	Oz.	Grs.
1. Oxygen, a gas, and supporter of combustion, weighs	103	2	335
2. Carbon, a solid; found most nearly pure in charcoal. Carbon in the body combines with other elements to produce carbonic-acid gas, and by its burning sets heat free. Its weight is	18	11	150
3. Hydrogen, a gas, is a part of all bone, blood, and muscle, and weighs	4	14	0
4. Nitrogen, a gas, is also part of all muscle, blood, and bone; weighing	4	14	0
5. Phosphorus, a solid, found in brain and bones, weighs	1	12	25
6. Sulphur, a solid, found in all parts of the body, weighs	0	8	0
7. Chlorine, a gas, found in all parts of the body, weighs	0	4	150
8. Fluorine, supposed to be a gas, is found with calcium in teeth and bones, and weighs	0	3	300
9. Silicon, a solid, found united with oxygen in the hair, skin, bile, bones, blood, and saliva, weighs	0	0	14
10. Magnesium, a metal found in union with phosphoric acid in the bones	0	2	250
11. Potassium, a metal, the basis of potash, is found as phosphate and chloride; weighs	0	3	340
12. Sodium, a metal, basis of soda; weighs	0	3	217
13. Calcium, a metal, basis of lime, found chiefly in bones and teeth; weighs	3	13	190
14. Iron, a metal essential in the coloring of the blood, and found everywhere in the body; weighs	0	0	65
15. Manganese. } Faint traces of both these metals }			
16. Copper metals.} are found in brain and blood, but in too minute portions to be given by weight.			
Total	154	0	0

The second table gives the combinations of these elements; and, though a knowledge of such combinations is not as absolutely essential as the first, we still can not well dispense with it. The same weight--one hundred and fifty-four pounds--is taken as the standard.

COMPOSITION OF THE BODY.

	Lbs.	Oz.	Grs.
1. Water, which is found in every part of the body, and amounts to	109	0	0
2. Fibrine, and like substances, found in the blood, and forming the chief solid materials of the flesh	15	10	0
3. Phosphate of lime, chiefly in bones and teeth, but in all liquids and tissues	8	12	0
4. Fat, a mixture of three chemical compounds, and distributed all through the body	4	8	0
5. Osseine, the organic framework of bones; boiled, gives gelatine. Weight	4	7	350
6. Keratine, a nitrogenous substance, forming the greater part of hair, nails, and skin. Weighs	4	2	0
7. Cartilagine resembles the osseine of bone, and is a nitrogenous substance, the chief constituent of cartilage, weighing	1	8	0
8. Haemoglobine gives the red color to blood, and is a nitrogenous substance containing iron, and weighing	1	8	0
9. Albumen is a soluble nitrogenous substance, found in the blood, chyle, lymph, and muscle, and weighs	1	1	0
10. Carbonate of lime is found in the bones chiefly, and weighs	1	1	0
11. Hephalin is found in nerves and brain, with cerebrine and other compounds	0	13	0
12. Fluoride of calcium is found in teeth and bones, and weighs	0	7	175

12. Fluoride of calcium is found in teeth and bones, and weighs	0	7	175
13. Phosphate of magnesia is also in teeth and bones, and weighs	0	7	0
14. Chloride of sodium, or common salt, is found in all parts of the body, and weighs	0	7	0
15. Cholesterine, glycogen, and inosite are compounds containing hydrogen, oxygen, and carbon, found in muscle, liver, and brain, and weighing	0	3	0
16. Sulphate phosphate, and salts of sodium, found in all tissues and liquids	0	2	107
17. Sulphate, phosphate, and chloride of potassium, are also in all tissues and liquids	0	1	300
18. Silica, found in hair, skin, and bone	0	0	30
	---	---	---
	154	0	0

With this basis, to give us some understanding of the complicated and delicate machinery with which we must work, the question arises, what food contains all these constituents, and what its amount and character must be. The answer to this question will help us to form an intelligent plan for providing a family with the right nutrition.

CHAPTER VIII.
FOOD AND ITS LAWS.

We have found, that, in analyzing the constituents of the body, water is the largest part; and turning to food, whether animal or vegetable, the same fact holds good. It forms the larger part of all the drinks, of fruits, of succulent vegetables, eggs, fish, cheese, the cereals, and even of fats.

Fat is found in butter, lard, drippings, milk, eggs, cheese, fish, meat, the cereals, leguminous vegetables,--such as pease and beans,--nuts, cocoa, and chocolate.

Sugar abounds in fruits and vegetables, and is found in milk and cereals.

Starch, which under the action of the saliva changes into glucose or grape-sugar, is present in vegetables and cereals.

Flesh foods, called as often nitrogenous foods, from containing so large a proportion of nitrogen, are made up of fibrine, albumen, caseine, gelatine, and gluten; the first four elements being present in flesh, the latter in vegetables.

Salts of various forms exist in both animal and vegetable food. In meat, fish, and potatoes are found phosphorus, lime, and magnesia. Common salt is largely made up of soda, but is found with potash in many vegetables. This last element is also in meat, fish, milk, vegetables, and fruits. Iron abounds in flesh and vegetables; and sulphur enters into albumen, caseine, and fibrine.

The simplest division of food is into *flesh-formers* and *heat-producers*; the former being as often called nitrogenous food, or albumenoids; the latter, heat-giving or carbonaceous foods. Much minuter divisions could be made, but these two cover the ground sufficiently well. For a healthy body both are necessary, but climate and constitution will always make a difference in the amounts required. Thus, in a keen and long-continued winter, the most condensed forms of carbonaceous foods will be needed; while in summer a small portion of nitrogenous food to nourish muscle, and a large amount of cooling fruits and vegetables, are indicated; both of these, though more or less carbonaceous in character, containing so much water as to neutralize any heat-producing effects.

Muscle being the first consideration in building up a strong body, we need first to find out the values of different foods as flesh-formers, healthy flesh being muscle in its most perfect condition. Flesh and fat are never to be confounded, fat being really a species of disease,--the overloading of muscle and tissue with what has no rightful place there. There should be only enough fat to round over the muscle, but never hide its play. The table given is the one in use in the food-gallery of the South Kensington Museum, and includes not only the nutritive value, but the cost also, of each article; taking beef as the standard with which other animal foods are to be compared, beef being the best-known of all meats. Among vegetables, lentils really contain most nourishment; but wheat is chosen as being much more familiar, lentils being very little used in this country save by the German part of the population, and having so strong and peculiar a flavor that we are never likely to largely adopt their use.

About an equal amount of nourishment is found in the varied amounts mentioned in the table which follows:--

TABLE.

	Cost about
Eight ounces of lean beef (half-pound)	6 cts.
Ten ounces of dried lentils	7 cts.
Eleven ounces of pease or beans	5 cts.
Twelve ounces of cocoa-nibs	20 cts.
Fourteen ounces of tea	40 cts.
Fifteen ounces of oatmeal	5 cts.
One pound and one ounce of wheaten flour	4 cts.
One pound and one ounce of coffee	30 cts.
One pound and two ounces of rye-flour	5 cts.
One pound and three ounces of barley	5 cts.

One pound and five ounces Indian meal	5 cts.
One pound and thirteen ounces of buckwheat-flour	10 cts.
Two pounds of wheaten bread	10 cts.
Two pounds and six ounces of rice	20 cts.
Five pounds and three ounces of cabbage	10 cts.
Five pounds and three ounces of onions	15 cts.
Eight pounds and fifteen ounces of turnips	9 cts.
Ten pounds and seven ounces of potatoes	10 cts.
Fifteen pounds and ten ounces of carrots	15 cts.

Now, because tea, coffee, and cocoa approach so nearly in value as nutriment to beef and lentils, we must not be misled. Fourteen ounces of tea are equivalent to half a pound of meat; but a repast of dry tea not being very usual, in fact, being out of the question altogether, it becomes plain, that the principal value of these foods, used as we must use them, in very small quantities, is in the warmth and comfort they give. Also, these weights (except the bread) are of uncooked food. Eight ounces of meat would, if boiled or roasted, dwindle to five or six, while the ten ounces of lentils or beans would swell to twice the capacity of any ordinary stomach. So, ten pounds of potatoes are required to give you the actual benefit contained in the few ounces of meat; and only the Irishman fresh from his native cabin can calmly consider a meal of that magnitude, while, as to carrots, neither Irishman nor German, nor the most determined and enterprising American, could for a moment face the spectacle of fifteen pounds served up for his noonday meal.

The inference is plain. Union is strength, here as elsewhere; and the perfect meal must include as many of these elements as will make it not too bulky, yet borrowing flavor and substance wherever necessary.

As a rule, the food best adapted to climate and constitution seems to have been instinctively decided upon by many nations; and a study of national dishes, and their adaptation to national needs, is curious and interesting. The Esquimaux or Greenlander finds his most desirable meal in a lump of raw blubber, the most condensed form of carbonaceous food being required to preserve life. It is not a perverted taste, but the highest instinct; for in that cruel cold the body must furnish the food on which the keen air draws, and the lamp of life there has a very literal supply.

Take now the other extreme of temperature,--the East Indies, China, Africa, and part even of the West Indies and America,--and you find rice the universal food. There is very little call, as you may judge, for heat-producers, but rather for flesh-formers; and starch and sugar both fulfill this end, the rice being chiefly starch, which turns into sugar under the action of the saliva. Add a little melted butter, the East Indian *ghee*, or olive-oil used in the West Indies instead, and we have all the elements necessary for life under those conditions.

A few degrees northward, and the same rice is mingled with bits of fish or meat, as in the Turkish *pilau*, a dish of rice to which mutton or poultry is added.

The wandering Arab finds in his few dates, and handful of parched wheat or maize, the sugar and starch holding all the heat required, while his draught of mare's or camel's milk, and his occasional *pilau* of mutton, give him the various elements which seem sufficient to make him the model of endurance, blitheness, and muscular power. So the Turkish burden-bearers who pick up a two-hundred-pound bag of coffee as one picks up a pebble, use much the same diet, though adding melons and cucumbers, which are eaten as we eat apples.

The noticeable point in the Italian dietary is the universal and profuse use of macaroni. Chestnuts and Indian corn, the meal of which is made into a dish called *polenta*, something like our mush, are also used, but macaroni is found at every table, noble or peasant's. No form of wheat presents such condensed nourishment, and it deserves larger space on our own bills of fare than we have ever given it.

In Spain we find the *olla podrida*, a dish containing, as chief ingredient, the *garbanzo* or field-pea: it is a rich stew, of fowls or bacon, red peppers, and pease. Red pepper enters into most of the dishes in torrid climates, and there is a good and sufficient reason for this apparent mistake. Intense and long-continued heat weakens the action of the liver, and thus lessens the supply of bile; and red pepper has the power of stimulating the liver, and so assisting digestion. East Indian curries, and the Mexican and Spanish *olla*, are therefore founded on common-sense.

In France the *pot-au-feu*, or soup-pot, simmers in every peasant or middle-class home, and is not to be despised even in richer ones. In this dish, a small portion of meat is cooked so judiciously as to flavor a large mass of vegetables and broth; and this, served with salad and oil and bread, forms a meal which can hardly be surpassed in its power of making the most of every constituent offered. In Germany soups are a national dish also; but their extreme fondness for pork, especially raw ham and sausage, is the source of many diseases. Sweden, Norway, Russia,--all the far northern countries,--tend more and more to the oily diet of the Esquimaux, fish being a large part of it. There is no room for other illustrations; but, as you learn the properties of food, you will be able to read national dietaries, from the Jewish down, with a new understanding of what power food had and has in forming national peculiarities.

It is settled, then, that to renew our muscles which are constantly wearing out, we must eat the food containing the same constituents; and these we find in meat, milk, eggs, and the entire gluten of grains, &c, as in wheaten-grits or oatmeal.

Fat and heat must come to us from the starches and sugars, in sufficient supply to "put a layer of wadding between muscles and skin, fill out the wrinkles, and keep one warm." To find out the proportion needed for one's own individual constitution, is the first work for all of us. The laborer requires one thing, the growing child another, the man or woman whose labor is purely intellectual another; and to understand how best to meet these needs, demands a knowledge to which most of us have been indifferent. If there is excess or lack of any necessary element, that excess or lack means disease, and for such disease we are wholly responsible. Food is not the only and the universal elixir of life; for weak or poor blood is often an inheritance, and comes to one tainted by family diseases, or by defects in air or climate in general. But, even when outward conditions are most disastrous, perfect food has power to avert or alter their effects; and the child who begins life burdened with scrofulous or other diseases, and grows to a pale, weak, unwholesome youth, and either a swift passing into the next world, or a life here of hopeless invalidism, can, nine times out of ten, have this course of things stopped by scientific understanding of what foods are necessary for such conditions.

I propose to take the life of one who from babyhood up has been fed on the best food, perfectly prepared, and to give the tables of such food for different periods in that life, allowing only such digression as will show the effects of an opposite course of treatment; thus showing the relations of food to health,--a more necessary and vital form of knowledge than any other that the world owns.

CHAPTER IX.
THE RELATIONS OF FOOD TO HEALTH.

We begin, then, with a typical baby, born of civilized parents, and living in the midst of the best civilization to be had. Savage or even partially civilized life could never furnish the type we desire. It is true, as we have seen, that natural laws, so deeply planted that they have become instincts, have given to many wild nations a dietary meeting their absolute needs; but only civilization can find the key to these modes, and make past experience pay tribute to present knowledge. We do not want an Indian baby, bound and swathed like a little mummy, hanging from the pole of a wigwam, placidly sucking a fish's tail, or a bone of boiled dog; nor an Esquimaux baby, with its strip of blubber; nor the Hottentot, with its rope of jerked beef; nor the South-sea Islander, with its half-cocoanut. Nor will we admit the average Irish baby, among the laboring classes in both city and country, brought to the table at three months old to swallow its portion of coffee or tea; nor the small German, whom at six months I have seen swallowing its little mug of lager as philosophically as its serious-faced father. That these babies have fevers and rashes, and a host of diseases peculiar to that age, is a matter of course; and equally a matter of course that the round-eyed mother wonders where it got its dreadful disposition, but scorns the thought that lager or coffee can be irritants, or that the baby stomach requires but one food, and that one the universal food of all young animal life,--milk.

Take, then, our typical baby, lying fresh and sweet in the well aired and lighted room we suppose to be his birthright. The bones are still soft, the tender flesh and skin with little or no power of resistance. Muscles, nerves, all the wonderful tissues, are in process of formation; and in the strange growth and development of this most helpless yet most precious of all God's creations, there are certain elements which must be had,--phosphates to harden the delicate bones; nitrogen for flesh, which is only developed muscle; carbon,--or sugar and fat, which represent carbon,--for the whole wonderful course of respiration and circulation. Water, too, must be in abundance to fill the tiny stomach, which in the beginning can hold but a spoonful; and to float the blood-corpuscles through the winding channels whose mysteries, even now, no man has fully penetrated. Caseine, which is the solid, nourishing, cheesy part of milk, and abounds in nitrogen, is also needed; and all the salts and alkalies that we have found to be necessary in forming perfect blood. Let us see if milk will meet these wants.

COMPOSITION OF COW'S MILK.

(_Supposed to contain 1,000 parts._)

Water	870.2
Caseine	44.8
Butter	31.3
Sugar	47.7

Carried forward	994.0
Brought forward	994.0

Soda	}	
Chloride of sodium and potassium	}	
Phosphate of soda and potassa	}	
Phosphate of lime	}	6.0
Magnesia	}	
Iron	}	
Alkaline carbonates	}	

	1,000.0	

Mother's milk being nearly the same, having only a larger proportion of water, will for the first year of our baby's life meet every demand the system can make. Even the first teeth are no sign, as ignorant mothers believe, that the stomach calls for stronger food. They are known, with reason, as milk-teeth, and the grinders delay their appearance for months afterward. A little oatmeal, bread and milk, and various porridges, come in here, that the bones may harden more rapidly; but that is all. The baby is in constant motion; and eyes and ears are taking in the mysteries of the new life, and busy hands testing properties, and little feet walking into mischief, all day. This is hardly the place to dwell upon the amount of knowledge acquired from birth to five years of age; yet when you consider how the mind is reaching in every direction, appropriating, investigating, drawing conclusions which are the foundation of all our after-knowledge, you will see that the brain is working with an intensity never afterwards equaled; and, as brain-work means actual destruction of brain-fiber, how vital it is that food should be furnished in the right ratio, and made up of the right elements!

With the coming of the grinders, and the call of the muscles and tissues for stronger food, begins the necessity for a more varied dietary. Our baby now, from two and a half to seven years of age, will require daily:--

Bread, not less than	12 ounces.
Butter	1 ounce.
Milk	1/2 pint.
Meat	2 ounces.
Vegetables	6 ounces.
Pudding or gruel	6 ounces.

This table is made from the dietaries of various children's hospitals, where long experiment has settled the quantities and qualities necessary to health, or, as in these cases, recovery from sickness, at which time the appetite is always keener.

In many cases physicians who have studied the laws of food, and kept pace with modern experiments in dietetics, strike out meat altogether till the child is seven or eight years old, and allow it but once daily after this time, and in very limited amount. Sir Henry Thompson, one of the most distinguished of English physicians, and a man noted for his popularity as diner out and giver of dinners, writes strenuously against the prevailing excessive use of meat, and especially protests against its over use for children; and his opinion is shared by most thoughtful medical men. The nitrogenous vegetables advantageously take its place; and cheese, as prepared after the formulas given in Mattieu Williams's "Chemistry of Cookery," is a food the value of which we are but just beginning to appreciate.

As to quantity, with the healthy child, playing at will, there need be very little restraint. Few children will eat too much of perfectly simple food, such as this table includes. Let cake or pastry or sweetmeats enter in, and of course, as long as the thing tastes good, the child will beg for more. English children are confined to this simple diet; and though of course a less exacting climate has much to do with the greater healthfulness of the English than the American people, the plain but hearty and regular diet of childhood has far more.

Our young American of seven, at a hotel breakfast, would call for coffee and ham and eggs and sausages and hot cakes. His English cousin would have no liberty to call for anything. In fact, it is very doubtful if he would be brought to table at all; and if there, bread and milk or oatmeal and milk would form his meal.

By this time I do not doubt our baby has your heartiest pity, and you are saying, "What! no snacks? no cooky nor cake nor candy? no running to aunt or grandmother or tender-hearted cook for goodies? If that must be so, half the pleasure of childhood is lost."

Perhaps; but suppose that with that pleasure some other things are also lost. Suppose our baby to have begun life with a nervous, irritable, sensitive organization, keenly alive to pain, and this hard regimen to have covered these nerves with firm flesh, and filled the veins with clean, healthy blood. Suppose headache is unknown, and loss of appetite, and a bad taste in the mouth, and all the evils we know so well; and that work and play are easy, and food of the simplest eaten with solid satisfaction. The child would choose the pleasant taste, and let health go, naturally; for a child has small reason, and life must be ordered for it. But if the mother or father has no sense or understanding of the laws of food, it is useless to hope for the wholesome results that under the diet of our baby are sure to follow.

By seven some going to school has begun; and from this time on the diet, while of the same general character, may vary more from day to day. Habits of life are fixed during this time; and even if parents dislike certain articles of food themselves, it is well to give no sign, but as far as possible, accustom the child to eat any wholesome food. We are a wandering people, and sooner or later are very likely to have circumnavigated the globe, at least in part. Our baby must have no antipathies, but every good thing given by Nature shall at least be tolerated. "I never eat this," or "I never eat that," is a formula that no educated person has a right to use save when some food actually hurtful or to which he has a natural repulsion is presented to him. Certain articles of diet are often strangely and unaccountably harmful to some. Oysters are an almost deadly poison to certain constitutions; milk to others. Cheese has produced the same effect, and even strawberries; yet all these are luxuries to the ordinary stomach.

Usually the thing to guard against most carefully is gluttony, so far as boys are concerned. With girls the tendency often is to eat far too little. A false delicacy, a feeling that paleness and fragility are beautiful and feminine, inclines the young girl often to eat less than she desires; and the stomach accustoms itself to the insufficient supply, till the reception of a reasonable meal is an impossibility. Or if they eat improper food (hot breads and much fat and sweets), the same result follows. Digestion, or rather assimilation, is impossible; and pasty face and lusterless eyes become the rule. A greedy woman is the exception; and yet all schoolgirls know the temptation to over-eating produced by a box of goodies from home, or the stronger temptation, after a school-term has ended, to ravage all cake-boxes and preserve-jars. Then comes the pill or powder, and the habit of going to them for a relief which if no excess had been committed, would have been unnecessary. Patent medicines are the natural sequence of unwholesome food, and both are outrages on common-sense.

We will take it for granted, then, that our baby has come to boyhood and youth in blissful ignorance of their names or natures. But as we are not in the least certain what personal tastes he may have developed, or what form his life-work is to take,--whether professional or mercantile or artisan in one of the many trades,--we can now only give the regimen best adapted for each.

Supposing his tastes to be scholarly, and a college and professional career to be chosen, the time has come for slight changes in the system of diet,--very slight, however. It has become a popular saying among thinkers upon these questions,

"Without phosphorus, no thinking;" and like all arbitrary utterances it has done more harm than good. The amount of phosphorus passing through the system bears no relation whatever to the intensity of thought. "A captive lion," to quote from Dr. Chambers, one of the most distinguished living authorities on diet, "a leopard, or hare, which can have wonderfully little to think about, assimilates and parts with a greater quantity of phosphorus than a professor of chemistry working hard in his laboratory; while a beaver, who always seems to be contriving something, excretes so little phosphorus that chemical analysis cannot detect it."

Phosphatic salts are demanded, but so are other salts, fat, and water; and the dietaries that order students to live upon fish, eggs, and oysters, because they are rich in phosphorus, without which the brain starves, err just so far as they make this the sole reason,--the real reason being that these articles are all easily digested, and that the student, leading an inactive muscular life, does not require the heavy, hearty food of the laborer.

The most perfect regimen for the intellectual life is precisely what would be advised for the growing boy: frequent *small* supplies of easily-digested food, that the stomach may never be overloaded, or the brain clouded by the fumes of half-assimilated food. If our boy trains for a foot-race, rows with the college crew, or goes in for base-ball, his power as a brain-worker at once diminishes. Strong muscular action and development hinder continuous mental work; and the literary life, as a rule, allows no extremes, demanding only mild exercise and temperance as its foundation-stones. But our boy can well afford to develop his muscular system so perfectly that his mild exercise would seem to the untrained man tolerably heavy work.

The rower in a college crew requires six weeks of training before his muscular power and endurance have reached their height. Every particle of superfluous fat must be removed, for fat is not strength, but weakness. There is a vast difference between the plumpness of good muscular development and the flabby, heavy over-loading of these muscles with rolls of fat. The chest must be enlarged, that the lungs may have full play, and be capable of long-continued, extra draughts upon them; and special diet and special exercise alone can accomplish these ends. All fat-producing foods are struck out, sugar and all starchy foods coming under this head, as well as all puddings, pies, cakes, and sweets in general. Our boy, after a short run, would breakfast on lean, under-done beef or mutton, dry toast, or the crust of bread, and tea without milk or sugar; would dine on meat and a little bread and claret, and sup on more meat and toast, with cresses or some acid fruit, having rowed twice over the course in the afternoon, steadily increasing the speed, and following it by a bath and rub. At least nine hours sleep must be had; and with this diet, at the end of the training-time the muscles are hard and firm, the skin wonderfully pure and clear, and the capacity for long, steady breathing under exertion, almost unlimited. No better laws for the reduction of excessive fat can be laid down for any one.

Under such a course, severe mental exertion is impossible; and the return to it requires to be gradual. But light exercise with dumb-bells, &c., fresh air, walking, and good food are the conditions of all sound mental work, whether done by man or woman.

For the clerk or bookkeeper closely confined to desk or counter, much the same regimen is needed, with brisk exercise at the beginning and end of the day,--at least always walking rather than riding to and from the office or store; while in all the trades where hard labor is necessary, heartier food must be the rule. And for all professions or trades, the summing-up is the same: suitable food, fresh air, sunlight, and perfect cleanliness,--the following of these laws insuring the perfect use of every power to the very end.

As old age advances, the food-demand lessens naturally. Nourishing food is still necessary, but taken in much smaller quantities and more often, in order that the waning powers of the stomach may not be overtaxed. Living on such principles, work can go on till the time for work is over, and the long sleep comes as quietly as to a tired child. Simple common-sense and self-control will free one once for all from the fear, too often hanging over middle life, of a paralytic and helpless invalidism, or the long train of apoplectic symptoms often the portion even of middle life.

I omit detail as to the character and effects of tea, coffee, alcohol, &c, such details coming in the chapters on the chemistry of food.

CHAPTER X.
THE CHEMISTRY OF ANIMAL FOOD.

Animal food has a wider range than is usually included under that head. The vegetarian who announces that no animal food is allowed upon his table offers a meal in which one finds milk, eggs, butter, and cheese,--all forms of animal food, and all strongly nourishing. A genuine vegetarian, if consistent, would be forced to reject all of these; and it has already been attempted in several large water-cures by enthusiasts who have laid aside their common-sense, and resigned with it some of the most essential forces for life and work. Meat may often be entirely renounced, or eaten only at rare intervals, with great advantage to health and working power, but the dietary for the varied nourishment which seems demanded must include butter, cheese, eggs, and milk.

Meats will be regarded as essential by the majority, and naturally they come first in considering food; and beef is taken as the standard, being identical in composition with the structures of the human body.

BEEF, if properly fed, is in perfection at seven years old. It should then be a light red on the cut surface, a darker red near the bone, and slightly marbled with fat. Beef contains, in a hundred parts, nearly twenty of nitrogen, seventy-two of water, four of fat, and the remainder in salts of various descriptions. The poorer the quality of the beef, the more it will waste in cooking; and its appearance before cooking is also very different from that of the first quality, which, though looking moist, leaves no stain upon the hand. In poor beef, the watery part seems to separate from the rest, which lies in a pool of serous bloody fluid. The gravy from such beef is pale and poor in flavor; while the fat, which in healthy beef is firm and of a delicate yellow, in the inferior quality is dark yellow and of rank smell and taste. Beef is firmer in texture and more satisfying to the stomach than any other form of meat, and is usually considered more strengthening.

MUTTON is a trifle more digestible, however. A healthy person would not notice this, the digestive power in health being more than is necessary for the ordinary meal; but the dyspeptic will soon find that mutton gives his stomach less work. Its composition is very nearly the same as that of beef; and both when cooked, either by roasting or boiling, lose about a third of their substance, and come to us with twenty-seven parts of nitrogen, fifteen of fat, fifty-four of water, and three of salty matters.

Mountain sheep and cattle have the finest-flavored meat, and are also richest in nitrogenous matter. The mountain mutton of Virginia and North Carolina is as famous as the English Southdown; but proper feeding anywhere will make a new thing of the ordinary beef and mutton. When our cattle are treated with decent humanity,--not driven days with scant food and water, and then packed into cars with no food and no water, and driven at last to slaughter feverish and gasping in anguish that we have no right to permit for one moment,--we may expect tender, wholesome, well-flavored meat. It is astonishing that under present conditions it can be as good as it is.

In well-fed animals, the fat forms about a third of the weight, the largest part being in the loin. In mutton, one-half is fat; in pork, three-quarters; while poultry and game have very little.

The amount of bone varies very greatly. The loin and upper part of the leg have least; nearly half the entire weight being in the shin, and a tenth in the carcass. In the best mutton and pork, the bones are smaller, and fat much greater in proportion to size.

VEAL and LAMB, like all young meats, are much less digestible than beef or mutton. Both should have very white, clear fat; and if that about the kidneys is red or discolored, the meat should be rejected. Veal has but sixteen parts of nitrogenous matter to sixty-three of water, and the bones contain much more gelatine than is found in older animals. But in all bones much useful carbon and nitrogen is found; three pounds of bone yielding as much carbon, and six pounds as much nitrogen, as one pound of meat. Carefully boiled, this nutriment can all be extracted, and flavored with vegetables, form the basis of an endless variety of soups.

PORK is of all meats the most difficult to digest, containing as it does so large a proportion of fat. In a hundred parts of the meat, only nine of nitrogen are found, fat being forty-eight and water thirty-nine, with but two of salty matters. Bacon properly cured is much more digestible than pork, the smoke giving it certain qualities not existing in uncured pork. No food has yet been found which can take its place for army and navy use or in pioneering. Beef when salted or smoked loses much of its virtue, and eight ounces of fat pork will give nearly three times as much carbon or heat-food as the same amount of beef; but its use is chiefly for the laborer, and it should have only occasional place in the dietary of sedentary persons.

The pig is liable to many most unpleasant diseases, measles and trichina spiralis being the most fatal to the eaters of meat thus affected; but the last--a small animalcule of deadly effect if taken alive into the human stomach, as is done in eating raw ham or sausage--becomes harmless if the same meat is long and thoroughly boiled. Never be tempted into eating raw ham or sausage; and in using pork in any form, try to have some knowledge of the pig. A clean, well-fed pig in a well-kept stye is a wonderfully different object from the hideous beast grunting its way in many a Southern or Western town, feeding on offal and sewage, and rolling in filth. Such meat is unfit for human consumption, and the eating of it insures disease.

We come now to another form of meat, that of edible ENTRAILS. This includes *Tripe*, *Haslet*, or lights, &c. More nitrogen is found here than in any other portion of the meat. The cheap and abundant supply in this country has made us, as a people, reject all but the liver. In the country, the sweetbreads or pancreas are often thrown away, and tripe also. The European peasant has learned to utilize every scrap; and while such use should not be too strongly urged, it is certain that this meat is far better than *no* meat. Fully one-third of the animals' weight comes under this head,--that is, feet, tail, head, and tongue, lungs, liver, spleen, omentum, pancreas, and heart, together with the intestines. The rich man is hardly likely to choose much of this food, the tongue and sweetbreads being the only dainty bits; but there are wholesome and savory dishes to be made from every part, and the knowledge of their preparation may be of greatest value to a poorer neighbor. Both ox-tails and head make excellent soup. Tripe, the inner lining of the stomach, is, if properly prepared, not only appetizing but pleasant to the eye. Calves' feet make good jelly; and pigs' feet, ears, and head are soused or made into scrapple. Blood-puddings are much eaten by Germans, but we are not likely to adopt their use. Fresh blood has, however, been found of wonderful effect for consumptive patients; and there are certain slaughter-houses in our large cities where every day pale invalids are to be found waiting for the goblet of almost living food from the veins of the still warm animal. Horrible as it seems, the taste for it is soon acquired; and certainly the good results warrant at least the effort to acquire it.

VENISON comes next in the order of meats, but is more like game than any ordinary butchers' meat. It is lean, dark in color, and savory, and if well cooked, very digestible.

POULTRY are of more importance to us than game, and the flesh, containing less nitrogen, is not so stimulating as beef or mutton. Old fowls are often tough and indigestible, and have often, also, a rank flavor like a close hen-house, produced by the absorption into the flesh of the oil intended by nature to lubricate the feathers.

GAME contains even less fat than poultry, and is considered more strengthening. The flesh of rabbits and hares is more like poultry or game than meat, but is too close in fiber to be as digestible. Pigeons and many other birds come under none of the heads given. As a rule, flesh is tender in proportion to the smallness of the animal, and many varieties are eaten for the description of which we have no room here.

FISH forms the only animal food for a large part of the world. It does not possess the satisfying or stimulating properties belonging to flesh, yet the inhabitants of fishing-towns are shown to be unusually strong and healthy. The flesh of some fish is white, and of others red; the red holding much more oil, and being therefore less digestible. In *Salmon*, the most nutritious of all fishes, there are, in a hundred parts, sixteen of nitrogen, six of fat, nearly two of saline matter, and seventy-seven of water. *Eels* contain thirteen parts of fat. *Codfish*, the best-known of all the white fish, vary greatly, according to the time of year in which they are taken, being much more digestible in season than out (i.e., from October to May). *Mackerel* and *Herring* both abound in oil, the latter especially, giving not only relish to the Irishman's potato, but the carbon he needs as heat-food. *Shell-fish* are far less digestible, the *Oyster* being the only exception. The nitrogenous matter in oysters is fourteen parts, of fatty matter one and a half, of saline matter two, and of water eighty. At the time of spawning--from May to September--they lose their good condition, and become unwholesome. *Lobsters* rank next in importance, and are more delicate and finer-flavored than *Crabs*. Both are, however, very difficult of digestion, and should only be used occasionally. The many forms of pickled and smoked fish are convenient, but always less wholesome than fresh.

MILK comes next, and has already been considered in a previous chapter. It is sometimes found to disagree with the stomach, but usually because looked upon as drink and not as real food, the usual supply of which is taken, forgetful of the fact that a glass or two of milk contains as much nourishment as two-thirds of the average meal. The nitrogenous matter in milk is known as caseine, and it is this which principally forms cheese.

CHEESE is commonly considered only a relish, but is in reality one of the most condensed forms of nitrogenous food; and a growing knowledge of its value has at last induced the Army Department to add it to the army ration list. Mattieu Williams, after giving the chemical formulas of caseine and the other elements of cheese, writes; "I have good and sufficient reasons for thus specifying the properties of this constituent of food. I regard it as the most important of all that I have to describe in connection with my subject,--The Science of Cookery. It contains, as I shall presently show, more nutritious material than any other food that is ordinarily obtainable, and its cookery is singularly neglected,--practically an unknown art, especially in this country. We commonly eat it raw, although in its raw state it is peculiarly indigestible, and in the only cooked form familiarly known among us here, that of Welsh rabbit or rare-bit, it is too often rendered still more indigestible, though this need not be the case. Cream-cheese is the richest form, but keeps less well than that of milk. Stilton, the finest English brand, is made partly of cream, partly of milk, and so with various other foreign brands, Gruyere, &c. Parmesan is delicately flavored with fine herbs, and retains this flavor almost unaltered by age. Our American cheeses now rank with the best foreign ones, and will grow more and more in favor as their value is understood, this being their strongly nitrogenous character. A cheese of twenty pounds weight contains as much food as a sheep weighing sixty pounds, as it hangs in the butcher's shop. In Dutch and factory cheeses, where the curd has been precipitated by hydrochloric acid, the food value is less than where rennet is used; but even in this case, it is far beyond meat in actual nutritive power."

BUTTER is a purely carbonaceous or heat-giving food, being the fatty part of the milk, which rises in cream. It is mentioned in the very earliest history, and the craving for it seems to be universal. Abroad it is eaten without salt; but to keep it well, salt is a necessity, and its absence soon allows the development of a rank and unpleasant odor. In other words, butter without it becomes rancid; and if any particle of whey is allowed to remain in it, the same effect takes place.

Perfect butter is golden in color, waxy in consistency, and with a sweetness of odor quite indescribable, yet unmistakable to the trained judge of butter. It possesses the property of absorption of odors in a curious degree; and if shut in a tight closet or a refrigerator with fish, meat, or vegetables of rank or even pronounced smell, exchanges its own delicate aroma for theirs, and reaches us bereft once for all of what is the real charm of perfect butter. For this reason absolute cleanliness and daintiness of vessels containing milk or cream, or used in any way in the manufacture of butter, is one of the first laws of the dairy.

Ghee, the East-Indian form of butter, is simply fresh butter clarified by melting, and is used as a dressing for the meal of rice. Butter, though counted as a pure fat, is in reality made up of at least six fatty principles, there being sixty-eight per cent of margarine and thirty per cent of oleine, the remainder being volatile compounds of fatty acids. In the best specimens of butter there is a slight amount of caseine, not over five per cent at most, though in poor there is much more. It is the only fat which may be constantly eaten without harm to the stomach, though if not perfectly good it becomes an irritant.

The *Drippings* of roasted meat, more especially of beef, rank next in value; and *Lard* comes last on the list, its excessive use being a serious evil. Eaten constantly, as in pastry or the New-England doughnut, it is not only indigestible, but becomes the source of forms of scrofulous disease. It is often a convenient substitute for butter, but if it must be used, would better be in connection with the harmless fat.

Eggs come last; and as a young animal is developed from them, it follows that they contain all that is necessary for animal life, though in the case of the chicken the shell also is used, all the earthy matter being absorbed. In a hundred parts are found fourteen of nitrogen, ten and a half of fatty matter, one and a half of saline matter, and seventy-four of water. Of this water the largest part is contained in the white, which is almost pure albumen, each particle of albumen being enclosed in very thin-walled cells; it is the breaking of these cells and the admission of air that enables one to beat the white of egg to a stiff froth. The fat is accumulated in the yolk, often amounting to thirty per cent. Raw and lightly-boiled eggs are easy of digestion, but hard-boiled ones decidedly not so. An egg loses its freshness within a day or so. The shell is porous; and the always-feeding and destroying oxygen of the air quickly gains admission, causing a gradual decomposition. To preserve them, they must be coated with lard or gum, or packed in either salt or oats, points down. In this way they keep good a long time, and while hardly desirable to eat as boiled eggs, answer for many purposes in cooking.

CHAPTER XI.
THE CHEMISTRY OF VEGETABLE FOOD.

We come now to the vegetable kingdom, the principal points that we are to consider arranging themselves somewhat as follows:-- Farinaceous seeds, Oleaginous seeds, Leguminous seeds, Tubers and roots, Herbaceous articles, Fruits, Saccharine and farinaceous preparations.

Under the first head, that of farinaceous seeds, are included wheat, rye, oats, Indian corn, rice, and a variety of less-known grains, all possessing in greater or less degree the same constituents. It will be impossible to more than touch upon many of them; and wheat must stand as the representative, being the best-known and most widely used of all grains. Each one is made up of nitrogenous compounds, gluten, albumen, caseine, and fibrine, gluten being the most valuable. Starch, dextrine, sugar, and cellulose are also found; fatty matter, which gives the characteristic odor of grain; mineral substances, as phosphates of lime and magnesia, salts of potash and soda, and silica, which we shall shortly mention again.

Hard Wheat, or that grown in hot climates and on fertile soil, has much more nitrogen than that of colder countries. In hard wheat, in a hundred parts, twenty-two will be of nitrogen, fifty-nine starch, ten dextrine, &c, four cellulose, two and a half of fatty matter, and three of mineral, thus giving many of the constituents found in animal food.

This wheat is taken as bread, white or brown, biscuits, crackers, various preparations of the grain whether whole or crushed, and among the Italians as *macaroni*, the most condensed form of cereal food. The best macaroni is made from the red wheat grown along the Mediterranean Sea, a hot summer and warm climate producing a grain, rich, as already mentioned, in nitrogen, and with a smaller proportion of water than farther north. The intense though short summer of our own far North-west seems to bring somewhat the same result, but the outer husk is harder. This husk was for years considered a necessity in all really nutritious bread; and a generation of vegetarians taking their name from Dr. Graham, and known as Grahamites, conceived the idea of living upon the wheaten flour in which husk and kernel were ground together. Now, to stomachs and livers brought to great grief by persistent pie and doughnuts and some other New-England wickednesses, these husks did a certain office of stimulation, stirring up jaded digestions, and really seeming to arrest or modify long-standing dyspepsia. But they did not know what we do, that this outer husk is a layer of pure silica, one of the hardest of known minerals. Boil it six weeks, and it comes out unchanged. Boil it six years, or six centuries, and the result would be the same. You can not stew a grindstone or bring granite to porridge, and the wheat-husk is equally obstinate. So long as enthusiasts ate husk and kernel ground together, little harm was done. But when a more progressive soul declared that in bran alone the true nutriment lay, and a host of would-be healthier people proceeded to eat bran and preach bran, there came a time when eating and preaching both stopped, from sheer want of strength to go on. The enthusiasts were literally starving themselves to death--for starvation is by no means mere deprivation of food: on the contrary, a man may eat heartily to the day of his death, and feel no inconvenience, so far as any protest of the stomach is concerned, yet the verdict of the wise physician would be, "Died of starvation." If the food was unsuitable, and could not be assimilated, this was inevitable. Blood, muscle, nerve--each must have its fitting food; and thus it is easy to see why knowledge is the first condition of healthful living. The moral is: Never rashly experiment in diet till sure what you are about, and, if you can not for yourselves find out the nature of your projected food, call upon some one who can.

Where wheat is ground whole, it includes six and a half parts of heat-producers to one of flesh-formers. The amount of starch varies greatly. Two processes of making flour are now in use,--one the old, or St. Louis process; the other, the "new process," giving Haxall flour. In the former, grindstones were used, which often reached so great a degree of heat as to injure the flour; and repeated siftings gave the various grades. In the new, the outer husk is rejected, and a system of knives is used, which chop the grain to powder, and it is claimed do not heat it. The product is more starchy, and for this reason less desirable. We eat far too much heat-producing food, and any thing which gives us the gluten of the grain is more wholesome, and thus "seconds" is really a more nutritious flour than the finer grades. Try for yourselves a small experiment, and you will learn the nature of flour better than in pages of description.

Take a little flour; wet it with cold water enough to form a dough. Place it on a sieve, and, while working it with one hand, pour a steady stream of water over it with another. Shortly you will find a grayish, tough, elastic lump before you, while in the pan below, when the water is carefully poured off, will be pure wheat-starch, the water itself containing all the sugar, dextrine or gum, and mineral matter. This toughness and elasticity of gluten is an important quality; for in bread-making, were it not for the gluten, the carbonic-acid gas formed by the action of yeast on dough would all escape. But, though it works its way out vigorously enough to swell up each cell, the gluten binds it fast, and enables us to have a panful of light "sponge," where a few hours before was only a third of a pan.

Starch, as you have seen, will not dissolve in the cold water. Dry it, after the water is poured on, and minute grains remain. Look at these grains under a microscope, and each one is cased in a thick skin, which cold water can not dissolve. In boiling water, the skins crack, and the inside swells and becomes gummy. Long boiling is thus an essential for all starchy foods.

Bread proper is simply flour, water, and salt, mixed to a firm dough and baked. Such bread as this, Abram gave to his angelic guests, and at this day the Bedouin Arab bakes it on his heated stone. But bread, as we understand it, is always lightened by the addition of yeast or some form of baking-powder, yeast making the most wholesome as well as most palatable bread. Carbonic-acid gas is the active agent required; and yeast so acts upon the little starch-granules, which the microscope shows as forming the finest flour, that this gas is formed and evenly distributed through the whole dough. The process is slow, and in the action some of the natural sweetness of the flour is lost. In what is known as aerated bread, the gas made was forced directly into the dough, by means of a machine invented for the purpose; and a very scientific and very good bread it is. But it demands an apparatus not to be had save at great expense, and the older fashions give a sufficiently sweet and desirable bread.

Rye and *Indian Corn* form the next best-known varieties of flour in bread-making; but barley and oats are also used, and beans, pease, rice, chestnuts, in short, any farinaceous seed, or legume rich in starch, can fill the office.

Oatmeal may take rank as one of the best and most digestible forms of farinaceous food. Some twenty-eight per cent of the grain is husk, seventy-two being kernel; and this kernel forms a meal containing twelve parts of nitrogenous matter, sixty-three of carbo-hydrates, five and a half of fatty matter, three of saline, and fifteen of water. So little gluten is found, that the flour of oats can not be made into loaves of bread; although, mixed and baked as thin cakes, it forms a large part of the Scotchman's food. It requires thorough cooking, and is then slightly laxative and very easily digested.

Buckwheat is very rich in nitrogenous substances, and as we eat it, in the form of cakes with butter and sirup, so heating a food, as to be only suitable for hard workers in cold weather.

Indian corn has also a very small proportion of gluten, and thus makes a bread which crumbles too readily. But it is the favorite form of bread, not only for South and West in our own country, but in Spanish America, Southern Europe, Germany, and Ireland. It contains a larger amount of fatty matter than any other grain, this making it a necessity in fattening animals. In a hundred parts are eleven of nitrogen, sixty-five of carbo-hydrates, eight of fatty matter, one and a half of saline, and fourteen of water. The large amount of fatty matter makes it difficult to keep much meal on hand, as it grows rancid and breeds worms; and it is best that it should be ground in small quantities as required.

Rice abounds in starch. In a hundred parts are found seven and a half of nitrogen, eighty-eight of starch, one of dextrine, eight-tenths of fatty matter, one of cellulose, and nine-tenths of mineral matter. Taken alone it can not be called a nutritive food; but eaten with butter or milk and eggs, or as by the East Indians in curry, it holds an important place.

We come now to OLEAGINOUS SEEDS; nuts, the cocoanut, almonds, &c, coming under this head. While they are rich in oil, this very fact makes them indigestible, and they should be eaten sparingly.

Olive-oil must find mention here. No fat of either the animal or vegetable kingdom surpasses this in delicacy and purity. Palm-oil fills its place with the Asiatics in part; but the olive has no peer in this respect, and we lose greatly in our general distaste for this form of food. The liking for it should be encouraged as decidedly as the liking for butter. It is less heating, more soothing to the tissues, and from childhood to old age its liberal use prevents many forms of disease, as well as equalizes digestion in general.

LEGUMINOUS SEEDS are of more importance, embracing as they do the whole tribe of beans, pease, and lentils. Twice as much nitrogen is found in beans as in wheat; and they rank so near to animal food, that by the addition of a little fat they practically can take its place. Bacon and beans have thus been associated for centuries, and New England owes to Assyria the model for the present Boston bean-pot. In the best table-bean, either Lima or the butter-bean, will be found in a hundred parts, thirty of nitrogen, fifty-six of starch, one and a half of cellulose, two of fatty matter, three and a half of saline, and eight and a half of water. The proportion of nitrogen is less in pease, but about the same in lentils. The chestnut also comes under this head, and is largely eaten in Spain and Italy, either boiled, or dried and ground into flour.

TUBERS and ROOTS follow, and of these the *Potato* leads the van. Low as you may have noticed their standing on the food-table to be, they are the most economical and valuable of foods, combining as well with others, and as little cloying to the palate, as bread itself. Each pound of potatoes contains seven hundred and seventy grains of carbon, and twenty-four grains of nitrogen; each pound of wheat-flour, two thousand grains of carbon, and one hundred and twenty of nitrogen. But the average cost of the pound of potatoes is but one cent; that of the pound of wheat, four. It is obtainable at all seasons, and thus invaluable as a permanent store, though best in the winter. Spring, the germinating season, diminishes its nutritive value. New potatoes are less nutritious than older ones, and in cooking, if slightly underdone, are said to satisfy the appetite better; this being the reason why the laboring classes prefer them, as they say, "with a bone in them."

In a hundred parts are found but two of nitrogen, eighteen of starch, three of sugar, two-tenths of fat, seven-tenths of saline matter, and seventy-five parts of water. The *Sweet-potato*, *Yam*, and *Artichoke* are all of the same character. Other *Tubers*, the *Turnip*, *Beet*, *Carrot*, and *Parsnip*, are in ordinary use. The turnip is nine-tenths water, but possesses some valuable qualities. The beet, though also largely water, has also a good deal of sugar, and is excellent food. Carrots and parsnips are much alike in composition. Carrots are generally rejected as food, but properly cooked are very appetizing, their greatest use, however, being in soups and stews.

HERBACEOUS ARTICLES follow; and, though we are not accustomed to consider *Cabbage* as an herb, it began existence as cole-wort, a shrub or herb on the south coast of England. Cultivation has developed it into a firm round head; and as a vegetable, abounding as it does in nitrogen, it ranks next to beans as a food. *Cauliflower* is a very delicate and highly prized form of cabbage, but cabbage itself can be so cooked as to strongly resemble it.

Onions are next in value, being much milder and sweeter when grown in a warm climate, but used chiefly as a flavoring. *Lettuce* and *Celery* are especially valuable; the former for salads, the latter to be eaten without dressing though it is excellent cooked. *Tomatoes* are really a fruit, though eaten as a vegetable, and are of especial value as a cooling food. Egg-plant, cucumbers, &c., all demand space; and so with edible fungi, mushrooms, and truffles, the latter the property of the epicure, and really not so desirable as that fact would indicate.

FRUITS are last in order; and among these stands first of all the apple. While in actual analysis fruits have less nutritive value than vegetables, their acids and salts give to them the power of counteracting the unhealthy states brought about by the long use of dried or salted provisions. They are a corrective also of the many evils arising from profuse meat-eating, the citric acid of lemons and grape-fruit being an antidote to rheumatic and gouty difficulties. Cold storage now enables one to command grapes long after their actual season has ended, and they are invaluable food. The brain-worker is learning to depend more and more on fruit in all its forms; and apples lead the list, containing more solid nutriment than any other form. While considered less digestible raw than baked, they are still one of the most attractive, life-giving forms of food, and if eaten daily would prove a standard antidote to patent medicine. The list of fruits is too long for mention here; but all have their specific uses, and are necessary to perfect health.

SUGAR and HONEY follow in the stores of the vegetable kingdom. Cane-sugar and glucose, or grape-sugar, are the two recognized varieties, though the making of beet-sugar has become an industry here as well as in France. Grape-sugar requires to be used in five times the amount of cane, to secure the same degree of sweetness. Honey also is a food,--a concentrated solution of sugar, mixed with odorous, gummy, and waxy matters. It possesses much the same food value as sugar, and is easily digested.

With the various FARINACEOUS PREPARATIONS, *Sago*, *Tapioca*, *Arrow-root*, &c, the vegetable dietary ends. All are light, digestible foods, principally starchy in character, but with little nutriment unless united with milk or eggs. Their chief use is in the sick-room.

Restricted as comment must be, each topic introduced will well reward study; and the story of each of these varied ingredients in cookery, if well learned, will give one an unsuspected range of thought, and a new sense of the wealth that may be hidden in very common things.

CHAPTER XII.
CONDIMENTS AND BEVERAGES.

Condiments are simply seasoning or flavoring agents, and, though hardly coming under the head of food, yet have an important part to play. As food by their use is rendered more tempting, a larger amount is consumed, and thus a delicate or uncertain appetite is often aided. In some cases they have the power of correcting the injurious character of some foods.

Salt stands foremost. Vinegar, lemon-juice, and pickles owe their value to acidity; while mustard, pepper black and red, ginger, curry-powder, and horse-radish all depend chiefly upon pungency. Under the head of aromatic condiments are ranged cinnamon, nutmegs, cloves, allspice, mint, thyme, fennel, sage, parsley, vanilla, leeks, onions, shallots, garlic, and others, all of them entering into the composition of various sauces in general use.

Salt is the one thing indispensable. The old Dutch law condemned criminals to a diet of unsalted food, the effects being said to be those of the severest physical torture. Years ago an experiment tried near Paris demonstrated the necessity of its use. A number of cattle were fed without the ration of salt; an equal number received it regularly. At the end of a specified time, the unsalted animals were found rough of coat, the hair falling off in spots, the eyes wild, and the flesh hardly half the amount of those naturally fed.

A class of extreme Grahamites in this country decry the use of salt, as well as of any form of animal food; and I may add that the expression of their thought in both written and spoken speech is as savorless as their diet.

Salt exists, as we have already found, in the blood: the craving for it is a universal instinct, even buffaloes making long journeys across the plains to the salt-licks; and its use not only gives character to insipid food, but increases the flow of the gastric juice.

Black pepper, if used profusely as is often done in American cooking, becomes an irritant, and produces indigestion. Red pepper, or cayenne, on the contrary, is a useful stimulant at times; but, as with mustard, any over-use irritates the lining of the stomach.

So with spices and sweet herbs. There should be only such use of them as will flavor well, delicately, and almost imperceptibly. No one flavor should predominate, and only a sense of general savoriness rule. Extracts, as of vanilla, lemon, bitter almond, &c., should be used with the greatest care, and if possible always be added to an article after it cools, as the heat wastes the strength.

BEVERAGES.

Tea and coffee are the most universal drinks, after water. The flavor of both is due to a principle, *theine* in tea, *caffeine* in coffee, in which both the good and the ill effects of these drinks are bound up. It is hardly necessary the principles should have different names, as they have been found by chemists to be identical; the essential spirit of cocoa and chocolate,-- *theobromine*,--though not identical, having many of the same properties.

Tea is valuable chiefly for its warming and comforting qualities. Taken in moderation, it acts partly as a sedative, partly as a stimulant, arresting the destruction of tissue, and seeming to invigorate the whole nervous system. The water in it, even if impure, is made wholesome by boiling, and the milk and sugar give a certain amount of real nourishment. Nervous headaches are often cured by it, and it has, like coffee, been used as an antidote in opium-poisoning.

Pass beyond the point of moderation, and it becomes an irritant, precisely in the same way that an overdose of morphine will, instead of putting to sleep, for just so much longer time prevent any sleep at all. The woman who can not eat, and who braces her nerves with a cup of green tea,--the most powerful form of the herb,--is doing a deeper wrong than she may be able to believe. The immediate effect is delightful. Lightness, exhilaration, and sense of energy are all there; but the re-action comes surely, and only a stronger dose next time accomplishes the end desired. Nervous headaches, hysteria in its thousand forms, palpitations, and the long train of nervous symptoms, own inordinate tea and coffee drinking as their parent. Taken in reasonable amounts, tea can not be said to be hurtful; and the medium qualities, carefully prepared, often make a more wholesome tea than that of the highest price, the harmful properties being strongest in the best. If the water is soft, it should be used as soon as boiled, boiling causing all the gases which give flavor to water to escape. In hard water, boiling softens it. In all cases the water must be fresh, and poured boiling upon the proper portion of tea,--the teapot having first been well scalded with boiling water. Never boil any tea but English-breakfast tea; for all others, simple steeping gives the drink in perfection.

A disregard of these rules gives one the rank, black, unpleasant infusion too often offered as tea; while, if boiled in tin, it becomes a species of slow poison,--the tannic acid in the tea acting upon the metal, and producing a chemical compound whose character it is hard to determine. Various other plants possess the essential principle of tea, and are used as such; as in Paraguay, where the Brazilian holly is dried, and makes a tea very exhilarating in quality, but much more astringent.

The use of *Coffee* dates back even farther than that of tea. Of the many varieties, Mocha and Java are finest in flavor, and a mixture of one-third Mocha with two-thirds Java gives the drink at its best. As in tea, there are three chief constituents: (1) A volatile oil, giving the aroma it possesses, but less in amount than that in tea. (2) Astringent matter,--a modification of tannin, but also less than in tea. (3) Caffeine, now found identical with theine, but varying in amount in different varieties of coffee,--being in some three or four per cent, in others less.

The most valuable property of coffee is its power of relieving the sensation of hunger and fatigue. To the soldier on active service, nothing can take its place; and in our own army it became the custom often, not only to drink the infusion, but, if on a hard march, to eat the grounds also. In all cases it diminishes the waste of tissue. In hot weather it is too heating and stimulating, acting powerfully upon the liver, and, by producing over-activity of that organ, bringing about a general disturbance.

So many adulterations are found in ground coffee, that it is safest for the real coffee-lover to buy the bean whole. Roasting is usually more perfectly done at the grocers', in their rotary roasters, which give every grain its turn; but, by care and constant stirring, it can be accomplished at home. Too much boiling dissipates the delicious aroma we all know; and the best methods are considered to be those which allow no boiling, after boiling water has been poured upon it, but merely a standing, to infuse and settle. The old fashion, however, of mixing with an egg, and boiling a few minutes, makes a coffee hardly inferior in flavor. In fact, the methods are many, but results, under given conditions, much the same; and we may choose urn, or old-fashioned tin pot, or a French biggin, with the certainty that good coffee, well roasted, boiling water, and good judgment as to time, will give always a delicious drink. Make a note of the fact that long boiling sets free tannic acid, powerful enough to literally tan the coats of the stomach, and bring on incurable dyspepsia. Often coffee without milk can be taken, where, with milk, it proves harmful; but, in all cases, moderation must rule. Taken too strong, palpitation of the heart, vertigo, and fainting are the usual consequences.

Cocoa, or, literally, cacao, from the cacao-tree, comes in the form of a thick seed, twenty or thirty of which make up the contents of a gourd-like fruit, the spaces between being filled with a somewhat acid pulp. The seeds, when freed from this pulp by various processes, are first dried in the sun, and then roasted; and from these roasted seeds come various forms of cocoa.

Cocoa-shells are the outer husk, and by long boiling yield a pleasant and rather nutritious drink. Cocoa itself is the nut ground to powder, and sometimes mixed with sugar, the husk being sometimes ground with it.

In *Chocolate*--a preparation of cocoa--the cocoa is carefully dried and roasted, and then ground to a smooth paste, the nuts being placed on a hot iron plate, and so keeping the oily matter to aid in forming a paste. Sugar and flavorings, as vanilla, are often added, and the whole pressed into cakes. The whole substance of the nut being used, it is exceedingly nutritious, and made more so by the milk and sugar added. Eaten with bread it forms not only a nourishing but a hearty meal; and so condensed is its form, that a small cake carried in traveling, and eaten with a cracker or two, will give temporarily the effect of a full meal.

In a hundred parts of chocolate are found forty-eight of fatty matter or cocoa-butter, twenty-one of nitrogenous matter, four of theobromine, eleven of starch, three of cellulose, three of mineral matter, and ten of water; there being also traces of coloring matter, aromatic essence, and sugar. Twice as much nitrogenous, and twenty-five times as much fatty matter as wheaten flour, make it a valuable food, though the excess of fat will make it disagree with a very delicate stomach.

Alcohol is last upon our list, and scientific men are still uncertain whether or not it can in any degree be considered as a food; but we have no room for the various arguments for and against. You all know, in part at least, the effects of intemperance; and even the moderate daily drinker suffers from clouded mind, irritable nerves, and ruined digestion.

This is not meant as an argument for total abstinence; but there are cases where such abstinence is the only rule. In an inherited tendency to drink, there is no other safe road; but to the man or woman who lives by law, and whose body is in the best condition, wine in its many forms is a permissible *occasional* luxury, and so with beer and cider and the wide range of domestic drinks. In old age its use is almost essential, but always in moderation, individual temperament modifying every rule, and making the best knowledge an imperative need. A little alcoholic drink increases a delicate appetite: a great deal diminishes or takes it away entirely, and also hinders and in many cases stops digestion altogether. In its constant overuse the membranes of the stomach are gradually destroyed, and every organ in the body suffers. In ales and beers there is not only alcohol, but much nitrogenous and sugary matter, very fattening in its nature. A light beer, well flavored with hops, is an aid to digestion, but taken in excess produces biliousness. The long list of alcoholic products it is not necessary to give, nor is it possible to enter into much detail regarding alcohol itself; but there are one or two points so important that they can not be passed by.

You will recall in a preceding chapter the description of the circulation of the blood, and of its first passage through veins and arteries for cleansing, before a second round could make it food for the whole complex nervous system. Alcohol taken in excess, it has been proved in countless experiments by scientific men, possesses the power of coagulating the blood. The little corpuscles adhere in masses, and cannot force themselves through the smaller vessels, and circulation is at once hindered. This, however, is the secondary stage. At first, as many of you have had occasion to notice, the face flushes, the eyes grow brighter, and thought and word both come more freely. The heart beats far more rapidly, and the speed increases in proportion to the amount of alcohol absorbed. The average number of beats of the heart, allowing for its slower action during sleep, is 100,000 beats per day. Under a small supply of alcohol this rose to 127,000, and in actual intoxication to 131,000.

The flush upon the cheek is only a token of the same fact within; every organ is congested. The brain has been examined under such circumstances, and "looked as if injected with vermilion ... the membrane covering both brains resembling a delicate web of coagulated red blood, so tensely were its fine vessels engorged."

At a later stage the muscular power is paralyzed, the rule of mind over body suspended, and a heavy, brutal sleep comes, long or short according to the amount taken. This is the extreme of alcoholism, and death the only ending to it, as a habitual condition. Alcohol seems a necessary evil; for that its occasional beneficence can modify or neutralize the long list of woe and crime and brutality following in its train, is more than doubtful.

"Whatever good can come from alcohol, or whatever evil, is all included in that primary physiological and luxurious action of the agent upon the nervous supply of the circulation.... If it be really a luxury for the heart to be lifted up by alcohol, for the blood to course more swiftly through the brain, for the thoughts to flow more vehemently, for words to come more fluently, for emotions to rise ecstatically, and for life to rush on beyond the pace set by nature; then those who enjoy the luxury must enjoy it--with the consequences."

And now, at the end of our talks together, friends, there is yet another word. Much must remain unsaid in these narrow limits; but they are wide enough, I hope, to have given the key by which you may find easy entrance to the mysteries we all may know, indeed must, if our lives are truly lived. If through intemperance, in meat or drink, in feeling or thought, you lessen bodily or mental power, you alone are accountable, whether ignorant or not. Only in a never-failing self-control can safety ever be. Temperance is the foundation of high living; and here is its definition, by one whose own life holds it day by day:--

"Temperance is personal cleanliness; is modesty; is quietness; is reverence for one's elders and betters; is deference to one's mother and sisters; is gentleness; is courage; is the withholding from all which leads to excess in daily living; is the eating and drinking only of that which will insure the best body which the best soul is to inhabit: nay, temperance is all these, and more."

PART II.
STOCK AND SEASONING.

The preparation called STOCK is for some inscrutable reason a stumbling-block to average cooks, and even by experienced housekeepers is often looked upon as troublesome and expensive. Where large amounts of fresh meat are used in its preparation, the latter adjective might be appropriate; but stock in reality is the only mode by which every scrap of bone or meat, whether cooked or uncooked, can be made to yield the last particle of nourishment contained in it. Properly prepared and strained into a stone jar, it will keep a week, and is as useful in the making of hashes and gravies as in soup itself.

The first essential is a tightly-covered kettle, either tinned iron or porcelain-lined, holding not less than two gallons; three being a preferable size. Whether cooked or uncooked meat is used, it should be cut into small bits, and all bones broken or sawn into short pieces, that the marrow may be easily extracted.

To every pound of meat and bone allow one quart of cold water, one even teaspoon of salt, and half a saltspoon of pepper. Let the meat stand till the water is slightly colored with its juice; then put upon the fire, and let it come slowly to a boil, skimming off every particle of scum as it rises. The least neglect of this point will give a broth in which bits of dark slime float about, unpleasant to sight and taste. A cup of cold water, thrown in as the kettle boils, will make the scum rise more freely. Let it boil steadily, but very slowly, allowing an hour to each pound of meat. The water will boil away, leaving, at the end of the time specified, not more than half or one-third the original amount. In winter this will become a firm jelly, which can be used by simply melting it, thus obtaining a strong, clear broth; or can be diluted with an equal quantity of water, and vegetables added for a vegetable soup.

The meat used in stock, if boiled the full length of time given, has parted with all its juices, and is therefore useless as food. If wanted for hashes or croquettes, the portion needed should be taken out as soon as tender, and a pint of the stock with it, to use as gravy. Strain, when done, into a stone pot or crock kept for the purpose, and, when cold, remove the cake of fat which will rise to the top. This fat, melted and strained, serves for many purposes better than lard. If the stock is to be kept several days, leave the fat on till ready to use it.

Fresh and cooked meat may be used together, and all remains of poultry or game, and trimmings of chops and steaks, may be added, mutton being the only meat which can not as well be used in combination; though even this, by trimming off all the fat, may also be added. If it is intended to keep the stock for some days, no vegetables should be added, as vegetable juices ferment very easily. For clear soups they must be cooked with the meat; and directions will be given under that head for amounts and seasonings.

The secret of a savory soup lies in many flavors, none of which are allowed to predominate; and, minutely as rules for such flavoring may be given, only careful and frequent *tasting* will insure success. Every vegetable, spice, and sweet herb, curry-powders, catchups, sauces, dried or fresh lemon-peel, can be used; and the simple stock, by the addition of these various ingredients, becomes the myriad number of soups to be found in the pages of great cooking manuals like Gouffee's or Francatelli's.

Brown soups are made by frying the meat or game used in them till thoroughly brown on all sides, and using dark spices or sauces in their seasoning.

White soups are made with light meats, and often with the addition of milk or cream.

Purees are merely thick soups strained carefully before serving, and made usually of some vegetable which thickens in boiling, as beans, pease, &c, though there are several forms of fish *purees* in which the foundation is thickened milk, to which the fish is added, and the whole then rubbed through a common sieve, if a regular puree-sieve is not to be had.

Browned flour is often used for coloring, but does not thicken a soup, as, in browning it, the starchy portion has been destroyed; and it will not therefore mix, but settles at the bottom. Burned sugar or caramel makes a better coloring, and also adds flavor. With clear soups grated cheese is often served, either Parmesan or any rich cheese being used. Onions give a better flavor if they are fried in a little butter or dripping before using, and many professional cooks fry all soup vegetables lightly. Cabbage and potatoes should be parboiled in a separate water before adding to a soup. In using wine or catchup, add only at the last moment, as boiling dissipates the flavor. Unless a thick vegetable soup is desired, always strain into the tureen. Rice, sago, macaroni, or any cereal may be used as thickening; the amounts required being found under the different headings. Careful skimming, long boiling, and as careful removing of fat, will secure a broth especially desirable as a food for children and the old, but almost equally so for any age; while many fragments, otherwise entirely useless, discover themselves as savory and nutritious parts of the day's supply of food.

*   *   *   *   *

SOUPS.
BEEP SOUP WITH VEGETABLES.
For this very excellent soup take two quarts of stock prepared beforehand, as already directed. If the stock is a jelly, as will usually be the case in winter, an amount sufficient to fill a quart-measure can be diluted with a pint of water, and will then be rich enough. Add to this one small carrot, a turnip, a small parsnip, and two onions, all chopped fine; a cupful of chopped cabbage; two tablespoonfuls of barley or rice; and either six fresh tomatoes sliced, or a small can of sealed ones. Boil gently at least one hour; then add one saltspoonful each of pepper, curry-powder, and clove. If the stock has been salted properly, no more will be needed; but tasting is essential to secure just the right flavors. Boil a few minutes longer, and serve without straining.

This is an especially savory and hearty soup, and the combinations of vegetables may be varied indefinitely. A cup of chopped celery is an exceedingly nice addition, or, if this is not to be had, a teaspoonful of celery salt, or a saltspoonful of celery-seed. A lemon may also be sliced thin, and added at the last. Where tomatoes are used, a little sugar is always an improvement; in this case an even tablespoonful being sufficient. If a thicker broth is desired, one heaped tablespoonful of corn-starch or flour may be first dissolved in a little cold water; then a cup of the hot broth gradually mixed with it, and the whole added to the soup and boiled for five minutes.

CLEAR OR AMBER SOUP.

This soup needs careful attention. It may be made of beef alone, but, if desired very rich for a special dinner, requires the addition of either a chicken or a knuckle of veal. Allow, then, for the best soup, a soup-bone,--the shin of beef being most desirable,--weighing from two to three pounds; a chicken; a slice of fat ham; two onions, each stuck with three cloves; one small carrot and parsnip; one stalk of celery; one tablespoonful of salt; half a saltspoonful of pepper; and four quarts of cold water.

Cut all the meat from the beef bone in small pieces; slice the onions; fry the ham (or, if preferred, a thick slice of salt pork weighing not less than two ounces); fry the onions a bright brown in this fat; add the pieces of beef, and brown them also. Now put all the materials, bones included, into the soup-kettle; add the cold water, and let it very gradually come to a boil. Skim with the utmost care, and then boil slowly and steadily for not less than five hours, six or even seven being preferable. Strain, and set in a cold place. Next day remove the fat, and put the soup on the fire one hour before it will be wanted. Break the white and shell of an egg into a bowl; add a spoonful of cold water, and beat a moment; add a little of the hot soup, that the white may mix more thoroughly with the soup, and then pour it into the kettle. Let all boil slowly for ten minutes; then strain, either through a jelly-bag, or through a thick cloth laid in a sieve or colander. Do not stir, as this would cloud the soup; and, if not clear and sparkling, strain again. Return to the fire, and heat to boiling-point, putting a lemon cut in thin slices, and, if liked, a glass of sherry, into the tureen before serving. A poached egg, or a boiled egg from which the shell has been peeled, is often served with each plate of this soup, which must be clear to deserve its name.

WHITE SOUP.

Veal or chicken must be used for this soup; and the stock must always be prepared the day beforehand, having been flavored with two chopped onions and a cup of cut celery, or celery-seed and other seasoning, in the proportions already given. On the day it is to be used, heat a quart of milk; stir one tablespoonful of butter to a cream; add a heaping tablespoonful of flour or corn-starch, a saltspoonful of mace, and the same amount of white pepper. Stir into the boiling milk, and add to the soup. Let all boil a moment, and then pour into the tureen. Three eggs, beaten very light and stirred into the hot milk without boiling, make a still richer soup. The bones of cold roast chicken or turkey may be used in this way; and the broth of any meat, if perfectly clear, can serve as foundation, though veal or chicken is most delicate.

MOCK TURTLE SOUP.

A calf's head is usually taken for this soup; but a set of calf's feet and a pound of lean veal answer equally well. In either case, boil the meat in four quarts of water for five hours, reducing the amount to two quarts, and treating as stock for clear soup.

Remove all fat, and put on the fire next day, half an hour before dinner, seasoning it with a saltspoonful each of mace, powdered thyme, or sweet marjoram and clove. Melt a piece of butter the size of a walnut in a small saucepan; add a heaping tablespoonful of flour, and stir both till a bright brown. Add soup till a smooth thickening is made, and pour it into the soup-kettle. Cut about half a pound of the cold meat into small square pieces,-- *dice* they are called,--and put into the tureen. Make forcemeat balls by chopping a large cup of meat very fine; season with a saltspoonful each of pepper and thyme; mix in the yolk of a raw egg; make into little balls the size of a hickory-nut, and fry brown in a little butter. Squeeze the juice of half a lemon into the tureen with (or without) a wine-glass of sherry. Pour in the soup, and serve. If egg-balls are desired, make them of the yolks of two hard-boiled eggs rubbed fine. Add the yolk of a raw egg, a tablespoonful of melted butter, a saltspoon of salt and half a one of pepper, and flour enough to make a dough which can be easily handled. Roll out; cut into little dice, and make each into a ball by rolling between the palms of the hands. Boil five minutes in the soup.

MUTTON BROTH.

Prepare and boil as directed for stock. The broth from a boiled leg of mutton can be used, or any cheap pieces and trimmings from chops. One small turnip and an onion will give flavoring enough. On the day it is to be used, add to two quarts of broth half a cup of rice, and boil for half an hour.

CHICKEN BROTH.

Even an old fowl which is unusable in any other way makes excellent broth. Prepare as in any stock, and, when used, add a tablespoonful of rice to each quart of broth, boiling till tender. A white soup will be found the most savory mode of preparation, the plain broth with rice being best for children and invalids.

TOMATO SOUP WITHOUT MEAT.

Materials for this soup are: one large can, or twelve fresh tomatoes; one quart of boiling water; two onions; a small carrot; half a small turnip; two or three sprigs of parsley, or a stalk of celery,--all cut fine, and boiled one hour. As the water boils away, add more to it, so that the quantity may remain the same. Season with one even tablespoonful each of salt and sugar, and half a teaspoonful of pepper. Cream a tablespoonful of butter with two heaping ones of flour, and add hot soup till it will pour easily. Pour into the soup; boil all together for five minutes; then strain through a sieve, and serve with toasted crackers or bread.

HASTY TOMATO SOUP.

Simple but excellent. One large can of tomatoes and one pint of water brought to the boiling-point, and rubbed through a sieve. Return to the fire. Add half a tea-spoonful of soda, and stir till it stops foaming. Season with one even tablespoonful of salt, two of sugar, one saltspoonful of cayenne. Thicken with two heaping table-spoonfuls of flour, and one of butter rubbed to a cream, with hot soup added till it pours easily. Boil a pint of milk separately, and, when ready to use, pour into the boiling tomato, and serve at once, as standing long makes the milk liable to curdle.

OYSTER SOUP.

Two quarts of perfectly fresh oysters. Strain off the juice, and add an equal amount of water, or, if they are solid, add one pint of water, and then strain and boil. Skim carefully. Add to one quart of milk one tablespoonful of salt, and half a teaspoonful of pepper, and, if thickening is liked, use same proportions as in hasty tomato soup, and set to boil. When the milk boils, put in the oysters. The moment the edges curl a little, which will be when they have boiled one minute, they are done, and should be served at once. Longer boiling toughens and spoils them. This rule may be used also for stewed oysters, omitting the thickening; or they may be put simply into the boiling juice, with the same proportions of butter, salt, and pepper, and cooked the same length of time.

CLAM SOUP.

Fifty clams (hard or soft), boiled in a quart of water one hour. Take out, and chop fine. Add one quart of milk, half a teaspoonful of pepper, and one teaspoonful of salt. It will be necessary to taste, however, as some clams are salter than others. Rub one tablespoonful of butter to a cream with two of flour, and use as thickening. Add the chopped clams, and boil five minutes. If the clams are disliked, simply strain through a sieve, or cut off the hard part and use the soft only.

PUREE, OF FISH, VEGETABLES, ETC.

One pound of fresh boiled salmon, or one small can of the sealed.

Pick out all bone and skin, and, if the canned is used, pour off every drop of oil. Shred it as fine as possible. Boil one quart of milk, seasoning with one teaspoonful of salt, and one saltspoonful each of mace and white pepper, increasing the amount slightly if more is liked. Thicken with two tablespoonfuls of flour, and one of butter rubbed to a cream, with a cup of boiling water; add thickening and salmon, and boil two minutes. Strain into the tureen through a puree sieve, rubbing as much as possible of the salmon through with a potato-masher, and *serve very hot*. All that will not go through can be mixed with an equal amount of cracker-crumbs or mashed potato, made into small cakes or rolls, and fried in a little butter for breakfast, or treated as croquettes, and served at dinner.

This thickened milk is the foundation for many forms of fish and vegetable purees. A pint of green pease, boiled, mashed, and added; or asparagus or spinach in the same proportions can be used. *Lobster* makes a puree as delicious as that of salmon. Dry the "coral" in the oven; pound it fine, and add to the milk before straining, thus giving a clear pink color. Cut all the meat and green fat into dice, and put into the tureen, pouring the hot milk upon it. Boiled *cod* or *halibut* can be used; but nothing is so nice as the salmon, either fresh or canned. For a *Puree of Celery* boil one pint of cut celery in water till tender; then add to boiling milk, and rub through the sieve. For *Potato Puree* use six large or ten medium sized potatoes, boiled and mashed fine; then stirred into the milk, and strained; a large tablespoonful of chopped parsley being put in the tureen. For a *Green-Corn Soup* use the milk without straining; adding a can of corn, or the corn cut from six ears of fresh boiled corn, and an even tablespoonful of sugar, and boiling ten minutes. *Salsify* can also be used, the combinations being numberless, and one's own taste a safe guide in making new ones.

TURTLE-BEAN SOUP.

Wash and soak over-night, in cold water, one pint of the black or turtle beans. In the morning put on the fire in three quarts of cold water, which, as it boils away, must be added to, to preserve the original quantity. Add quarter of a pound of salt pork and half a pound of lean beef; one carrot and two onions cut fine; one table-spoonful of salt; one saltspoonful of cayenne. Cover closely, and boil four or five hours. Rub through a colander, having first put in the tureen three hard-boiled eggs cut in slices, one lemon sliced thin, and half a glass of wine. This soup is often served with small sausages which have been boiled in it for ten minutes, and then skinned, and used either whole or cut in bits. Cold baked beans can also be used, in which case the meat, eggs, and wine are omitted.

PEA SOUP.

One quart of dried pease, washed and soaked over-night; split pease are best. In the morning put them on the fire with six quarts of cold water; half a pound of salt pork; one even tablespoonful of salt; one saltspoonful of cayenne; and one teaspoonful of celery-seed. Fry till a bright brown three onions cut small, and add to the pease; cover closely, and boil four or five hours. Strain through a colander, and, if not perfectly smooth, return to fire, and add a thickening made of one heaping teaspoonful of flour and an even one of butter, stirred together with a little hot water and boiled five minutes. Beans can be used in precisely the same way; and both bean and pea soups are nicer served with *croutons*, or a thick slice of bread cut in dice, and fried brown and crisp, or simply browned in the oven, and put into the tureen at the moment of serving.

ONION SOUP.

Take three large onions, slice them very thin, and then fry to a bright brown in a large spoonful of either butter or stock-fat, the latter answering equally well. When brown, add half a teacupful of flour, and stir constantly until red. Then pour in slowly one pint of boiling water, stirring steadily till it is all in. Boil and mash fine four large potatoes, and stir into one quart of boiling milk, taking care that there are no lumps. Add this to the fried onions, with one teaspoonful of salt and half a teaspoonful of white pepper. Let all boil for five minutes, and then serve with toasted or fried bread. Simple as this seems, it is one of the best of the vegetable soups, though it is made richer by the use of stock instead of water.

BROWNED FLOUR FOR SOUPS.

Put a pint of sifted flour into a perfectly clean frying-pan, and stir and turn constantly as it darkens, till the whole is an even dark brown. If scorched at all, it is ruined, and should not be used for any purpose. As a coloring for soups and gravies it is by no means as good as caramel or burned sugar.

CARAMEL.

Half a pound of brown sugar; one tablespoonful of water. Put into a frying-pan, and stir steadily over the fire till it becomes a deep dark brown in color. Then add one cup of boiling water and one teaspoonful of salt. Boil a minute longer, bottle, and keep corked. One tablespoonful will color a clear soup, and it can be used for many jellies, gravies, and sauces.

*   *   *   *   *

FISH.

The most essential point in choosing fish is their *freshness*, and this is determined as follows: if the gills are red, the eyes prominent and full, and the whole fish stiff, they are good; but if the eyes are sunken, the gills pale, and the fish flabby, they are stale and unwholesome, and, though often eaten in this condition, lack all the fine flavor of a freshly-caught fish.

The fish being chosen, the greatest care is necessary in cleaning. If this is properly done, one washing will be sufficient: the custom of allowing fresh fish to lie in water after cleaning, destroys much of their flavor.

Fresh-water fish, especially the cat-fish, have often a muddy taste and smell. To get rid of this, soak in water strongly salted; say, a cupful of salt to a gallon of water, letting it heat gradually in this, and boiling it for one minute; then drying it thoroughly before cooking.

All fish for boiling should be put into cold water, with the exception of salmon, which loses its color unless put into boiling water. A tablespoonful each of salt and vinegar to every two quarts of water improves the flavor of all boiled fish, and also makes the flesh firmer. Allow ten minutes to the pound after the fish begins to boil, and test with a knitting-needle or sharp skewer. If it runs in easily, the fish can be taken off. If a fish-kettle with strainer is used, the fish can be lifted out without danger of breaking. If not, it should be thoroughly dredged with flour, and served in a cloth kept for the purpose. In all cases drain it perfectly, and send to table on a folded napkin laid upon the platter.

In frying, fish should, like all fried articles, be *immersed* in the hot lard or drippings. Small fish can be fried whole; larger ones boned, and cut in small pieces. If they are egged and crumbed, the *egg* will form a covering, hardening at once, and absolutely impervious to fat.

Pan-fish, as they are called,--flounders and small fish generally,--can also be fried by rolling in Indian meal or flour, and browning in the fat of salt pork.

Baking and broiling preserve the flavor most thoroughly.

Cold boiled fish can always be used, either by spicing as in the rule to be given, or by warming again in a little butter and water. Cold fried or broiled fish, can be put in a pan, and set in the oven till hot, this requiring not over ten minutes; a longer time giving a strong, oily taste, which spoils it. Plain boiled or mashed potatoes are always served with fish where used as a dinner-course. If fish is boiled whole, do not cut off either tail or head. The tail can be skewered in the mouth if liked; or a large fish may be boiled in the shape of the letter S by threading a trussing-needle, fastening a string around the head, then passing the needle through the middle of the body, drawing the string tight and fastening it around the tail.

BAKED FISH.

Bass, fresh shad, blue-fish, pickerel, &c., can be cooked in this way:--

See that the fish has been properly cleaned. Wash in salted water, and wipe dry. For stuffing for a fish weighing from four to six pounds, take four large crackers, or four ounces of bread-crumbs; quarter of a pound of salt pork; one teaspoonful of salt, and half a teaspoonful of pepper; a tablespoonful of chopped parsley, or a teaspoonful of thyme. Chop half the pork fine, and mix with the crumbs and seasoning, using half a cup of hot water to mix them, or, if preferred, a beaten egg. Put this dressing into the body of the fish, which is then to be fastened together with a skewer. Cut the remainder of the pork in narrow strips, and lay it in gashes cut across the back of the fish about two inches apart. Dredge thickly with flour, using about two tablespoonfuls. Put a tin baking-sheet in the bottom of a pan, as without it the fish can not be easily taken up. Lay the fish on this; pour a cup of boiling water into the pan, and bake in a hot oven for one hour, basting it very often that the skin may not crack; and, at the end of half an hour, dredging again with flour, repeating this every ten minutes till the fish is done. If the water dries away, add enough to preserve the original quantity. When the fish is done, slide it carefully from the tin sheet on to a hot platter. Set the baking-pan on top of the stove. Mix a teaspoonful of flour with quarter of a cup of cold water, and stir into the boiling gravy. A tablespoonful of walnut or mushroom catchup, or of Worcestershire sauce, may be added if liked. *Serve very hot.*

Before sending a baked fish to table, take out the skewer. When done, it should have a handsome brown crust. If pork is disliked, it may be omitted altogether, and a tablespoonful of butter substituted in the stuffing. Basting should be done as often as once in ten minutes, else the skin will blister and crack. Where the fish is large, it will be better to sew the body together after stuffing, rather than to use a skewer. The string can be cut and removed before serving.

If any is left, it can be warmed in the remains of the gravy, or, if this has been used, make a gravy of one cup of hot water, thickened with one teaspoonful of flour or corn-starch stirred smooth first in a little cold water. Add a tablespoonful of butter and any catchup or sauce desired. Take all bones from the fish; break it up in small pieces, and stew not over five minutes in the gravy. Or it can be mixed with an equal amount of mashed potato or bread-crumbs, a cup of milk and an egg added, with a teaspoonful of salt and a saltspoonful of pepper, and baked until brown-- about fifteen minutes--in a hot oven.

TO BOIL FISH.

General directions have already been given. All fish must boil *very* gently, or the outside will break before the inside is done. In all cases salt and a little vinegar, a teaspoonful each, are allowed to each quart of water. Where the fish has very little flavor, Dubois' receipt for boiling will be found exceedingly nice, and much less trouble than the name applied by professional cooks to this method-- *au court bouillon* --would indicate. It is as follows:--

Mince a carrot, an onion, and one stalk of celery, and fry them in a little butter. Add two or three sprigs of parsley, two tablespoonfuls of salt, six pepper-corns, and three cloves. Pour on two quarts of boiling water and one pint of vinegar, and boil for fifteen minutes. Skim as it boils, and use, when cold, for boiling the fish. Wine can be used instead of vinegar; and, by straining carefully and keeping in a cold place, the same mixture can be used several times.

TO BROIL FISH.

If the fish is large, it should be split, in order to insure its being cooked through; though notches may be cut at equal distances, so that the heat can penetrate. Small fish may be broiled whole. The gridiron should be well greased with dripping or olive oil. If a double-wire gridiron is used, there will be no trouble in turning either large or small fish. If a single-wire or old-fashioned iron one, the best way is to first loosen with a knife any part that sticks; then, holding a platter over the fish with one hand, turn the gridiron with the other, and the fish can then be returned to it without breaking.

Small fish require a hot, clear fire; large ones, a more moderate one, that the outside may not be burned before the inside is done. Cook always with the *skin-side* down at first, and broil to a golden brown,--this requiring, for small fish, ten minutes; for large ones, from ten to twenty, according to size. When done, pepper and salt lightly; and to a two-pound fish allow a tablespoonful of butter spread over it. Set the fish in the oven a moment, that the butter may soak in, and then serve. A teaspoonful of chopped parsley, and half a lemon squeezed over shad or any fresh fish, is a very nice addition. Where butter, lemon, and parsley are blended beforehand, it makes the sauce known as *maitre d'hotel* sauce, which is especially good for broiled shad.

In broiling steaks or cutlets of large fish,--say, salmon, halibut, fresh cod, &c.,--the same general directions apply. Where very delicate broiling is desired, the pieces of fish can be wrapped in buttered paper before laying on the gridiron; this applying particularly to salmon.

TO FRY FISH.

Small fish--such as trout, perch, smelts, &c.--may simply be rolled in Indian meal or flour, and fried either in the fat of salt pork, or in boiling lard or drippings. A nicer method, however, with fish, whether small or in slices, is to dip them first in flour or fine crumbs, then in beaten egg,--one egg, with two tablespoonfuls of cold water and half a teaspoonful of salt, being enough for two dozen smelts; then rolling again in crumbs or meal, and dropping into hot lard. The egg hardens instantly, and not a drop of fat can penetrate the inside. Fry to a golden brown. Take out with a skimmer; lay in the oven on a double brown paper for a moment, and then serve.

Filets of fish are merely flounders, or any flat fish with few bones, boned, skinned, and cut in small pieces; then egged and fried.

To bone a fish of this sort, use a very sharp knife. The fish should have been scaled, but not cleaned or cut open. Make a cut down the back from head to tail. Now, holding the knife pressed close to the bone, cut carefully till the fish is free on one side; then turn, and cut away the other. To skin, take half the fish at a time firmly in one hand; hold the blade of the knife flat as in boning, and run it slowly between skin and flesh. Cut the fish in small diamond-shaped pieces; egg, crumb, and put into shape with the knife; and then fry. The operation is less troublesome than it sounds, and the result most satisfactory.

The *bones and trimmings* remaining can either be stewed in a pint of water till done, adding half a teaspoonful of salt, a saltspoonful of pepper, and a tablespoonful of catchup; straining the gravy off, and thickening with one heaping teaspoonful of flour dissolved in a little cold water: or they can be broiled. For broiled bones, mix one saltspoonful of mustard, as much cayenne as could be taken up on the point of a penknife, a saltspoonful of salt, and a tablespoonful of vinegar. A tablespoonful of olive-oil may be added, if liked. Lay the bone in this, turning it till all is absorbed; broil over a quick fire; and *serve very hot*.

Fish may also be fried in batter (p. 182), or these pieces, or *filets*, may be laid on a buttered dish; a simple drawn butter or cream sauce (p. 182) poured over them; the whole covered with rolled bread or cracker-crumbs, dotted with bits of butter, and baked half an hour. A cup of canned mushrooms is often added.

TO STEW FISH.

Any fresh-water fish is good, cooked in this way; cat-fish which have been soaked in salted water, to take away the muddy taste, being especially nice. Cut the fish in small pieces. Boil two sliced onions in a cup of water. Pour off this water; add another cup, and two tablespoonfuls of wine, a saltspoonful of pepper, and salt to taste (about half a teaspoonful). Put in the fish, and cook for twenty minutes. Thicken the gravy with a heaping teaspoonful of flour, rubbed to a cream with a teaspoonful of butter. If wine is not used, add a sprig of chopped parsley and the juice of half a lemon.

These methods will be found sufficient for all fresh fish, no other special rules being necessary. Experience and individual taste will guide their application. If the fish is oily, as in the case of mackerel or herring, broiling will always be better than frying. If fried, let it be with very little fat, as their own oil will furnish part.

TO BOIL SALT CODFISH.

The large, white cod, which cuts into firm, solid slices, should be used. If properly prepared, there is no need of the strong smell, which makes it so offensive to many, and which comes only in boiling. The fish is now to be had boned, and put up in small boxes, and this is by far the most desirable form. In either case, lay in tepid water *skin-side up*, and soak all night. If the skin is down, the salt, instead of soaking out, settles against it, and is retained. Change the water in the morning, and soak two or three hours longer; then, after scraping and cleaning thoroughly, put in a kettle with tepid water enough to well cover it, and set it where it will heat to the scalding-point, but *not boil*. Keep it at this point, but never let it boil a moment. Let it cook in this way an hour: two will do no harm. Remove every particle of bone and dark skin before serving, sending it to table in delicate pieces, none of which need be rejected. With egg sauce (p. 169), mashed or mealy boiled potatoes, and sugar-beets, this makes the New-England "fish dinner" a thing of terror when poorly prepared, but both savory and delicate where the above rule is closely followed.

Fish-balls, and all the various modes of using salted cod, require this preparation beforehand.

SALT COD WITH CREAM.

Flake two pounds of cold boiled salt cod very fine. Boil one pint of milk. Mix butter the size of a small egg with two tablespoonfuls of flour, and stir into it. Add a few sprigs of parsley or half an onion minced very fine, a pinch of cayenne pepper, and half a teaspoonful of salt. Butter a quart pudding-dish. Put in alternate layers of dressing and fish till nearly full. Cover the top with sifted bread or cracker crumbs, dot with bits of butter, and brown in a quick oven about twenty minutes. The fish may be mixed with an equal part of mashed potato, and baked; and not only codfish, but any boiled *fresh* fish, can be used, in which case double the measure of salt given will be required.

SPICED FISH.

Any remains of cold fresh fish may be used. Take out all bones or bits of skin. Lay in a deep dish, and barely cover with hot vinegar in which a few cloves and allspice have been boiled. It is ready for use as soon as cold.

POTTED FISH.

Fresh herring or mackerel or shad may be used. Skin the fish, and cut in small pieces, packing them in a small stone jar. Just cover with vinegar. For six pounds of fish allow one tablespoonful of salt, and a dozen each of whole allspice, cloves, and pepper-corns. Tie a thick paper over the top of the cover, and bake five hours. The vinegar dissolves the bones perfectly, and the fish is an excellent relish at supper.

FISH CHOWDER.

Three pounds of any sort of fresh fish may be taken; but fresh cod is always best. Six large potatoes and two onions, with half a pound of salt pork.

Cut the pork into dice, and fry to a light brown. Add the onions, and brown them also. Pour the remaining fat into a large saucepan, or butter it, as preferred. Put in a layer of potatoes, a little onion and pork, and a layer of the fish cut in small pieces, salting and peppering each layer. A tablespoonful of salt and one teaspoonful of pepper will be a mild seasoning. A pinch of cayenne may be added, if liked. Barely cover with boiling water, and boil for half an hour. In the meantime boil a pint of milk, and, when at boiling-point, break into it three ship biscuit or half a dozen large crackers; add a heaping tablespoonful of butter. Put the chowder in a platter, and pile the softened crackers on top, pouring the milk over all. Or the milk may be poured directly into the chowder; the crackers laid in, and softened in the steam; and the whole served in a tureen. Three or four tomatoes are sometimes added. In clam chowder the same rule would be followed, substituting one hundred clams for the fish, and using a small can of tomatoes if fresh ones were not in season.

STEWED OYSTERS.

The rule already given for *oyster soup* is an excellent one, omitting the thickening. A simpler one is to strain the juice from a quart of oysters, and add an equal amount of water. Bring it to boiling-point; skim carefully; season with salt to taste, this depending on the saltness of the oysters, half a teaspoonful being probably enough. Add a saltspoonful of pepper, a tablespoonful of butter, and a cup of milk. The milk may be omitted, if preferred. Add the oysters. Boil till the edges curl, and no longer. Serve at once, as they toughen by standing.

FRIED OYSTERS.

Choose large oysters, and drain thoroughly in a colander. Dry in a towel. Dip first in sifted cracker-crumbs; then in egg, one egg beaten with a large spoonful of cold water, half a teaspoonful of salt, and a saltspoonful of pepper, being enough for two dozen oysters. Roll again in crumbs, and drop into boiling lard. If a wire frying-basket is used, lay them in this. Fry to a light brown. Lay them on brown paper a moment to drain, and serve at once on a *hot platter*. As they require hardly more than a minute to cook, it is better to wait till all are at the table before beginning to fry. Oysters are very good, merely fried in a little hot butter; but the first method preserves their flavor best.

SCALLOPED OYSTERS.

One quart of oysters; one large breakfast cup of cracker or bread crumbs, the crackers being nicer if freshly toasted and rolled hot; two large spoonfuls of butter; one teaspoonful of salt; half a teaspoonful of pepper; one saltspoonful of mace. Mix the salt, pepper, and mace together. Butter a pudding-dish; heat the juice with the seasoning and butter, adding a teacup of milk or cream if it can be had, though water will answer. Put alternate layers of crumbs and oysters, filling the dish in this way. Pour the juice over, and bake in a quick oven twenty minutes. If not well browned, heat a shovel red-hot, and brown the top with that; longer baking toughening the oysters.

OYSTERS FOR PIE OR PATTIES.

One quart of oysters put on to boil in their own liquor. Turn them while boiling into a colander to drain. Melt a piece of butter the size of an egg in the saucepan, add a tablespoonful of sifted flour, and stir one minute. Pour in the oyster liquor slowly, which must be not less than a large cupful. Beat the yolks of two eggs thoroughly with a saltspoonful of salt, a pinch of cayenne pepper, and one of mace. Add to the boiling liquor, but do not let it boil. Put in the oysters, and either use them to fill a pie, the form for which is already baked, for patties for dinner, or serve them on thin slices of buttered toast for breakfast or tea.

SPICED OR PICKLED OYSTERS.

To a gallon of large, fine oysters, allow one pint of cider or white-wine vinegar; one tablespoonful of salt; one grated nutmeg; eight blades of mace; three dozen cloves, and as many whole allspice; and a saltspoon even full of cayenne pepper. Strain the oyster juice, and bring to the boiling-point in a porcelain-lined kettle. Skim carefully as it boils up. Add the vinegar, and skim also, throwing in the spices and salt when it has boiled a moment. Boil all together for five minutes, and then pour over the oysters, adding a lemon cut in very thin slices. They are ready for the table next day, but will keep a fortnight or more in a cold place. If a sharp pickle is desired, use a quart instead of a pint of vinegar.

SMOTHERED OYSTERS (*Maryland fashion*).

Drain all the juice from a quart of oysters. Melt in a frying-pan a piece of butter the size of an egg, with as much cayenne pepper as can be taken up on the point of a penknife, and a saltspoonful of salt. Put in the oysters, and cover closely. They are done as soon as the edges ruffle. Serve on thin slices of buttered toast as a breakfast or supper dish. A glass of sherry is often added.

OYSTER OR CLAM FRITTERS.

Chop twenty-five clams or oysters fine, and mix them with a batter made as follows: One pint of flour, in which has been sifted one heaping teaspoonful of baking-powder and half a teaspoonful of salt; one large cup of milk, and two eggs well beaten. Stir eggs and milk together; add the flour slowly; and, last, the clams or oysters. Drop by spoonfuls into boiling lard. Fry to a golden brown, and serve at once; or they may be fried like pancakes in a little hot fat. Whole clams or oysters may be used instead of chopped ones, and fried singly.

TO BOIL LOBSTERS OR CRABS.

Be sure that the lobster is alive, as, if dead, it will not be fit to use. Have water boiling in a large kettle, and, holding the lobster or crab by the back, drop it in head foremost; the reason for this being, that the animal dies instantly when put in in this way. An hour is required for a medium-sized lobster, the shell turning red when done. When cold, the meat can be used either plain or in salad, or cooked in various ways. A can-opener will be found very convenient in opening a lobster.

STEWED OR CURRIED LOBSTER.

Cut the meat into small bits, and add the green fat, and the coral which is found only in the hen-lobster. Melt in a saucepan one tablespoonful of butter and a heaping tablespoonful of flour. Stir smoothly together, adding slowly one large cup of either stock or milk, a saltspoonful of mace, a pinch of cayenne pepper, and half a teaspoonful of salt. Put in the lobster, and cook for ten minutes. For curry, simply add one teaspoonful of curry-powder. This stewed lobster may also be put in the shell of the back, which has been cleaned and washed, bread or cracker crumbs sprinkled over it, and browned in the oven; or it may be treated as a scallop, buttering a dish, and putting in alternate layers of crumbs and lobster, ending with crumbs. Crabs, though more troublesome to extract from the shell, are almost equally good, treated in any of the ways given.

*   *   *   *   *

MEATS.

The qualities and characteristics of meats have already been spoken of in Part I., and it is necessary here to give only a few simple rules for marketing.

The best BEEF is of a clear red color, slightly marbled with fat, and the fat itself of a clear white. Where the beef is dark red or bluish, and the fat yellow, it is too old, or too poorly fed, to be good. The sirloin and ribs, especially the sixth, seventh, and eighth, make the best roasting-pieces. The ribs can be removed and used for stock, and the beef rolled or skewered firmly, making a piece very easily carved, and almost as presentable the second day as the first. For steaks sirloin is nearly as good, and much more economical, than porter-house, which gives only a small eatable portion, the remainder being only fit for the stock-pot. If the beef be very young and tender, steaks from the round may be used; but these are usually best stewed. Other pieces and modes of cooking are given under their respective heads.

MUTTON should be a light, clear red, and the fat very white and firm. It is always improved by keeping, and in cold weather can be hung for a month, if carefully watched to see that it has not become tainted. Treated in this way, well-fed mutton is equal to venison. If the fat is deep yellow, and the lean dark red, the animal is too old; and no keeping will make it really good eating. Four years is considered the best age for prime mutton.

VEAL also must have clear white fat, and should be fine in grain. If the kidney is covered with firm white fat, it indicates health, and the meat is good; if yellow, it is unwholesome, and should not be eaten. The loin and fillet are used in roasting, and are the choice pieces, the breast coming next, and the neck and ribs being good for stewing and fricassees.

PORK should have fine, white fat, and the meat should be white and smooth. Only country-fed pork should ever be eaten, the pig even then being liable to diseases unknown to other animals, and the meat, even when carefully fed, being at all times less digestible than any sort. *Bacon*, carefully cured and smoked, is considered its most wholesome form.

POULTRY come last. The best *Turkeys* have black legs; and, if young, the toes and bill are soft and pliable. The combs of fowls should be bright colored, and the legs smooth.

Geese, if young and fine, are plump in the breast, have white soft fat, and yellow feet.

Ducks are chosen by the same rule as geese, and are firm and thick on the breast.

Pigeons should be fresh, the breast plump, and the feet elastic. Only experience can make one familiar with other signs; and a good butcher can usually be trusted to tide one over the season of inexperience, though the sooner it ends the better for all parties concerned.

BOILED MEATS AND STEWS.

All meats intended to be boiled and served whole at table must be put into *boiling water*, thus following an entirely opposite rule from those intended for soups. In the latter, the object being to extract all the juice, cold water must always be used first, and then heated with the meat in. In the former, all the juice is to be kept in; and, by putting into boiling water, the albumen of the meat hardens on the surface and makes a case or coating for the meat, which accomplishes this end. Where something between a soup and plain boiled meat is desired, as in *beef bouilli*, the meat is put on in cold water, which is brought to a boil *very quickly*, thus securing good gravy, yet not robbing the meat of all its juices. With corned or salted meats, tongue, &c., cold water must be used, and half an hour to the pound allowed. If to be eaten cold, such meats should always be allowed to cool in the water in which they were boiled; and this water, if not too salt, can be used for dried bean or pea soups.

BEEF A LA MODE.

Six or eight pounds of beef from the round, cut thick. Take out the bone, trim off all rough bits carefully, and rub the meat well with the following spicing: One teaspoonful each of pepper and ground clove, quarter of a cup of brown sugar, and three teaspoonfuls of salt. Mix these all together, and rub thoroughly into the beef, which must stand over-night.

Next morning make a stuffing of one pint of bread or cracker crumbs; one large onion chopped fine; a tablespoonful of sweet marjoram or thyme; half a teaspoonful each of pepper and ground clove, and a heaping teaspoonful of salt. Add a large cup of hot water, in which has been melted a heaping tablespoonful of butter, and stir into the crumbs. Beat an egg light, and mix with it. If there is more than needed to fill the hole, make gashes in the meat, and stuff with the remainder. Now bind into shape with a strip of cotton cloth, sewing or tying it firmly. Put a trivet or small iron stand into a soup-pot, and lay the beef upon it. Half cover it with cold water; put in two onions stuck with three cloves each, a large tablespoonful of salt, and a half tea-spoonful of pepper; and stew very slowly, allowing half an hour to the pound, and turning the meat twice while cooking. At the end of this time take off the cloth, and put the meat, which must remain on the trivet, in a roasting-pan. Dredge it quickly with flour, set into a hot oven, and brown thoroughly. Baste once with the gravy, and dredge again, the whole operation requiring about half an hour. The water in the pot should have been reduced to about a pint. Pour this into the roasting-pan after the meat is taken up, skimming off every particle of fat. Thicken with a heap-ing tablespoonful of browned flour, stirred smooth in a little cold water, and add a tablespoonful of catchup and two of wine, if desired, though neither is necessary. Taste, as a little more salt may be required.

The thick part of a leg of veal may be treated in the same manner, both being good either hot or cold; and a round of beef may be also used without spicing or stuffing, and browned in the same way, the remains being either warmed in the gravy or used for hashes or croquettes.

BEEF A LA MODE (*Virginia fashion*).

Use the round, as in the foregoing receipt, and remove the bone; and for eight pounds allow half a pint of good vinegar; one large onion minced fine; half a tea-spoonful each of mustard, black pepper, clove, and allspice; and two tablespoonfuls of brown sugar. Cut half a pound of fat salt pork into lardoons, or strips, two or three inches long and about half an inch square. Boil the vinegar with the onion and seasoning, and pour over the strips of pork, and let them stand till cold. Then pour off the liquor, and thicken it with bread or cracker crumbs. Make incisions in the beef at regular intervals,--a carving-steel being very good for this purpose,--and push in the strips of pork. Fill the hole from which the bone was taken with the rest of the pork and the dressing, and tie the beef firmly into shape. Put two tablespoon-fuls of dripping or lard in a frying-pan, and brown the meat on all sides. This will take about half an hour. Now put the meat on a trivet in the kettle; half cover with boiling water; and add a tablespoonful of salt, a teaspoonful of pepper, an onion and a small carrot cut fine, and two or three sprigs of parsley. Cook very slowly, allow-ing half an hour to a pound, and make gravy by the directions given for it in the preceding receipt.

Braised beef is prepared by either method given here for *a la mode* beef, but cooked in a covered iron pan, which comes for the purpose, and which is good also for beef *a la mode*, or for any tough meat which requires long cooking, and is made tenderer by keeping in all the steam.

BOILED MUTTON.

A *shoulder*, or *fore-quarter*, of mutton, weighing five or six pounds, will boil in an hour, as it is so thin. The *leg*, or *hind-quarter*, requires twenty minutes to the pound; though, if very young and tender, it will do in less. It can be tried with a knitting-needle to see if it is tender. It is made whiter and more delicate by boil-ing in a cloth, but should be served without it. Boil in well-salted water according to the rule already given. Boiled or mashed turnips are usually served with it, and either drawn butter or caper sauce as on p. 169.

Lamb may be boiled in the same manner, but is better roasted; and so also with *veal*.

BOILED CORNED BEEF.

If to be eaten hot, the *round* is the best piece. If cold and pressed, what are called "*plate pieces*"--that is, the brisket, the flank, and the thin part of the ribs--may be used. Wash, and put into cold water, allowing half an hour to a pound after it begins to boil. If to be eaten cold, let it stand in the water till nearly cold, as this makes it richer. Take out all bones from a thin piece; wrap in a cloth, and put upon a large platter. Lay a tin sheet over it, and set on a heavy weight,--flat-irons will do,--and let it stand over-night. Or the meat may be picked apart with a knife and fork; the fat and lean evenly mixed and packed into a pan, into which a smaller pan is set on top of the meat, and the weight in this. Thus marbled slices may be had. All corned beef is improved by pressing, and all trimmings from it can be used in hash or croquettes.

BOILED TONGUE.

Smoked tongue will be found much better than either fresh or pickled tongues.

Soak it over night, after washing it. Put on in cold water, and boil steadily four hours. Then take out; peel off the skin, and return to the water to cool. Cut in *lengthwise* slices, as this makes it tenderer. The root of the tongue may be chopped very fine, and seasoned like deviled ham (p. 265).

BOILED HAM.

Small hams are better in flavor and quality than large ones. A brush should be kept to scrub them with, as it is impossible to get them clean without it. Soak overnight in plenty of cold water. Next morning, scrape, and trim off all the hard black parts, scrubbing it well. Put on to boil in cold water. Let it heat very gradually. Allow half an hour to the pound. When done, take from the water, skin, and return, letting it remain till cold. Dot with spots of black pepper, and cover the knuckle with a frill of white paper. It is much nicer, whether eaten hot or cold, if covered with bread or cracker crumbs and browned in the oven. The fat is useless, save for soap-grease. In carving, cut down in thin slices through the middle. The knuckle can always be deviled (p. 265). A *leg of pork* which has simply been corned is boiled in the same way as ham, soaking over-night, and browning in the oven or not, as liked.

IRISH STEW.

This may be made of either beef or mutton, though mutton is generally used. Reject all bones, and trim off all fat and gristle, reserving these for the stock-pot. Cut the meat in small pieces, not over an inch square, and cover with cold water. Skim carefully as it boils up, and see that the water is kept at the same level by adding as it boils away. For two pounds of meat allow two sliced onions, eight good-sized potatoes, two teaspoonfuls of salt, and half a teaspoonful of pepper. Cover closely, and cook for two hours. Thicken the gravy with one tablespoonful of flour stirred smooth in a little cold water, and serve very hot. The trimmings from a fore-quarter of mutton will be enough for a stew, leaving a well-shaped roast besides. If beef is used, add one medium-sized carrot cut fine, and some sprigs of parsley. Such a stew would be called by a French cook a *ragout*, and can be made of any pieces of meat or poultry.

WHITE STEW, OR FRICASSEE.

Use *veal* for this stew, allowing an hour to a pound of meat, and the same proportions of salt and pepper as in the preceding receipt, adding a saltspoonful of mace. Thicken, when done, with one heaping tablespoonful of flour rubbed smooth with a piece of butter the size of an egg, and one cup of hot milk added just at the last. A cauliflower nicely boiled, cut up, and stewed with it a moment, is very nice.

This stew becomes a *pot-pie* by making a nice biscuit-crust, as on p. 164; cutting it out in rounds, and laying in the kettle half an hour before the stew is done. Cover closely, and do not turn them. Lay them, when done, around the edge of the platter; pile the meat in the centre, and pour over it the thickened gravy. Two beaten eggs are sometimes added, and it is then called a *blanquette* of veal.

BROWN STEW OR FRICASSEE.

To make these stews the meat is cut in small pieces, and browned on each side in a little hot dripping; or, if preferred, quarter of a pound of pork is cut in thin slices and fried crisp, the fat from it being used for browning. Cover the meat with warm water when done. If a stew, any vegetables liked can be added; a fricassee never containing them, having only meat and a gravy, thickened with browned flour and seasoned in the proportions already given. Part of a can of mushrooms may be used with a beef stew, and a glass of wine added; this making a *ragout with mushrooms*. The countless receipts one sees in large cook-books for ragouts and fricassees are merely variations in the flavoring of simple stews; and, after a little experimenting, any one can improvise her own, remembering that the strongly-flavored vegetables (as carrots) belong especially to dark meats, and the more delicate ones to light. Fresh pork is sometimes used in a white fricassee, in which case a little powdered sage is better than mace as a seasoning.

Curries can be made by adding a heaping teaspoonful of curry-powder to a brown fricassee, and serving with boiled rice; put the rice around the edge of the platter, and pour the curry in the middle. Chicken makes the best curry; but veal is very good. In a genuine East-Indian curry, lemon-juice and grated cocoa-nut are added; but it is an unwholesome combination.

BEEF ROLLS.

Two pounds of steak from the round, cut in very thin slices. Trim off all fat and gristle, and cut into pieces about four inches square. Now cut *very thin* as many slices of salt pork as you have slices of steak, making them a little smaller. Mix together one teaspoonful of salt and one of thyme or summer savory, and one salt-spoonful of pepper. Lay the pork on a square of steak; sprinkle with the seasoning; roll up tightly, and tie. When all are tied, put the bits of fat and trimmings into a hot frying-pan, and add a tablespoonful of drippings. Lay in the rolls, and brown on all sides, which will require about ten minutes; then put them in a saucepan. Add to the fat in the pan a heaping tablespoonful of flour, and stir till a bright brown. Pour in gradually one quart of boiling water, and then strain it over the beef rolls. Cover closely, and cook two hours, or less if the steak is tender, stirring now and then to prevent scorching. Take off the strings before serving. These rolls can be prepared without the pork, and are very nice; or a whole beefsteak can be used, covering it with a dressing made as for stuffed veal, and then rolling; tying at each end, browning, and stewing in the same way. This can be eaten cold or hot; while the small rolls are much better hot. If wanted as a breakfast dish, they can be cooked the day beforehand, left in the gravy, and simply heated through next morning.

BRUNSWICK STEW.

Two squirrels or small chickens; one quart of sliced tomatoes; one pint of sweet corn; one pint of lima or butter beans; one quart of sliced potatoes; two onions; half a pound of fat salt pork.

Cut the pork in slices, and fry brown; cut the squirrels or chickens in pieces, and brown a little, adding the onion cut fine. Now put all the materials in a soup-pot; cover with two quarts of boiling water, and season with one tablespoonful of salt, one of sugar, and half a teaspoonful of cayenne pepper. Stew slowly for four hours. Just before serving, cream a large spoonful of butter with a heaping table-spoonful of flour; thin with the broth, and pour in, letting all cook five minutes longer. To be eaten in soup-plates.

ROASTED MEATS.

Our roasted meats are really *baked* meats; but ovens are now so well made and ventilated, that there is little difference of flavor in the two processes.

Allow ten minutes to the pound if the meat is liked rare, and from twelve to fifteen, if well done. It is always better to place the meat on a trivet or stand made to fit easily in the roasting-pan, so that it may not become sodden in the water used for gravy. Put into a hot oven, that the surface may soon sear over and hold in the juices, enough of which will escape for the gravy. All rough bits should have been trimmed off, and a joint of eight or ten pounds rubbed with a tablespoonful of salt. Dredge thickly with flour, and let it brown on the meat before basting it, which must be done as often as once in fifteen minutes. Pepper lightly. If the water in the pan dries away, add enough to have a pint for gravy in the end. Dredge with flour at least twice, as this makes a crisp and relishable outer crust. Take up the meat, when done, on a hot platter. Make the gravy in the roasting-pan, by setting it on top of the stove, and first scraping up all the browning from the corners and bottom. If there is much fat, pour it carefully off. If the dredging has been well managed while roasting, the gravy will be thick enough. If not, stir a teaspoonful of browned flour smooth in cold water, and add. Should the gravy be too light, color with a teaspoonful of caramel, and taste to see that the seasoning is right.

Mutton requires fifteen minutes to the pound, unless preferred rare, in which case ten will be sufficient. If a tin kitchen is used, fifteen minutes for beef, and twenty for mutton, will be needed.

STUFFED LEG OF MUTTON.

Have the butcher take out the first joint in a leg of mutton; or it can be done at home by using a very sharp, narrow-bladed knife, and holding it close to the bone. Rub in a tablespoonful of salt, and then fill with a dressing made as follows: One pint of fine bread or cracker crumbs, in which have been mixed dry one even tablespoonful of salt and one of summer savory or thyme, and one teaspoonful of pepper. Chop one onion very fine, and add to it, with one egg well beaten. Melt a piece of butter the size of an egg in a cup of hot water, and pour on the crumbs. If not enough to thoroughly moisten them, add a little more. Either fasten with a skewer, or sew up, and roast as in previous directions. Skim all the fat from the gravy, as the flavor of mutton-fat is never pleasant. A tablespoonful of currant jelly may be put into the gravy-tureen, and the gravy strained upon it. The meat must be basted, and dredged with flour, as carefully as beef. Both the shoulder and saddle are roasted in the same way, but without stuffing; and the leg may be also, though used to more advantage with one.

Lamb requires less time; a leg weighing six pounds needing but one hour, or an hour and a quarter if roasted before an open fire.

ROAST VEAL.

Veal is so dry a meat, that a moist dressing is almost essential. This dressing may be made as in the previous receipt; or, instead of butter, quarter of a pound of salt pork can be chopped fine, and mixed with it. If the loin is used,--and this is always best,--take out the bone to the first joint, and fill the hole with dressing, as in the leg of mutton. In using the breast, bone also, reserving the bones for stock; lay the dressing on it; roll, and tie securely. Baste often. Three or four thin slices of salt pork may be laid on the top; or, if this is not liked, melt a tablespoonful of butter in a cup of hot water, and baste with that. Treat it as in directions for roasted meats, but allow a full half-hour to the pound, and make the gravy as for beef. Cold veal makes so many nice dishes, that a large piece can always be used satisfactorily.

ROAST PORK.

Bone the leg as in mutton, and stuff; substituting sage for the sweet marjoram, and using two onions instead of one. Allow half an hour to the pound, and make gravy as for roast beef. Spare-ribs are considered most delicate; and both are best eaten cold, the hot pork being rather gross, and, whether hot or cold, less digestible than any other meat.

ROAST VENISON.

In winter venison can be kept a month; and, in all cases, it should hang in a cold place at least a month before using. Allow half an hour to a pound in roasting, and baste very often. Small squares of salt pork are sometimes inserted in incisions made here and there, and help to enrich the gravy. In roasting a haunch it is usually covered with a thick paste of flour and water, and a paper tied over this, not less than four hours being required to roast it. At the end of three, remove the paper and paste, dredge and baste till well browned. The last basting is with a glass of claret; and this, and half a small glass of currant jelly are added to the gravy. Venison steaks are treated as in directions for broiled meats.

BAKED PORK AND BEANS.

Pick over one quart of dried beans, what is known as "navy beans" being the best, and soak over-night in plenty of cold water.

Turn off the water in the morning, and put on to boil in cold water till tender,--at least one hour. An earthen pot is always best for this, as a shallow dish does not allow enough water to keep them from drying. Drain off the water. Put the beans in the pot. Take half a pound of salt pork, fat and lean together being best. Score the skin in small squares with a knife, and bury it, all but the surface of this rind, in the beans. Cover them completely with boiling water. Stir in one tablespoonful of salt, and two of good molasses. Cover, and bake slowly,--not less than five hours,--renewing the water if it bakes away. Take off the cover an hour before they are done, that the pork may brown a little. If pork is disliked, use a large spoonful of butter instead. Cold baked beans can be warmed in a frying-pan with a little water, and are even better than at first, or they can be used in a soup as in directions given. A teaspoonful of made mustard is sometimes stirred in, and gives an excellent flavor to a pot of baked beans. Double the quality if the family is large, as they keep perfectly well in winter, the only season at which so hearty a dish is required, save for laborers.

BROILED AND FRIED MEATS.

If the steak is tender, never pound or chop it. If there is much fat, trim it off, or it will drop on the coals and smoke. If tough, as in the country is very likely to be the case, pounding becomes necessary, but a better method is to use the chopping-knife; not chopping through, but going lightly over the whole surface. Broken as it may seem, it closes at once on the application of a quick heat.

The best *broiler* is by all means a light wire one, which can be held in the hand and turned quickly. The fire should be quick and hot. Place the steak in the centre of the broiler, and hold it close to the coals an instant on each side, letting both sear over before broiling really begins.

Where a steak has been cut three-quarters of an inch thick, ten minutes will be sufficient to cook it rare, and fifteen will make it well done. Turn almost constantly, and, when done, serve at once on a *hot dish*. Never salt broiled meats beforehand, as it extracts the juices. Cut up a tablespoonful of butter, and let it melt on the hot dish, turning the steak in it once or twice. Salt and pepper lightly, and, if necessary to have it stand at all, cover with an earthen dish, or stand in the open oven. *Chops* and *cutlets* are broiled in the same way. Veal is so dry a meat that it is better fried.

Where broiling for any reason cannot be conveniently done, the next best method is to heat a frying-pan very hot; grease it with a bit of fat cut from the steak, just enough to prevent it from sticking. Turn almost as constantly as in broiling, and season in the same way when done. Venison steaks are treated in the same manner.

VEAL CUTLETS.

Fry four or five slices of salt pork till brown, or use drippings instead, if this fat is disliked. Let the cutlets, which are best cut from the leg, be made as nearly of a size as possible; dip them in well-beaten egg and then in cracker-crumbs, and fry to a golden brown. Where the veal is tough, it is better to parboil it for ten or fifteen minutes before frying.

PORK STEAK.

Pork steaks or chops should be cut quite thin, and sprinkled with pepper and salt and a little powdered sage. Have the pan hot; put in a tablespoonful of dripping, and fry the pork slowly for twenty minutes, turning often. A gravy can be made for these, and for veal cutlets also, by mixing a tablespoonful of flour with the fat left in the pan, and stirring it till a bright brown, then adding a large cup of boiling water, and salt to taste; a saltspoonful being sufficient, with half the amount of pepper.

Pigs' liver, which many consider very nice, is treated in precisely the same way, using a teaspoonful of powdered sage to two pounds of liver.

FRIED HAM OR BACON.

Cut the ham in very thin slices. Take off the rind, and, if the ham is old or hard, parboil it for five minutes. Have the pan hot, and, unless the ham is quite fat, use a teaspoonful of drippings. Turn the slices often, and cook from five to eight minutes. They can be served dry, or, if gravy is liked, add a tablespoonful of flour to the fat, stir till smooth, and pour in slowly a large cup of milk or water. Salt pork can be fried in the same way. If eggs are to be fried with the ham, take up the slices, break in the eggs, and dip the boiling fat over them as they fry. If there is not fat enough, add half a cup of lard. To make each egg round, put muffin-rings into the frying-pan, and break an egg into each, pouring the boiling fat over them from a spoon till done, which will be in from three to five minutes. Serve one on each slice of ham, and make no gravy. The fat can be strained, and used in frying potatoes.

FRIED TRIPE.

The tripe can be merely cut in squares, rolled in flour, salted and peppered, and fried brown in drippings, or the pieces may be dipped in a batter made as for clam fritters, or egged and crumbed like oysters, and fried. In cities it can be bought already prepared. In the country it must first be cleaned, and then boiled till tender.

TO WARM COLD MEATS.

Cold roast beef should be cut in slices, the gravy brought to boiling-point, and each slice dipped in just long enough to heat, as stewing in the gravy toughens it. Rare mutton is treated in the same way, but is nicer warmed in a chafing-dish at table, adding a tablespoonful of currant jelly and one of wine to the gravy. Venison is served in the same manner. Veal and pork can cook in the gravy without toughening, and so with turkey and chicken. Cold duck or game is very nice warmed in the same way as mutton, the bones in all cases being reserved for stock.

*   *   *   *   *

POULTRY.

TO CLEAN POULTRY.

First be very careful to singe off all down by holding over a blazing paper, or a little alcohol burning in a saucer. Cut off the feet and ends of the wings, and the neck as far as it is dark. If the fowl is killed at home, be sure that the head is chopped off, and never allow the neck to be wrung as is often done. It is not only an unmerciful way of killing, but the blood has thus no escape, and settles about all the vital organs. The head should be cut off, and the body hang and bleed thoroughly before using.

Pick out all the pin-feathers with the blade of a small knife. Turn back the skin of the neck, loosening it with the finger and thumb, and draw out the windpipe and crop, which can be done without making any cut. Now cut a slit in the lower part of the fowl, the best place being close to the thigh. By working the fingers in slowly, keeping them close to the body, the whole intestines can be removed in a mass. Be especially careful not to break the gall-bag, which is near the upper part of the breastbone, and attached to the liver. If this operation is carefully performed, it will be by no means so disagreeable as it seems. A French cook simply wipes out the inside, considering that much flavor is lost by washing. I prefer to wash in one water, and dry quickly, though in the case of an old fowl, which often has a strong smell, it is better to dissolve a teaspoonful of soda in the first water, which should be warm, and wash again in cold, then wiping dry as possible. Split and wash the gizzard, reserving it for gravy.

DRESSING FOR POULTRY.

One pint of bread or cracker crumbs, into which mix dry one teaspoonful of pepper, one of thyme or summer savory, one even tablespoonful of salt, and, if in season, a little chopped parsley. Melt a piece of butter the size of an egg in one cup of boiling water, and mix with the crumbs, adding one or two well-beaten eggs. A slice of salt pork chopped fine is often substituted for the butter.

For *ducks* two onions are chopped fine, and added to the above; or a potato dressing is made, as for geese, using six large boiled potatoes, mashed hot, and seasoned with an even tablespoonful of salt, a teaspoonful each of sage and pepper, and two chopped onions.

Game is usually roasted unstuffed; but grouse and prairie-chickens may have the same dressing as chickens and turkeys, this being used also for boiled fowls.

ROAST TURKEY.

Prepare by cleaning, as in general directions above, and, when dry, rub the inside with a teaspoonful of salt. Put the gizzard, heart, and liver on the fire in a small saucepan, with one quart of boiling water and one teaspoonful of salt, and boil two hours. Put a little stuffing in the breast, and fold back the skin of the neck, holding it with a stitch or with a small skewer. Put the remainder in the body, and sew it up with darning-cotton. Cross and tie the legs down tight, and run a skewer through the wings to fasten them to the body. Lay it in the roasting-pan, and for an eight-pound turkey allow not less than three hours' time, a ten or twelve pound one needing four. Put a pint of boiling water with one teaspoonful of salt in the pan, and add to it as it dries away. Melt a heaping tablespoonful of butter in the water, and baste very often. The secret of a handsomely-browned turkey, lies in this frequent basting. Dredge over the flour two or three times, as in general roasting directions, and turn the turkey so that all sides will be reached. When done, take up on a hot platter. Put the baking-pan on the stove, having before this chopped the gizzard and heart fine, and mashed the liver, and put them in the gravy-tureen. Stir a tablespoonful of brown flour into the gravy in the pan, scraping up all the brown, and add slowly the water in which the giblets were boiled, which should be about a pint. Strain on to the chopped giblets, and taste to see if salt enough. The gravy for all roast poultry is made in this way. Serve with cranberry sauce or jelly.

ROAST OR BOILED CHICKENS.

Stuff and truss as with turkeys, and to a pair of chickens weighing two and a half pounds each, allow one hour to roast, basting often, and making a gravy as in preceding receipt.

Boil as in rule for turkeys.

ROAST DUCK.

After cleaning, stuff as in rule given for poultry dressing, and roast,--if game, half an hour; if tame, one hour, making gravy as in directions given, and serving with currant jelly.

ROAST GOOSE.

No fat save its own is needed in basting a goose, which, if large, requires two hours to roast. Skim off as much fat as possible before making the gravy, as it has a strong taste.

BIRDS.

Small birds may simply be washed and wiped dry, tied firmly, and roasted twenty minutes, dredging with flour, basting with butter and water, and adding a little currant jelly or wine to the gravy. They may be served on toast.

FRIED CHICKEN.

Cut the chicken into nice pieces for serving. Roll in flour, or, if preferred, in beaten egg and crumbs. Heat a cupful of nice dripping or lard; add a teaspoonful of salt and a saltspoonful of pepper; lay in the pieces, and fry brown on each side, allowing not less than twenty minutes for the thickest pieces and ten for the thin ones. Lay on a hot platter, and make a gravy by adding one tablespoonful of flour to the fat, stirring smooth, and adding slowly one cupful of boiling water or stock. Strain over the chicken. Milk or cream is often used instead of water.

BROWN FRICASSEE.

Fry one or two chickens as above, using only flour to roll them in. Three or four slices of salt pork may be used, cutting them in bits, and frying brown, before putting in the chicken. When fried, lay the pieces in a saucepan, and cover with warm water, adding one teaspoonful of salt and a saltspoonful of pepper. Cover closely, and stew one hour, or longer if the chickens are old. Take up the pieces, and thicken the gravy with one tablespoonful of flour, first stirred smooth in a little cold water. Or the flour may be added to the fat in the pan after frying, and water enough for a thin gravy, which can all be poured into the saucepan, though with this method there is more danger of burning. If not dark enough, color with a teaspoonful of caramel. By adding a chopped onion fried in the fat, and a teaspoonful of curry-powder, this becomes a curry, to be served with boiled rice.

WHITE FRICASSEE.

Cut up the chicken as in brown fricassee, and stew without frying for an hour and a half, reducing the water to about one pint. Take up the chicken on a hot plat-ter. Melt one tablespoonful of butter in a saucepan, and add a heaping tablespoon-ful of flour, stirring constantly till smooth. Pour in slowly one cup of milk, and, as it boils and thickens, add the chicken broth, and serve. This becomes a pot-pie by adding biscuit-crust as in rule for veal pot-pie, p. 150, and serving in the same way. The same crust may also be used with a brown fricassee, but is most customary with a white.

CHICKEN PIE.

Make a fricassee, as above directed, either brown or white, as best liked, and a nice pie-crust, as on p. 224, or a biscuit-crust if pie-crust is considered too rich. Line a deep baking-dish with the crust; a good way being to use a plain biscuit-crust for the lining, and pie-crust for the lid. Lay in the cooked chicken; fill up with the gravy, and cover with pastry, cutting a round hole in the centre; and bake about three-quarters of an hour. The top can be decorated with leaves made from pastry, and in this case will need to have a buttered paper laid over it for the first twenty minutes, that they need not burn. Eat either cold or hot. Game pies can be made in the same way, and veal is a very good substitute for chicken. Where veal is used, a small slice of ham may be added, and a little less salt; both veal and ham being cut very small before filling the pie.

BOILED TURKEY.

Clean, stuff, and truss the fowl selected, as for a roasted turkey. The body is sometimes filled with oysters. To truss in the tightest and most compact way, run a skewer under the leg-joint between the leg and the thigh, then through the body and under the opposite leg-joint in the same way; push the thighs up firmly close to the sides; wind a string about the ends of the skewer, and tie it tight. Treat the wings in the same way, though in boiled fowls the points are sometimes drawn under the back, and tied there. The turkey may be boiled with or without cloth around it. In either case use *boiling* water, salted as for stock, and allow twenty minutes to the pound. It is usually served with oyster sauce, but parsley or capers may be used instead.

CHICKEN CROQUETTES.

Take all the meat from a cold roast or boiled chicken, and chop moderately fine. Mince an onion very small, and fry brown in a piece of butter the size of an egg. Add one small cup of stock or water; one saltspoonful each of pepper and mace; one teaspoonful of salt; the juice of half a lemon; two well-beaten eggs; and, if liked, a glass of wine. Make into small rolls like corks, or mold in a pear shape, sticking in a clove for the stem when fried. Roll in sifted cracker-crumbs; dip in an egg beaten with a spoonful of water, and again in crumbs; put in the frying-basket, and fry in boiling lard. Drain on brown paper, and pile on a napkin in serving.

A more delicate croquette is made by using simply the white meat, and adding a set of calf's brains which have been boiled in salted water. A cupful of boiled rice mashed fine is sometimes substituted for the brains. Use same seasoning as above, adding quarter of a saltspoonful of cayenne, omitting the wine, and using instead half a cup of cream or milk. Fry as directed. Veal croquettes can hardly be distinguished from those of chicken.

PHILADELPHIA CHICKEN CROQUETTES.

The croquette first given is dry when fried, and even the second form is somewhat so, many preferring them so. For the creamy delicious veal, sweetbread, or chicken croquette one finds in Philadelphia, the following materials are necessary: one pint of hot cream; two even tablespoonfuls of butter; four heaping tablespoonfuls of sifted flour; half a teaspoonful of salt; half a saltspoonful of white pepper; a dust of cayenne; half a teaspoonful of celery salt; and one teaspoonful of onion juice. Scald the cream in a double boiler. Melt the butter in an enameled or granite saucepan, and as it boils, stir in the flour, stirring till perfectly smooth. Add the cream very slowly, stirring constantly as it thickens, adding the seasoning at the last. An egg may also be added, but the croquettes are more creamy without it. To half a pound of chicken chopped fine, add one teaspoonful of lemon juice and one of minced parsley, one beaten egg and the pint of cream sauce. Spread on a platter to cool, and when cool make into shapes, either corks or like pears; dip in egg and crumbs, and fry in boiling fat. Oyster, sweetbread, and veal croquettes are made by the same form, using a pint of chopped oysters. To the sweetbreads a small can of mushrooms may be added cut in bits.

SALMI OF DUCKS OR GAME.

Cut the meat from cold roast ducks or game into small bits. Break the bones and trimmings, and cover with stock or cold water, adding two cloves, two pepper-corns, and a bay-leaf or pinch of sweet herbs. Boil till reduced to a cupful for a pint of meat. Mince two small onions fine, and fry brown in two tablespoonfuls of butter; then add two tablespoonfuls of flour and stir till deep brown, adding to it the strained broth from the bones. Put in the bits of meat with one tablespoonful of lemon juice and one of Worcestershire sauce. Simmer for fifteen minutes, and at the last add, if liked, six or eight mushrooms and a glass of claret. Serve on slices of fried bread, and garnish with fried bread and parsley.

CASSEROLE OF RICE AND MEAT.

This can be made of any kind of meat, but is nicest of veal or poultry. Boil a large cup of rice till tender, and let it cool. Chop fine half a pound of meat, and sea-son with half a teaspoonful of salt, a small grated onion, and a teaspoonful of minced parsley and a pinch of cayenne. Add a teacupful of cracker crumbs and a beaten egg, and wet with stock or hot water enough to make it pack easily. Butter a tin mould, quart size best, and line the bottom and sides with rice about half an inch thick. Pack in the meat; cover with rice, and steam one hour. Loosen at edges; turn out on hot platter, and pour tomato sauce around it.

ITALIA'S PRIDE.

This is a favorite dish in the writer's family, having been sent many years ago from Italy by a friend who had learned its composition from her Italian cook. Its name was bestowed by the children of the house. One large cup of chopped meat; two onions minced and fried brown in butter; a pint of cold boiled macaroni or spaghetti; a pint of fresh or cold stewed tomatoes; one teaspoonful of salt; half a tea-spoonful of white pepper. Butter a pudding dish, and put first a layer of macaroni, then tomato, then meat and some onion and seasoning, continuing this till the dish is full. Cover with fine bread crumbs, dot with bits of butter, and bake for half an hour. Serve very hot.

DEVILED HAM.

For this purpose use either the knuckle or any odds and ends remaining. Cut off all dark or hard bits, and see that at least a quarter of the amount is fat. Chop as finely as possible, reducing it almost to a paste. For a pint-bowl of this, make a dressing as follows:--

One even tablespoonful of sugar; one even teaspoonful of ground mustard; one saltspoonful of cayenne pepper; one spoonful of butter; one teacupful of boiling vinegar. Mix the sugar, mustard, and pepper thoroughly, and add the vinegar little by little. Stir it into the chopped ham, and pack it in small molds, if it is to be served as a lunch or supper relish, turning out upon a small platter and garnishing with parsley.

For sandwiches, cut the bread very thin; butter lightly, and spread with about a teaspoonful of the deviled ham. The root of a boiled tongue can be prepared in the same way. If it is to be kept some time, pack in little jars, and pour melted butter over the top.

BONED TURKEY.

This is a delicate dish, and is usually regarded as an impossibility for any ordinary housekeeper; and unless one is getting up a supper or other entertainment, it is hardly worth while to undertake it. If the legs and wings are left on, the boning becomes much more difficult. The best plan is to cut off both them and the neck, boiling all with the turkey, and using the meat for croquettes or hash.

Draw only the crop and windpipe, as the turkey is more easily handled before dressing. Choose a fat hen turkey of some six or seven pounds weight, and cut off legs up to second joint, with half the wings and the neck. Now, with a very sharp knife, make a clean cut down the entire back, and holding the knife close to the body, cut away the flesh, first on one side and then another, making a clean cut around the pope's nose. Be very careful, in cutting down the breastbone, not to break through the skin. The entire meat will now be free from the bones, save the pieces remaining in legs and wings. Cut out these, and remove all sinews. Spread the turkey skin-side down on the board. Cut out the breasts, and cut them up in long, narrow pieces, or as you like. Chop fine a pound and a half of veal or fresh pork, and a slice of fat ham also. Season with one teaspoonful of salt, a saltspoonful each of mace and pepper, half a saltspoonful of cayenne, and the juice of lemon. Cut half a pound of cold boiled smoked tongue into dice. Make layers of this force-meat, putting half of it on the turkey and then the dice of tongue, with strips of the breast between, using force meat for the last layer. Roll up the turkey in a tight roll, and sew the skin together. Now roll it firmly in a napkin, tying at the ends and across in two places to preserve the shape. Cover it with boiling water, salted as for stock, putting in all the bones and giblets, and two onions stuck with three cloves each. Boil four hours. Let it cool in the liquor. Take up in a pan, lay a tin sheet on it, and press with a heavy weight. Strain the water in which it was boiled, and put in a cold place.

Next day take off the napkin, and set the turkey in the oven a moment to melt off any fat. It can be sliced and eaten in this way, but makes a handsomer dish served as follows:

Remove the fat from the stock, and heat three pints of it to boiling-point, adding two-thirds of a package of gelatine which has been soaked in a little cold water. Strain a cupful of this into some pretty mold,--an ear of corn is a good shape,--and the remainder in two pans or deep plates, coloring each with caramel,--a teaspoonful in one, and two in the other. Lay the turkey on a small platter turned face down in a larger one, and when the jelly is cold and firm, put the molded form on top of it. Now cut part of the jelly into rounds with a pepper-box top or a small star-cutter, and arrange around the mold, chopping the rest and piling about the edge, so that the inner platter or stand is completely concealed. The outer row of jelly can have been colored red by cutting up, and boiling in the stock for it, half of a red beet. Sprigs of parsley or delicate celery-tops may be used as garnish, and it is a very elegant-looking as well as savory dish. The legs and wings can be left on and trussed outside, if liked, making it as much as possible in the original shape; but it is no better, and much more trouble.

JELLIED CHICKEN.

Tenderness is no object here, the most ancient dweller in the barnyard answering equally well, and even better than "broilers."

Draw carefully, and if the fowl is old, wash it in water in which a spoonful of soda has been dissolved, rinsing in cold. Put on in cold water, and season with a tablespoonful of salt and a half teaspoonful of pepper. Boil till the meat slips easily from the bones, reducing the broth to about a quart. Strain, and when cold, take off the fat. Where any floating particles remain, they can always be removed by laying a piece of soft paper on the broth for a moment. Cut the breast in long strips, and the rest of the meat in small pieces. Boil two or three eggs hard, and when cold, cut in thin slices. Slice a lemon very thin. Dissolve half a package of gelatine in a little cold water; heat the broth to boiling-point, and add a saltspoonful of mace, and if liked, a glass of sherry, though it is not necessary, pouring it on the gelatine. Choose a pretty mold, and lay in strips of the breast; then a layer of egg-slices, putting them close against the mold. Nearly fill with chicken, laid in lightly; then strain on the broth till it is nearly full, and set in a cold place. Dip for an instant in hot water before turning out. It is nice as a supper or lunch dish, and very pretty in effect.

*   *   *   *   *

SAUCES AND SALADS.

The foundation for a large proportion of sauces is in what the French cook knows as a *roux*, and we as "drawn butter." As our drawn butter is often lumpy, or with the taste of the raw flour, I give the French method as a security against such disaster.

TO MAKE A ROUX.

Melt in a saucepan a piece of butter the size of an egg, and add two even table-spoonfuls of sifted flour; one ounce of butter to two of flour being a safe rule. Stir till smooth, and pour in slowly one pint of milk, or milk and water, or water alone. With milk it is called *cream roux*, and is used for boiled fish and poultry. Where the butter and flour are allowed to brown, it is called a *brown roux*, and is thinned with the soup or stew which it is designed to thicken. Capers added to a *white roux*--which is the butter and flour, with water added--give *caper sauce*, for use with boiled mutton. Pickled nasturtiums are a good substitute for capers. Two hard-boiled eggs cut fine give egg sauce. Chopped parsley or pickle, and the variety of catchups and sauces, make an endless variety; the *white roux* being the basis for all of them.

BREAD SAUCE.

For this sauce boil one point of milk, with one onion cut in pieces. When it has boiled five minutes, take out the onion, and thicken the milk with half a pint of sifted bread-crumbs. Melt a teaspoonful of butter in a frying-pan; put in half a pint of coarser crumbs, stirring them till a light brown. Flavor the sauce with half a teaspoonful of salt, a saltspoonful of pepper, and a grate of nutmeg; and serve with game, helping a spoonful of the sauce, and one of the browned crumbs. The boiled onion may be minced fine and added, and the browned crumbs omitted.

CELERY SAUCE.

Wash and boil a small head of celery, which has been cut up fine, in one pint of water, with half a teaspoonful of salt. Boil till tender, which will require about half an hour. Make a *cream roux*, using half a pint of milk, and adding quarter of a saltspoonful of white pepper. Stir into the celery; boil a moment, and serve. A teaspoonful of celery salt can be used, if celery is out of season, adding it to the full rule for *cream roux*. Cauliflower may be used in the same way as celery, cutting it very fine, and adding a large cupful to the sauce. Use either with boiled meats.

MINT SAUCE.

Look over and strip off the leaves, and cut them as fine as possible with a sharp knife. Use none of the stalk but the tender tips. To a cupful of chopped mint allow an equal quantity of sugar, and half a cup of good vinegar. It should stand an hour before using.

CRANBERRY SAUCE.

Wash one quart of cranberries in warm water, and pick them over carefully. Put them in a porcelain-lined kettle, with one pint of cold water and one pint of sugar, and cook without stirring for half an hour, turning then into molds. This is the simplest method. They can be strained through a sieve, and put in bowls, forming a marmalade, which can be cut in slices when cold; or the berries can be crushed with a spoon while boiling, but left unstrained.

APPLE SAUCE.

Pare, core, and quarter some apples (sour being best), and stew till tender in just enough water to cover them. Rub them through a sieve, allowing a teacupful of sugar to a quart of strained apple, or even less, where intended to eat with roast pork or goose. Where intended for lunch or tea, do not strain, but treat as follows: Make a sirup of one large cupful of sugar and one of water for every dozen good-sized apples. Add half a lemon, cut in very thin slices. Put in the apple; cover closely, and stew till tender, keeping the quarters as whole as possible. The lemon may be omitted.

PLAIN PUDDING SAUCE.

Make a *white roux*, with a pint of either water or milk; but water will be very good. Add to it a large cup of sugar, a teaspoonful of lemon or any essence liked, and a wine-glass of wine. Vinegar can be substituted. Grate in a little nutmeg, and serve hot.

MOLASSES SAUCE.

This sauce is intended especially for apple dumplings and puddings. One pint of molasses; one tablespoonful of butter; the juice of one lemon, or a large spoonful of vinegar. Boil twenty minutes. It may be thickened with a tablespoonful of corn-starch dissolved in a little cold water, but is good in either case.

FOAMING SAUCE.

Cream half a cup of butter till very light, and add a heaping cup of sugar, beating both till white. Set the bowl in which it was beaten into a pan of boiling water, and allow it to melt slowly. Just before serving but *not before*, pour into it slowly half a cup or four spoonfuls of boiling water, stirring to a thick foam. Grate in nutmeg, or use a teaspoonful of lemon essence, and if wine is liked, add a glass of sherry or a tablespoonful of brandy. For a pudding having a decided flavor of its own, a sauce without wine is preferable.

HARD SAUCE

Beat together the same proportions of butter and sugar as in the preceding receipt; add a tablespoonful of wine if desired; pile lightly on a pretty dish; grate nutmeg over the top, and set in a cold place till used.

FRUIT SAUCES.

The sirup of any nice canned fruit may be used cold as sauce for cold puddings and blancmanges, or heated and thickened for hot, allowing to a pint of juice a heaping teaspoonful of corn-starch dissolved in a little cold water, and boiling it five minutes. Strawberry or raspberry sirup is especially nice.

PLAIN SALAD DRESSING.

Three tablespoonfuls of best olive-oil; one tablespoonful of vinegar; one salt-spoonful each of salt and pepper mixed together; and then, with three tablespoonfuls of best olive-oil, adding last the tablespoonful of vinegar. This is the simplest form of dressing. The lettuce, or other salad material, must be fresh and crisp, and should not be mixed till the moment of eating.

SPANISH TOMATO SAUCE.

One can of tomatoes or six large fresh ones; two minced onions fried brown in a large tablespoonful of butter. Add to the tomatoes with three sprigs of parsley and thyme, one teaspoonful of salt, and half a one of pepper; three cloves and two allspice, with a small blade of mace and a bit of lemon peel, and two lumps of sugar. Stew very slowly for two hours, then rub through a sieve, and return to the fire. Add two tablespoonfuls of flour, browned with a tablespoonful of butter, and boil up once. It should be smooth and thick. Keep on ice, and it will keep a week. Excellent.

MAYONNAISE SAUCE.

For this sauce use the yolks of three raw eggs; one even tablespoonful of mustard; one of sugar; one teaspoonful of salt; and a saltspoonful of cayenne.

Break the egg yolks into a bowl; beat a few strokes, and gradually add the mustard, sugar, salt, and pepper. Now take a pint bottle of best olive-oil, and stir in a few drops at a time. The sauce will thicken like a firm jelly. When the oil is half in, add the juice of one lemon by degrees with the remainder of the oil; and last, add quarter of a cup of good vinegar. This will keep for weeks, and can be used with either chicken, salmon, or vegetable salad.

A simpler form can be made with the yolk of one egg, half a pint of oil, and half the ingredients given above. It can be colored red with the juice of a boiled beet, or with the coral of a lobster, and is very nice as a dressing for raw tomatoes, cutting them in thick slices, and putting a little of it on each slice.

Mayonnaise may be varied in many ways, *sauce tartare* being a favorite one. This is simply two even tablespoonfuls of capers, half a small onion, and a tablespoonful of parsley, and two gherkins or a small cucumber, all minced fine and added to half a pint of mayonnaise. This keeps a long time, and is very nice for fried fish or plain boiled tongue.

DRESSING WITHOUT OIL.

Cream a small cup of butter, and stir into it the yolks of three eggs. Mix together one teaspoonful of mustard, one teaspoonful of salt, and quarter of a saltspoonful of cayenne, and add to the butter and egg. Stir in slowly, instead of oil, one cup of cream, and add the juice of one lemon and half a cup of vinegar.

BOILED DRESSING FOR COLD SLAW.

This is good also for vegetable salads. One small cup of good vinegar; two table-spoonfuls of sugar; half a teaspoonful each of salt and mustard; a saltspoonful of pepper; a piece of butter the size of a walnut; and two beaten eggs. Put these all in a small saucepan over the fire, and stir till it becomes a smooth paste. Have a firm, white cabbage, very cold, and chopped fine; and mix the dressing well through it. It will keep several days in a cold place.

CHICKEN SALAD.

Boil a tender chicken, and when cold, cut all the meat in dice. Cut up white tender celery enough to make the same amount, and mix with the meat. Stir into it a tablespoonful of oil with three of vinegar, and a saltspoonful each of mustard and salt, and let it stand an hour or two. When ready to serve, mix the whole with a mayonnaise sauce, leaving part to mask the top; or use the mayonnaise alone, without the first dressing of vinegar and oil. Lettuce can be substituted for celery; and where neither is obtainable, a crisp white cabbage may be chopped fine, and the meat of the chicken also, and either a teaspoonful of extract of celery or celery-seed used to flavor it The fat of the chicken, taken from the water in which it was boiled, carefully melted and strained, and cooled again, is often used by Southern housekeepers.

SALMON MAYONNAISE.

Carefully remove all the skin and bones from a pound of boiled salmon, or use a small can of the sealed, draining away all the liquid. Cut in small pieces, and season with two tablespoonfuls of vinegar, half a small onion minced fine, and half a teaspoonful each of salt and pepper. Cover the bottom of the salad dish with crisp lettuce-leaves; lay the salmon on it, and pour on the sauce. The meat of a lobster can be treated in the same way.

*   *   *   *   *

EGGS, CHEESE, AND BREAKFAST DISHES.

BOILED EGGS.

Let the water be boiling fast when the eggs are put in, that it may not be checked. They should have lain in warm water a few minutes before boiling, to prevent the shells cracking. Allow three minutes for a soft-boiled egg; four, to have the white firmly set; and ten, for a hard-boiled egg. Another method is to pour boiling water on the eggs, and let them stand for ten minutes where they will be nearly at boiling-point, though not boiling. The white and yolk are then perfectly cooked, and of jelly-like consistency.

POACHED EGGS.

Have a deep frying-pan full of boiling water,--simmering, not boiling furiously. Put in two teaspoonfuls of vinegar and a teaspoonful of salt. Break each egg into a cup or saucer, allowing one for each person; slide gently into the water, and let them stand five minutes, but without boiling. Have ready small slices of buttered toast which have been previously dipped quickly into hot water. Take up the eggs on a skimmer; trim the edges evenly, and slip off upon the toast, serving at once. For fried eggs, see *Ham and Eggs*, p. 158.

SCRAMBLED EGGS.

Break half a dozen eggs into a bowl, and beat for a minute. Have the frying-pan hot. Melt a tablespoonful of butter, with an even teaspoonful of salt and a saltspoonful of pepper, and turn in the eggs. Stir them constantly as they harden, until they are a firm yet delicate mixture of white and yellow, and turn into a hot dish, serving at once. A cup of milk may be added if liked. The whole operation should not exceed five minutes.

BAKED EGGS.

Break the eggs into a buttered pudding-dish. Salt and pepper them very lightly, and bake in a quick oven till set. Or turn over them a cupful of good gravy, that of veal or poultry being especially nice, and bake in the same way. Serve in the dish they were baked in.

STUFFED EGGS.

Boil eggs for twenty minutes. Drop them in cold water, and when cold, take off the shells, and cut the egg in two lengthwise. Take out the yolks carefully; rub them fine on a plate, and add an equal amount of deviled ham, or of cold tongue or chicken, minced very fine. If chicken is used, add a saltspoonful of salt and a pinch of cayenne. Roll the mixture into little balls the size of the yolk; fill each white with it; arrange on a dish with sprigs of parsley, and use cold as a lunch dish. They can also be served hot by laying them in a deep buttered pie-plate, covering with a cream *roux*, dusting thickly with bread-crumbs, and browning in a quick oven.

PLAIN OMELET.

The pan for frying an omelet should be clean and very smooth. Break the eggs one by one into a cup, to avoid the risk of a spoiled one. Allow from three to five, but never *over* five, for a single omelet. Turn them into a bowl, and give them twelve beats with whisk or fork. Put butter the size of an egg into the frying-pan, and let it run over the entire surface. As it begins to boil, turn in the eggs. Hold the handle of the pan in one hand, and with the other draw the egg constantly up from the edges as it sets, passing a knife underneath to let the butter run under. Shake the pan now and then to keep the omelet from scorching. It should be firm at the edges, and creamy in the middle. When done, either fold over one-half on the other, and turn on to a hot platter to serve at once, or set in the oven a minute to brown the top, turning it out in a round. A little chopped ham or parsley may be added. The myriad forms of omelet to be found in large cook-books are simply this plain one, with a spoonful or so of chopped mushrooms or tomatoes or green pease laid in the middle of it just before folding and serving. A variation is also made by beating whites and yolks separately, then adding half a cup of cream or milk; doubling the seasoning given above, and then following the directions for frying. Quarter of an onion and a sprig or two of parsley minced fine are a very nice addition. A cupful of finely minced fish, either fresh or salt, makes a fish omlet. Chopped oysters may also be used; and many persons like a large spoonful of grated cheese, though this is a French rather than American taste.

BAKED OMELET.

One large cup of milk; five eggs; a saltspoonful of salt; and half a one of white pepper mixed with the last. Beat the eggs well, a Dover egg-beater being the best possible one where yolks and whites are not separated; add the salt and pepper, and then the milk. Melt a piece of butter the size of an egg in a frying-pan, and when it boils, pour in the egg. Let it stand two minutes, or long enough to harden a little, but do not stir at all. When a little firm, put into a quick oven, and bake till brown. It will rise very high, but falls almost immediately. Serve at once on a very hot platter. This omelet can also be varied with chopped ham or parsley. The old-fashioned iron spider with short handle is best for baking it, as a long-handled pan cannot be shut up in the oven. This omelet can also be fried in large spoonfuls, like pancakes, rolling each one as done.

CHEESE FONDU.

This preparation of grated cheese and eggs can be made in a large dish for several people, or in "portions" for one, each in a small earthen dish. For one portion allow two eggs; half a saltspoonful of salt; a heaping tablespoonful of grated cheese; two of milk; and a few grains of cayenne. Melt a teaspoonful of butter in the dish, and when it boils, pour in the cheese and egg, and cook slowly till it is well set. It is served in the dish in which it is cooked, and should be eaten at once.

An adaptation of this has been made by Mattieu Williams, the author of the "Chemistry of Cookery." It is as follows:--

Soak enough slices of bread to fill a quart pudding-dish, in a pint of milk, to which half a teaspoonful of salt and two beaten eggs have been added. Butter the pudding-dish and lay in the bread, putting a thick coating of grated cheese on each slice. Pour what milk may remain over the top, and bake slowly about half an hour.

CHEESE SOUFFLE.

Melt in a saucepan two tablespoonfuls of butter, and add to it half a teaspoonful of dry mustard; a grain of cayenne; a saltspoonful of white pepper; a grate of nutmeg; two tablespoonfuls of flour; and stir all smooth, adding a gill of milk and a large cupful of grated cheese. Stir into this as much powdered bi-carbonate of potash as will stand on a three-cent piece, and then beat in three eggs, yolks and whites beaten separately. Pour this into a buttered earthen dish; bake in a quick oven, and serve at once. In all cases where cheese disagrees it will be found that the bi-carbonate of potash renders it harmless.

TO BOIL OATMEAL OR CRUSHED WHEAT.

Have ready a quart of boiling water in a farina-boiler, or use a small pail set in a saucepan of boiling water. If oatmeal or any grain is boiled in a single saucepan, it forms, no matter how often it is stirred, a thick crust on the bottom; and, as *never to stir* is a cardinal rule for all these preparations, let the next one be, a double boiler.

Add a teaspoonful of salt to the quart of water in the inside boiler. Be sure it is boiling, and then throw in one even cup of oatmeal or crushed wheat. Now *let it alone* for two hours, only being sure that the water in the outside saucepan does not dry away, but boils steadily. When done, each grain should be distinct, yet jelly-like. Stirring makes a mere mush, neither very attractive nor palatable. If there is not time for this long boiling in the morning, let it be done the afternoon before. Do not turn out the oatmeal, but fill the outer boiler next morning, and let it boil half an hour, or till heated through.

COARSE HOMINY.

Treat like oatmeal, using same amount to a quart of water, save that it must be thoroughly washed beforehand. Three hours' boiling is better than two.

FINE HOMINY.

Allow a cupful to a quart of boiling, salted water. Wash it in two or three waters, put over, and boil steadily for half an hour, or till it will pour out easily. If too thin, boil uncovered for a short time. Stir in a tablespoonful of butter before sending to table. Any of these preparations may be cut in slices when cold, floured on each side, and fried brown like mush.

FINE HOMINY CAKES.

One pint of cold boiled hominy; two eggs; a saltspoonful of salt; and a tablespoonful of butter melted. Break up the hominy fine with a fork, and add salt and butter. Beat the eggs,--whites and yolks separately; add the yolks first, and last the whites; and either fry brown in a little butter or drop by spoonfuls on buttered plates, and bake brown in a quick oven. This is a nice side-dish at dinner. Oatmeal and wheat can be used in the same way at breakfast.

HASTY PUDDING, OR MUSH.

One cup of sifted Indian meal, stirred smooth in a bowl with a little cold water. Have ready a quart of boiling water, with a teaspoonful of salt, and pour in the meal. Boil half an hour, or till it will just pour, stirring often. To be eaten hot with butter and sirup. Rye or graham flour can be used in the same way. If intended to fry, pour the hot mush into a shallow pan which has been wet with cold water to prevent its sticking. A spoonful of butter may be added while hot, but is not necessary. Cut in thin slices when cold; flour each side; and fry brown in a little butter or nice drippings, serving hot.

WHAT TO DO WITH COLD POTATOES.

Chop, as for hash; melt a tablespoonful of either butter or nice drippings in a frying-pan; add, for six or eight good-sized potatoes, one even teaspoonful of salt and a saltspoonful of pepper. When the fat boils, put in the potatoes, and fry for about ten minutes, or until well browned. As soon as they are done, if not ready to use, move to the back of the stove, that they may not burn.

Or cut each potato in lengthwise slices; dredge on a little flour; and fry brown on each side, watching carefully that they do not burn. The fat from two or three slices of fried salt pork may be used for these.

LYONNAISE POTATOES.

Slice six cold boiled potatoes. Mince very fine an onion and two or three sprigs of parsley,--enough to fill a teaspoon. Melt in a frying-pan a tablespoonful of butter; put in the onion, and fry light brown; then add the potatoes, and fry to a light brown also, turning them often. Put into a hot dish, stirring in the minced parsley, and pouring over them any butter that may be left in the pan.

STEWED POTATOES.

One pint of cold boiled potatoes cut in bits; one cup of milk; butter the size of an egg; a heaping teaspoonful of flour. Melt the butter in a saucepan; add the flour, and cook a moment; and pour in the milk, an even teaspoonful of salt, and a saltspoonful of white pepper. When it boils, add the potatoes. Boil a minute, and serve.

SARATOGA POTATOES.

Pare potatoes, and slice thin as wafers, either with a potato-slicer or a thin-bladed, very sharp knife. Lay in very cold water at least an hour before using. If for breakfast, over-night is better. Have boiling lard at least three inches deep in a frying kettle or pan. Dry the potatoes thoroughly in a towel, and drop in a few slices at a time, frying to a golden brown. Take out with a skimmer, and lay on a double brown paper in the oven to dry, salting them lightly. They may be eaten either hot or cold. Three medium-sized potatoes will make a large dishful; or, as they keep perfectly well, enough may be done at once for several meals, heating them a few minutes in the oven before using.

FISH BALLS.

One pint of cold salt fish, prepared as on page 136, and chopped very fine. Eight good-sized, freshly-boiled potatoes, or enough to make a quart when mashed. Mash with half a teaspoonful of salt, and a heaping tablespoonful of butter, and, if liked, a teaspoonful of made mustard. Mix in the chopped fish, blending both thoroughly. Make into small, round cakes; flour on each side; and fry brown in a little drippings or fat of fried pork. A nicer way is to make into round balls, allowing a large tablespoonful to each. Roll in flour; or they can be egged and crumbed like croquettes. Drop into boiling lard; drain on brown paper, and serve hot. Fresh fish can be used in the same way, and is very nice. Breadcrumbs, softened in milk, can be used instead of potato, but are not so good.

FISH HASH.

Use either fresh fish or salt. If the former, double the measure of salt will be needed. Prepare and mix as in fish balls, allowing always double the amount of fresh mashed potato that you have of fish. Melt a large spoonful of butter or drippings in a frying-pan. When hot, put in the fish. Let it stand till brown on the bottom, and then stir. Do this two or three times, letting it brown at the last, pressing it into omelet form, and turning out on a hot platter, or piling it lightly.

FISH WITH CREAM.

One pint of cold minced fish, either salt cod or fresh fish; always doubling the amount of seasoning given if fresh is used. Melt in a frying-pan a tablespoonful of butter; stir in a heaping one of flour, and cook a minute; then add a pint of milk and a saltspoonful each of salt and pepper. When it boils, stir in the fish, and add two well-beaten eggs. Cook for a minute, and serve very hot.

Cold salmon, or that put up unspiced, is nice done in this way. The eggs can be omitted, but it is not as good. If cream is plenty, use part cream. Any cold boiled fresh fish can be used in this way.

SALT MACKEREL OR ROE HERRING.

Soak over-night, the skin-side up. In the morning wipe dry, and either broil, as in general directions for broiling fish, page 133, or fry brown in pork fat or drippings.

Salted shad are treated in the same way. All are better broiled.

FRIED SAUSAGES.

If in skins, prick them all over with a large darning-needle or fork; throw them into a saucepan of boiling water and boil for one minute. Take out, wipe dry, and lay in a hot frying-pan, in which has been melted a tablespoonful of hot lard or drippings. Turn often. As soon as brown they are done. If gravy is wanted, stir a tablespoonful of flour into the fat in the pan; add a cup of boiling water, and salt to taste,--about a saltspoonful,--and pour, not *over*, but around the sausages. Serve hot.

FRIZZLED BEEF.

Half a pound of smoked beef cut very thin. This can be just heated in a table-spoonful of hot butter, and then served, or prepared as follows:--

Pour boiling water on the beef, and let it stand five minutes. In the meantime melt in a frying-pan one tablespoonful of butter; stir in a tablespoonful of flour, and add slowly half a pint of milk or water. Put in the beef which has been taken from the water; cook a few minutes, and add two or three well-beaten eggs, cooking only a minute longer. It can be prepared without eggs, or they may be added to the beef just heated in butter; but the last method is best.

VEAL LOAF.

Three pounds of lean veal and quarter of a pound of salt pork chopped very fine. Mince an onion as fine as possible. Grate a nutmeg, or use half a teaspoonful of powdered mace, mixing it with an even tablespoonful of salt, and an even salt-spoonful of cayenne pepper. Add three well-beaten eggs, a teacupful of milk, and a large spoonful of melted butter. Mix the ingredients very thoroughly; form into a loaf; cover thickly with sifted bread or cracker crumbs, and bake three hours, bast-ing now and then with a little butter and water. When cold, cut in thin slices, and use for breakfast or tea. It is good for breakfast with baked potatoes, and slices of it are sometimes served around a salad. A glass of wine is sometimes added before baking.

MEAT HASH.

The English hash is meat cut either in slices or mouthfuls, and warmed in the gravy; and the Southern hash is the same. A genuine hash, however, requires po-tato, and may be made of any sort of meat; cold roast beef being excellent, and cold corned beef best of all. Mutton is good; but veal should always be used as a mince, and served on toast as in the rule to be given.

Chop the meat fine, and allow one-third meat to two-thirds potato. For corned-beef hash the potatoes should be freshly boiled and mashed. For other cold meats finely-chopped cold potatoes will answer. To a quart of the mixture allow a tea-spoonful of salt and half a teaspoonful of pepper mixed together, and sprinkled on the meat before chopping. Heat a tablespoonful of butter or nice drippings in a frying-pan; moisten the hash with a little cold gravy or water; and heat slowly, stir-ring often. It may be served on buttered toast when hot, without browning, but is better browned. To accomplish this, first heat through, then set on the back of the stove, and let it stand twenty minutes. Fold like an omelet, or turn out in a round, and serve hot.

MINCED VEAL.

Chop cold veal fine, picking out all bits of gristle. To a pint-bowlful allow a large cup of boiling water; a tablespoonful of butter and one of flour; a teaspoonful of salt; and a saltspoonful each of pepper and mace. Make a *roux* with the butter and flour, and add the seasoning; put in the veal, and cook five minutes, serving it on buttered toast, made as in directions given for water toast.

TOAST, DRY OR BUTTERED.

Not one person in a hundred makes good toast; yet nothing can be simpler. Cut the slices of bread evenly, and rather thin. If a wire toaster is used, several can be done at once. Hold just far enough from the fire to brown nicely; and turn often, that there may be no scorching. Toast to an even, golden brown. No rule will secure this, and only experience and care will teach one just what degree of heat will do it. If to be buttered dry, butter each slice evenly as taken from the fire, and pile on a hot plate. If served without butter, either send to table in a toast-rack, or, if on a plate, do not pile together, but let the slices touch as little as possible, that they may not steam and lose crispness.

WATER TOAST.

Have a pan of boiling hot, well-salted water; a teaspoonful to a quart being the invariable rule. Dip each slice of toast quickly into this. It must not be *wet*, but only moistened. Butter, and pile on a hot plate. Poached eggs and minces are served on this form of toast, which is also nice with fricasseed chicken.

MILK TOAST.

Scald a quart of milk in a double boiler, and thicken it with two even table-spoonfuls of corn-starch dissolved in a little cold water, or the same amount of flour. Add a teaspoonful of salt, and a heaping tablespoonful of butter. Have ready a dozen slices of water toast, which, unless wanted quite rich, needs no butter. Pour the thickened milk into a pan, that each slice may be easily dipped into it, and pile them when dipped in a deep dish, pouring the rest of the milk over them. Serve very hot. Cream is sometimes used instead of milk, in which case no thickening is put in, and only a pint heated with a saltspoonful of salt.

*   *   *   *   *

TEA, COFFEE, ETC.

For these a cardinal rule has already been given in Part I., but can not be en-
forced too often; viz., the necessity of fresh water boiled, and used as soon as it boils,
that the gases which give it character and sparkle may not have had time to escape.
Tea and coffee both should be kept from the air, but the former even more carefully
than the latter, as the delicate flavor evaporates more quickly.

TEA.

To begin with, never use a tin teapot if an earthen one is obtainable. An even
teaspoonful of dry tea is the usual allowance for a person. Scald the teapot with
a little *boiling water*, and pour it off. Put in the tea, and pour on not over a cup of
boiling water, letting it stand a minute or two for the leaves to swell. Then fill with
the needed amount of *water still boiling*, this being about a small cupful to a person.
Cover closely, and let it stand five minutes. Ten will be required for English breakfast tea, but *never boil* either, above all in a tin pot. Boiling liberates the tannic acid
of the tea, which acts upon the tin, making a compound bitter and metallic in taste,
and unfit for human stomachs.

COFFEE.

The best coffee is made from a mixture of two-thirds Java and one-third Mocha; the Java giving strength, and the Mocha flavor and aroma. The roasting must be
very perfectly done. If done at home, constant stirring is necessary to prevent burning; but all good grocers use now rotary roasters, which brown each grain perfectly.
Buy in small quantities *unground*; keep closely covered; and if the highest flavor is
wanted, heat hot before grinding.

A noted German chemist claims to have discovered an effectual antidote to the
harmful effects of coffee,--an antidote for which he had searched for years. In his
experiments he discovered that the fibre of cotton, in its natural state before bleach-
ing, neutralizes the harmful principle of the caffein. To make absolutely harmless
coffee which yet has no loss of flavor, it is to be boiled in a bag of unbleached
cheese-cloth or something equally porous. In the coffee-pot of his invention, the
rounds of cotton are slipped between two cylinders of tin, and the boiling water is

poured through once or twice, on the same principle as French filtered coffee. The cloths must be rinsed in hot and then cold water daily and carefully dried; and none are to be used longer than one week, as at the end of that time, even with careful washing, the fibre is saturated with the harmful principle. The same proportions of coffee as those given below are used, and the pot must stand in a hot place while the water filters through.

For a quart of coffee allow four heaping tablespoonfuls of coffee when ground. Scald the coffee-pot; mix the ground coffee with a little cold water and two or three egg-shells, which can be dried and kept for this purpose. Part of a fresh egg with the shell is still better. Put into the hot coffee-pot, and pour on one quart of *boiling water*. Cover tightly, and boil five minutes; then pour out a cupful to free the spout from grounds, and return this to the pot. Let it stand a few minutes to settle, and serve with boiled milk, and cream if it is to be had. Never for appearance's sake decant coffee. Much of the flavor is lost by turning from one pot into another, and the shapes are now sufficiently pretty to make the block tin ones not at all unpresentable at table.

Where coffee is required for a large company, allow a pound and a half to a gallon of water.

Coffee made in a French filter or biggin is considered better by many; but I have preferred to give a rule that may be used with certainty where French cooking utensils are unknown.

COCOA, BROMA, AND SHELLS.

The directions found on packages of these articles are always reliable. The *cocoa* or *broma* should be mixed smoothly with a little boiling water, and added to that in the saucepan; one quart of either requiring a pint each of milk and water, about three tablespoonfuls of cocoa, and a small cup of sugar. A pinch of salt is always a great improvement. Boil for half an hour.

SHELLS are merely the husk of the cocoa-nut; and a cupful to a quart of boiling water is the amount needed. Boil steadily an hour, and use with milk and sugar.

CHOCOLATE.

This rule, though unlike that given in cook-books generally, makes a drink in consistency and flavor like that offered at Maillard's or Mendee's, the largest chocolate manufacturers in the country.

Scrape or grate fine two squares (two ounces) of Baker's or any unsweetened chocolate. Add to this one small cup of sugar and a pinch of salt, and put into a saucepan with a tablespoonful of water. Stir for a few minutes till smooth and glossy, and then pour in gradually one pint of milk and one of boiling water. Let all boil a minute. Dissolve one heaping teaspoonful of corn-starch or arrow-root in a little cold water, and add to the chocolate. Boil one minute, and serve. If cream can be had, whip to a stiff froth, allowing two tablespoonfuls of sugar and a few drops of vanilla essence to a cup of cream. Serve a spoonful laid on the top of the chocolate in each cup. The corn-starch may be omitted, but is necessary to the perfection of this rule, the following of which renders the chocolate not only smooth, but entirely free from any oily particles. Flavor is lost by any longer boiling, though usually half an hour has been considered necessary.

*   *   *   *   *

VEGETABLES.
POTATOES.

To be able to boil a potato perfectly is one of the tests of a good cook, there being nothing in the whole range of vegetables which is apparently so difficult to accomplish. Like the making of good bread, nothing is simpler when once learned. A good boiled potato should be white, mealy, and served very hot. If the potatoes are old, peel thinly with a sharp knife; cut out all spots, and let them lie in cold water some hours before using. It is more economical to boil before peeling, as the best part of the potato lies next the skin; but most prefer them peeled. Put on in boiling water, allowing a teaspoonful of salt to every quart of water. Medium-sized potatoes will boil in half an hour. Let them be as nearly of a size as possible, and if small and large are cooked at the same time, put on the large ones ten or fifteen minutes before the small. When done, pour off every drop of water; cover with a clean towel, and set on the back of the range to dry for a few minutes before serving. The poorest potato can be made tolerable by this treatment. Never let them wait for other things, but time the preparation of dinner so that they will be ready at the moment needed. New potatoes require no peeling, but should merely be well washed and rubbed.

MASHED POTATOES.

Boil as directed, and when dry and mealy, mash fine with a potato-masher or large spoon, allowing for a dozen medium-sized potatoes a piece of butter the size of an egg, half a cup of milk, a teaspoonful of salt, and half a teaspoonful of white pepper. The milk may be omitted if the potato is preferred dry. Pile lightly in a dish, or smooth over, and serve at once. Never brown in the oven, as it destroys the good flavor.

POTATO SNOW.

Mash as above, and rub through a colander into a very hot dish, being careful not to press it down in any way, and serve hot as possible.

BAKED POTATOES.

Wash and scrub carefully, as some persons eat the skin. A large potato requires an hour to bake. Their excellence depends upon being eaten the moment they are done.

POTATOES WITH BEEF.

Pare, and lay in cold water at least an hour. An hour before a roast of beef is done, lay in the pan, and baste them when the beef is basted. They are very nice.

POTATO CROQUETTES.

Cold mashed potatoes may be used, but fresh is better. To half a dozen potatoes, mashed as in directions given, allow quarter of a saltspoonful each of mace or nutmeg and cayenne pepper, and one beaten egg. Make in little balls or rolls; egg and crumb, and fry in boiling lard. Drain on brown paper, and serve like chicken croquettes.

SWEET POTATOES.

Wash carefully, and boil without peeling from three-quarters of an hour to an hour. Peel, and dry in the oven ten minutes. They are better baked, requiring about an hour for medium-sized ones.

BEETS.

Winter beets should be soaked over-night. Wash them carefully; but never peel or even prick them, as color and sweetness would be lost. Put in boiling, salted water. Young beets will cook in two hours; old ones require five or six. Peel, and if large, cut in slices, putting a little butter on each one. They can be served cold in a little vinegar.

PARSNIPS.

Wash, and scrape clean; cut lengthwise in halves, and boil an hour, or two if very old. Serve whole with a little drawn butter, or mash fine, season well, allowing to half a dozen large parsnips a teaspoonful of salt, a saltspoonful of pepper, and a tablespoonful of butter.

PARSNIP FRITTERS.

Three large parsnips boiled and mashed fine, adding two well-beaten eggs, half a teaspoonful of salt, a saltspoonful of pepper, two tablespoonfuls of milk, and one heaping one of flour. Drop in spoonfuls, and fry brown in a little hot butter. *Oyster-plant* fritters are made in the same way.

OYSTER-PLANT STEWED.

Scrape, and throw at once into cold water with a little vinegar in it, to keep them from turning black. Cut in small pieces, or boil whole for an hour. Mash fine, and make like parsnip fritters; or drain the pieces dry, and serve with drawn butter.

CARROTS.

Carrots are most savory boiled with corned beef for two hours. They may also be boiled plain, cut in slices, and served with drawn butter. For old carrots not less than two hours will be necessary. Plenty of water must be used, and when cold the carrots are to be cut in dice. Melt in a saucepan a spoonful of butter; add half a teaspoonful of salt, a saltspoonful of pepper, and a teaspoonful of sugar, and when the butter boils put in the carrots, and stir till heated through. Pile them in the centre of a platter, and put around them a can of French peas, which have been cooked in only a spoonful of water, with a teaspoonful of sugar, a spoonful of butter, half a teaspoonful of salt, and a dash of pepper. This is a pretty and excellent dish, and substantial as meat. A cup of stock can be added to the carrots if desired, but they are better without it.

TURNIPS.

Pare and cut in quarters. Boil in well-salted water for an hour, or until tender. Drain off the water, and let them stand a few minutes to dry; then mash fine, allowing for about a quart a teaspoonful of salt, half a one of pepper, and a piece of butter the size of a walnut.

Or they may be left in pieces, and served with drawn butter.

CABBAGE.

Wash, and look over very carefully, and lay in cold water an hour. Cut in quarters, and boil with corned beef an hour, or till tender, or with a small piece of salt pork. Drain, and serve whole as possible. A much nicer way is to boil in well-salted water, changing it once after the first half-hour. Boil an hour; take up and drain; chop fine, and add a teacupful of milk, a piece of butter the size of an egg, a teaspoonful of salt, and half a one of pepper. Serve very hot. For cabbage Virginia fashion, and the best of fashions, too, bake this last form in a buttered pudding-dish, having first stirred in two or three well-beaten eggs, and covered the top with bread-crumbs. Bake till brown.

CAULIFLOWER.

Wash and trim, and boil in a bag made of mosquito-netting to keep it whole. Boil steadily in well-salted water for one hour. Dish carefully, and pour over it a nice drawn butter. Any cold remains may be used as salad, or chopped and baked, as in rule for baked cabbage.

ONIONS.

If milk is plenty, use equal quantities of skim-milk and water, allowing a quart of each for a dozen or so large onions. If water alone is used, change it after the first half-hour, as this prevents their turning dark; salting as for all vegetables, and boiling young onions one hour; old ones, two. Either chop fine, and add a spoonful of butter, half a teaspoonful of salt, and a little pepper, or serve them whole in a dressing made by heating one cup of milk with the same butter and other seasoning as when chopped. Put the onions in a hot dish, pour this over them, and serve. They may also be half boiled; then put in a buttered dish, covered with this sauce and a layer of bread-crumbs, and baked for an hour.

WINTER SQUASH.

Cut in two, and take out the seeds and fiber. Half will probably be enough to cook at once. Cut this in pieces; pare off the rind, and lay each piece in a steamer. Never boil in water if it can be avoided, as it must be as dry as possible. Steam for two hours. Mash fine, or run through a vegetable sifter, and, for a quart or so of squash, allow a piece of butter the size of an egg, a teaspoonful of salt, and a salt-spoonful of pepper. Serve very hot.

SUMMER SQUASH, OR CIMLINS.

Steam as directed above, taking out the seeds, but not peeling them. Mash through a colander; season, and serve hot. If very young, the seeds are often cooked in them. Half an hour will be sufficient.

PEASE.

Shell, and put over in boiling, salted water, to which a teaspoonful of sugar has been added. Boil till tender, half an hour or a little more. Drain off the water; add a piece of butter the size of an egg, and a saltspoonful of salt. If the pease are old, put a bit of soda the size of a pea in the water.

FIELD PEASE.

These are generally used after drying. Soak over-night, and boil two hours, or till tender, with or without a small piece of bacon. If without, butter as for green pease. Or they can be mashed fine, rubbed through a sieve, and then seasoned, adding a pinch of cayenne pepper.

In Virginia they are often boiled, mashed a little, and fried in a large cake.

SUCCOTASH.

Boil green corn and beans separately. Cut the corn from the cob, and season both as in either alone. A nicer way, however, is to score the rows in half a dozen ears of corn; scrape off the corn; add a pint of lima or any nice green bean, and boil one hour in a quart of boiling water, with one teaspoonful each of salt and sugar, and a saltspoonful of pepper. Let the water boil away to about a cupful; add a spoonful of butter, and serve in a hot dish. Many, instead of butter, use with it a small piece of pork,--about quarter of a pound; but it is better without. A spoonful of cream may be added. Canned corn and beans may be used; and even dried beans and coarse hominy--the former well soaked, and both boiled together three hours--are very good.

STRING BEANS.

String, cut in bits, and boil an hour if very young. If old, an hour and an half, or even two, may be needed. Drain off the water, and season like green pease.

SHELLED BEANS.

Any green bean may be used in this way, lima and butter beans being the nicest. Put on in boiling, salted water, and boil not less than one hour. Season like string beans.

GREEN CORN.

Husk, and pick off all the silk. Boil in well-salted water, and serve on the cob, wrapped in a napkin, or cut off and seasoned like beans. Cutting down through each row gives, when scraped off, the kernel without the hull.

GREEN-CORN FRITTERS.

One pint of green corn grated. This will require about six ears. Mix with this, half a cup of milk, two well-beaten eggs, half a cup of flour, one teaspoonful of salt, half a teaspoonful of pepper, and a tablespoonful of melted butter. Fry in very small cakes in a little hot butter, browning well on both sides. Serve very hot.

CORN PUDDING.

One pint of cut or grated corn, one pint of milk, two well-beaten eggs, one tea-spoonful of salt, and a saltspoonful of pepper. Butter a pudding-dish, and bake the mixture half an hour. Canned corn can be used in the same way.

EGG-PLANT.

Peel, cut in slices half an inch thick, and lay them in well-salted water for an hour. Wipe dry; dip in flour or meal, and fry brown on each side. Fifteen minutes will be needed to cook sufficiently. The slices can be egged and crumbed before fry-ing, and are nicer than when merely floured.

EGG-PLANT FRITTERS.

Peel the egg-plant, and take out the seeds. Boil for an hour in well-salted water. Drain as dry as possible; mash fine, and prepare precisely like corn fritters.

BAKED EGG-PLANT.

Peel, and cut out a piece from the top; remove the seeds, and fill the space with a dressing like that for ducks, fitting in the piece cut out. Bake an hour, basting with a spoonful of butter melted in a cup of water, and dredging with flour between each basting. It is very nice.

ASPARAGUS.

Wash, and cut off almost all of the white end. Tie up in small bundles; put into boiling, salted water, and cook till tender,--about half an hour, or more if old.

Make some slices of water toast, as in rule given, using the water in which the asparagus was boiled; lay the slices on a hot platter, and the asparagus upon them, pouring a spoonful of melted butter over it. The asparagus may be cut in little bits, and, when boiled, a drawn butter poured over it, or served on toast, as when left whole. Cold asparagus may be cut fine, and used in an omelet, or simply warmed over.

SPINACH.

Not less than a peck is needed for a dinner for three or four. Pick over carefully, wash, and let it lie in cold water an hour or two. Put on in boiling, salted water, and boil an hour, or until tender. Take up in a colander, that it may drain perfectly. Have in a hot dish a piece of butter the size of an egg, half a teaspoonful of salt, a saltspoonful of pepper, and, if liked, a tablespoonful of vinegar. Chop the spinach fine, and put in the dish, stirring in this dressing thoroughly. A teacupful of cream is often added. Any tender greens, beet or turnip tops, kale, &c., are treated in this way; kale, however, requiring two hours' boiling.

ARTICHOKES.

Cut off the outside leaves; trim the bottom; throw into boiling, salted water, with a teaspoonful of vinegar in it, and boil an hour. Season, and serve like turnips, or with drawn butter poured over them.

TOMATOES STEWED.

Pour on boiling water to take off the skins; cut in pieces, and stew slowly for half an hour; adding for a dozen tomatoes a tablespoonful of butter, a teaspoonful of salt, a saltspoonful of pepper, and a teaspoonful of sugar. Where they are preferred sweet, two tablespoonfuls of sugar will be necessary. They may be thickened with a tablespoonful of flour or corn-starch dissolved in a little cold water, or with half a cup of rolled cracker or bread crumbs. Canned tomatoes are stewed in the same way.

BAKED TOMATOES.

Take off the skins; lay the tomatoes in a buttered pudding-dish; put a bit of butter on each one. Mix a teaspoonful of salt, and a saltspoonful of pepper, with a cup of bread or cracker crumbs, and cover the top. Bake an hour.

Or cut the tomatoes in bits, and put a layer of them and one of seasoned crumbs, ending with crumbs. Dot the top with bits of butter, that it may brown well, and bake in the same way. Canned tomatoes are almost equally good. Thin slices of well-buttered bread may be used instead of crumbs.

FRIED TOMATOES.

Cut in thick slices. Mix in a plate half a teacupful of flour, a saltspoonful of salt, and half a one of pepper; and dip each slice in this, frying brown in hot butter.

BROILED TOMATOES.

Prepare as for frying, and broil in a wire broiler, putting a bit of butter on each slice when brown, and serving on a hot dish or on buttered toast.

RICE.

Wash in cold water, changing it at least twice. It is better if allowed to soak an hour. Drain, and throw into a good deal of boiling, salted water, allowing not less than two quarts to a cupful of rice. Boil twenty minutes, stirring now and then. Pour into a colander, that every drop of water may drain off, and then set it at the back of the stove to dry for ten minutes. In this way every grain is distinct, yet perfectly tender. If old, half an hour's boiling may be required. Test by biting a grain at the end of twenty minutes. If tender, it is done.

RICE CROQUETTES.

Where used as a vegetable with dinner, to a pint of cold boiled rice allow a tablespoonful of melted butter and one or two well-beaten eggs. Mix thoroughly. A pinch of cayenne or a little chopped parsley may be added. Make in the shape of corks; egg and crumb, and fry a golden brown.

MACARONI.

Never wash macaroni if it can be avoided. Break in lengths of three or four inches and throw into boiling, salted water, allowing quarter of a pound for a dinner for three or four. Boil for half an hour, and drain off the water. It may be served plain with tomato sauce, or simply buttered, or with drawn butter poured over it.

MACARONI WITH CHEESE.

Boil as directed. Make a pint of white sauce or *roux*, as on p. 169, using milk if it can be had, though water answers. Have a cupful of good grated cheese. Butter a pudding-dish. Put in a layer of macaroni, one of sauce, and one of cheese, ending with cheese. Dust the top with sifted bread or cracker crumbs, dot with bits of butter, and bake fifteen minutes in a quick oven. It can be baked in the same way without cheese, or with simply a cup of milk and two eggs added, making a sort of pudding.

*   *   *   *   *

BREAD AND BREAKFAST CAKES.

BREAD-MAKING AND FLOUR.

Much of the health, and consequently much of the happiness, of the family depends upon good bread: therefore no pains should be spared in learning the best method of making, which will prove easiest in the end.

Yeast, flour, kneading, and baking must each be perfect, and nothing in the whole range of cooking is of such prime importance.

Once master the problem of yeast, and the first form of wheat bread, and endless varieties of both bread and breakfast cakes can be made.

The old and the new process flour--the former being known as the St. Louis, and the latter as Haxall flour--are now to be had at all good grocers; and from either good bread may be made, though that from the latter keeps moist longer. Potapsco flour is of the same quality as the St. Louis. It contains more starch than the St. Louis, and for this reason requires, even more than that, the use in the family of coarser or graham flour at the same time; white bread alone not being as nutritious or strengthening, for reasons given in Part I. Graham flour is fast being superseded by a much better form, prepared principally by the Health Food Company in New York, in which the entire grain, save the husk, is ground as fine as the ordinary flour, thus doing away with the coarseness that many have objected to in graham bread.

Flour made by the new process swells more than that by the old, and a little less quantity--about an eighth less--is therefore required in mixing and kneading. As definite rules as possible are given for the whole operation; but experience alone can insure perfect bread, changes of temperature affecting it at once, and baking being also a critical point.

Pans made of thick tin, or, better still, of Russia iron, ten inches long, four or five wide, and four deep, make the best-shaped loaf, and one requiring a reasonably short time to bake.

YEAST.

Ingredients: One teacupful of lightly broken hops; one pint of sifted flour; one cupful of sugar; one tablespoonful of salt; four large or six medium-sized potatoes; and two quarts of boiling water.

Boil the potatoes, and mash them fine. At the same time, having tied the hops in a little bag, boil them for half an hour in the two quarts of water, but in another saucepan. Mix the flour, sugar, and salt well together in a large mixing-bowl, and pour on the boiling hop-water, stirring constantly. Now add enough of this to the mashed potato to thin it till it can be poured, and mix all together, straining it through a sieve to avoid any possible lumps. Add to this, when cool, either a cupful of yeast left from the last, or of baker's yeast, or a Twin Brothers' yeast cake dissolved in a little warm water. Let it stand till partly light, and then stir down two or three times in the course of five or six hours, as this makes it stronger. At the end of that time it will be light. Keep in a covered stone jar, or in glass cans. By stirring in corn-meal till a dough is made, and then forming it in small cakes and drying in the sun, *dry yeast* is made, which keeps better than the liquid in hot weather. Crumb, and soak in warm water half an hour before using.

Potato yeast is made by omitting hops and flour, but mashing the potatoes fine with the same proportion of other ingredients, and adding the old yeast, when cool, as before. It is very nice, but must be made fresh every week; while the other, kept in a cool place, will be good a month.

BREAD.

For four loaves of bread of the pan-size given above, allow as follows: Four quarts of flour; one large cup of yeast; one tablespoonful of salt, one of sugar, and one of butter or lard; one pint of milk mixed with one of warm water, or one quart of water alone for the "wetting."

Sift the flour into a large pan or bowl. Put the sugar, salt, and butter in the bottom of the bread pan or bowl, and pour on a spoonful or two of boiling water, enough to dissolve all. Add the quart of wetting, and the yeast. Now stir in slowly two quarts of the flour; cover with a cloth, and set in a temperature of about 75 deg. to rise until morning. Bread mixed at nine in the evening will be ready to mould into loaves or rolls by six the next morning. In summer it would be necessary to find a cool place; in winter a warm one,--the chief point being to keep the temperature *even*. If mixed early in the morning, it is ready to mold and bake in the afternoon, from seven to eight hours being all it should stand.

This first mixture is called a *sponge*; and, if only a loaf of graham or rye bread is wanted, one quart of it can be measured, and thickened with other flour as in the rules given hereafter.

To finish as *wheat bread*, stir in enough flour from the two quarts remaining to make a dough. Flour the molding-board very thickly, and turn out. Now begin kneading, flouring the hands, but after the dough is gathered into a smooth lump, using as little flour as may be. Knead with the palm of the hand as much as possible. The dough quickly becomes a flat cake. Fold it over, and keep on, kneading not less than twenty minutes; half an hour being better.

Make into loaves; put into the pans; set them in a warm place, and let them rise from thirty to forty-five minutes, or till they have become nearly double in size. Bake in an oven hot enough to brown a teaspoonful of flour in one minute; spreading the flour on a bit of broken plate, that it may have an even heat. Loaves of this size will bake in from forty-five to sixty minutes. Then take them from the pans; wrap in thick cloths kept for the purpose and stand them, tilted up against the pans till cold. Never lay hot bread on a pine table, as it will sweat, and absorb the pitchy odor and taste; but tilt, so that air may pass around it freely. Keep well covered in a tin box or large stone pot, which should be wiped out every day or two, and scalded and dried thoroughly now and then. Pans for wheat bread should be greased very lightly; for graham or rye, much more, as the dough sticks and clings.

Instead of mixing a sponge, all the flour may be molded in and kneaded at once, and the dough set to rise in the same way. When light, turn out. Use as little flour as possible, and knead for fifteen minutes; less time being required, as part of the kneading has already been done.

GRAHAM BREAD.

One quart of wheat sponge; one even quart of graham flour; half a teacupful of brown sugar or molasses; half a teaspoonful of soda dissolved in a little hot water; and half a teaspoonful of salt.

Pour the sponge in a deep bowl; stir in the molasses, &c, and lastly the flour, which must never be sifted. The mixture should be so stiff, that the spoon moves with difficulty. Bake in two loaves for an hour or an hour and a quarter, graham requiring longer baking than wheat.

If no sponge can be spared, make as follows: One pint of milk or water; half a cup of sugar or molasses; half a cup of yeast; one teaspoonful of salt; one cup of wheat flour; two cups of graham. Warm the milk or water; add the yeast and other ingredients, and then the flour; and set in a cool place--about 60 deg. Fahrenheit--

over-night, graham bread souring more easily than wheat. Early in the morning stir well; put into two deep, well-greased pans; let it rise an hour in a warm place, and bake one hour.

GRAHAM MUFFINS.

These are made by the same rule as the bread. Fill the muffin-pans two-thirds full; let them rise till even with the top of the pans, which will take about an hour; and bake in a quick oven twenty minutes. To make them a little nicer, a large spoonful of melted butter may be added, and two beaten eggs. This will require longer to rise, as butter clogs the air-cells, and makes the working of the yeast slower. The quantities given for bread will make two dozen muffins.

RYE BREAD.

This bread is made by nearly the same rule as the graham, either using wheat sponge, or setting one over-night, but is kneaded slightly. Follow the rule just given, substituting rye for graham, but use enough rye to make a dough which can be turned out. It will take a quart. Use wheat flour for the molding-board and hands, as rye is very sticky; and knead only long enough to get into good shape. Raise, and bake as in rule for graham bread.

RYE MUFFINS.

Make by above rule, but use only one pint of rye flour, adding two eggs and a spoonful of melted butter, and baking in the same way. A set of earthen cups are excellent for both these and graham muffins, as the heat in baking is more even. They are used also for pop-overs, Sunderland puddings, and some small cakes.

BROWN BREAD.

Sift together into a deep bowl one even cup of Indian meal, two heaping cups of rye flour, one even teaspoonful of salt, and one of soda. To one pint of hot water add one cup of molasses, and stir till well mixed. Make a hole in the middle of the meal, and stir in the molasses and water, beating all till smooth. Butter a tin pudding-boiler, or a three-pint tin pail, and put in the mixture, setting the boiler into a kettle or saucepan of boiling water. Boil steadily for four hours, keeping the water always at the same level. At the end of that time, take out the boiler, and set in the oven for fifteen minutes to dry and form a crust. Turn out, and serve hot.

Milk may be used instead of water, or the same mixture raised over-night with half a cup of yeast, and then steamed.

PLAIN ROLLS.

A pint-bowlful of bread dough will make twelve small rolls. Increase amount of dough if more are desired. Flour the molding-board lightly, and work into the dough a piece of butter or lard the size of an egg. Knead not less than fifteen minutes, and cut into round cakes, which may be flattened and folded over, if folded or pocket rolls are wanted. In this case put a bit of butter or lard the size of a pea between the folds. For a cleft or French roll make the dough into small round balls, and press a knife-handle almost through the center of each. Put them about an inch apart in well-buttered pans, and let them rise an hour and a half before baking. They require more time to rise than large loaves, as, being small, heat penetrates them almost at once, and thus there is very little rising in the oven.

Bake in a quick oven twenty minutes.

PARKER-HOUSE ROLLS.

Two quarts of flour; one pint of milk; butter the size of an egg; one tablespoonful of sugar; one teacupful of good yeast; one teaspoonful of salt.

Boil the milk, and add the butter, salt, and sugar. Sift the flour into a deep bowl, and, when the milk is merely blood-warm, stir together with enough of the flour to form a batter or sponge. Do this at nine or ten in the evening, and set in a cool place, from 50 deg. to 60 deg.. Next morning about nine mix in the remainder of the flour; turn on to the molding-board; and knead for twenty minutes, using as little flour as possible. Return to the bowl, and set in cool place again till about four in the afternoon. Knead again for fifteen minutes; roll out, and cut into rounds, treating them as in plain rolls. Let them rise one hour, and bake twenty minutes. One kneading makes a good breakfast roll; but, to secure the peculiar delicacy of a "Parker-House," two are essential, and they are generally baked as a folded or pocket roll. If baked round, make the dough into a long roll on the board; cut off small pieces, and make into round balls with the hand, setting them well apart in the pan.

SODA AND CREAM OF TARTAR BISCUIT.

One quart of flour; one even teaspoonful of salt; one teaspoonful of soda, and two of cream of tartar; a piece of lard or butter the size of an egg; and a large cup of milk or water.

Mix the soda, cream of tartar, and salt with the flour, having first mashed them fine, and sift all together twice. Rub the shortening in with the hands till perfectly fine. Add the milk; mix and roll out as quickly as possible; cut in rounds, and bake in a quick oven. If properly made, they are light as puffs; but their success depends upon thorough and rapid mixing and baking.

BAKING-POWDER BISCUIT.

Make as above, using two heaping teaspoonfuls of baking powder, instead of the soda and cream of tartar.

BEATEN BISCUIT.

Three pints of sifted flour; one cup of lard; one teaspoonful of salt. Rub the lard and flour well together, and make into a very stiff dough with about a cup of milk or water: a little more may be necessary. Beat the dough with a rolling-pin for half an hour, or run through the little machine that comes for the purpose. Make into small biscuit, prick several times, and bake till brown.

WAFERS.

One pint of sifted flour; a piece of butter the size of a walnut; half a teaspoonful of salt.

Rub butter and flour together, and make into dough with half a cup of warm milk. Beat half an hour with the rolling-pin. Then take a bit of it no larger than a nut, and roll to the size of a saucer. They can not be too thin. Flour the pans lightly, and bake in a quick oven from five to ten minutes.

WAFFLES.

One pint of flour; one teaspoonful of baking powder; half a teaspoonful of salt; three eggs; butter the size of an egg; and one and a quarter cups of milk.

Sift salt and baking powder with the flour; rub in the butter. Mix and add the beaten yolks and milk, and last stir in the whites which have been beaten to a stiff froth. Bake at once in well-greased waffle-irons. By using two cups of milk, the mixture is right for pancakes. If sour milk is used, substitute soda for the baking powder. Sour cream makes delicious waffles.

RICE OR HOMINY WAFFLES.

One pint of warm boiled rice or hominy; one cup of sweet or sour milk; butter the size of a walnut; three eggs; one teaspoonful of salt and one of soda sifted with one pint of flour.

Stir rice and milk together; add the beaten yolks; then the flour, and last the whites beaten stiff. By adding a small cup more of milk, rice pancakes can be made.

Boiled oatmeal or wheaten grits may be substituted for the rice.

BREAKFAST PUFFS OR POP-OVERS.

One pint of flour, one pint of milk, and one egg. Stir the milk into the flour; beat the egg very light, and add it, stirring it well in. Meantime have a set of gem-pans well buttered, heating in the oven. Put in the dough (the material is enough for a dozen puffs), and bake for half an hour in a *very hot oven*. This is one of the simplest but most delicate breakfast cakes made. Ignorant cooks generally spoil several batches by persisting in putting in baking powder or soda, as they can not believe that the puffs will rise without.

SHORT-CAKE.

One quart of flour; one teaspoonful of salt and two of baking powder sifted with the flour; one cup of butter, or half lard and half butter; one large cup of hot milk. Rub the butter into the flour. Add the milk, and roll out the dough, cutting in small square cakes and baking to a light brown.

For a strawberry or peach short-cake have three tin pie-plates buttered; roll the dough to fit them, and bake quickly. Fill either, when done, with a quart of strawberries or raspberries mashed with a cup of sugar, or with peaches cut fine and sugared, and served hot.

CORN BREAD.

Two cups of corn meal; one cup of flour; one teaspoonful of soda and one of salt; one heaping tablespoonful of butter; a teacup full of sugar; three eggs; two cups of sour milk, the more creamy the better. If sweet milk is used, substitute baking powder for soda.

Sift meal, flour, soda, and salt together; beat the yolks of the eggs with the sugar; add the milk, and stir into the meal; melt the butter, and stir in, beating hard for five minutes. Beat the whites stiff, and stir in, and bake at once either in one large, round loaf, or in tin pie-plates. The loaf will need half an hour or a little more; the pie-plates, not over twenty minutes.

This can be baked as muffins, or, by adding another cup of milk, becomes a pancake mixture.

HOE-CAKE.

One quart of corn meal; one teaspoon full of salt; one tablespoonful of melted lard; one large cup of boiling water. Melt the lard in the water. Mix the salt with the meal, and pour on the water, stirring it into a dough. When cool, make either into one large oval cake or two smaller ones, and bake in the oven to a bright brown, which will take about half an hour; or make in small cakes, and bake slowly on a griddle, browning well on each side. Genuine hoe-cake is baked before an open fire on a board.

BUCKWHEAT CAKES.

Two cups of buckwheat flour; one of wheat flour; one of corn meal; half a cup of yeast; one teaspoonful of salt; one quart of boiling water. Mix the corn meal and salt, and pour on the boiling water very slowly, that the meal may swell. As soon as merely warm, stir in the sifted flour and yeast. All buckwheat may be used, instead of part wheat flour. Beat well, cover, and put in a cool place,--about 60 deg.. In the morning stir well, and add half a teaspoonful of soda dissolved in a little warm water. Grease the griddle with a bit of salt pork on a fork, or a *very little* drippings rubbed over it evenly, but never have it floating with fat, as many cooks do. Drop in large spoonfuls, and bake and serve *few at a time*, or they will become heavy and unfit to eat. If a cupful of the batter is saved, no yeast need be used for the next baking, and in cold weather this can be done for a month.

HUCKLEBERRY CAKE.

One quart of flour; one teaspoonful of salt and two of baking powder sifted with the flour; one pint of huckleberries; half a cup of butter; two eggs; two cups of sweet milk; two cups of sugar.

Cream the butter, and add the sugar and yolks of eggs; stir in the milk, and add the flour slowly; then beating the whites of the eggs stiff, and adding them. Have the huckleberries picked over, washed, dried, and well dusted with flour. Stir them in last of all; fill the pans three-quarters full, and bake in a moderate oven for about half an hour.

APPLE CAKE.

Make as above; but, instead of huckleberries, use one pint of sour, tender apples, cut in thin slices. It is a delicious breakfast or tea cake.

BROWN-BREAD BREWIS.

Dry all bits of crust or bread in the oven, browning them nicely. To a pint of these, allow one quart of milk, half a cup of butter, and a teaspoonful of salt. Boil the milk; add the butter and salt, and then the browned bread, and simmer slowly for fifteen minutes, or until perfectly soft. It is very nice. Bits of white bread or sea biscuit can be used in the same way.

CRISPED CRACKERS.

Split large soft crackers, what is called the "Boston cracker" being best; butter them well as for eating; lay the buttered halves in baking-pans, and brown in a quick oven. Good at any meal.

SOUR BREAD.

If, by any mishap, bread has soured a little, make into water toast or brewis, adding a teaspoonful of soda to the water or milk.

TO USE DRY BREAD.

Brown in the oven every scrap that is left, seeing that it does not scorch. Roll while hot and crisp, and sift, using the fine crumbs for croquettes, &c., and the coarser ones for puddings and pancakes. Keep dry in glass jars; or tin cans will answer.

BREAD PANCAKES.

One cup of coarse crumbs, soaked over-night in a quart of warm milk, or milk and water. In the morning mash fine, and run through a sieve. Add three eggs well beaten, half a cup of flour, a large spoonful of sugar, a teaspoonful of salt, and, if liked, a little nutmeg. If the bread was in the least sour, add a teaspoonful of soda dissolved in a little warm water. Bake like pancakes, but more slowly.

TO FRESHEN STALE BREAD OR ROLLS.

Wrap in a cloth, and steam for ten or fifteen minutes in a steamer. Then dry in the oven. Rolls or biscuits may have the top crust wet with a little melted butter, and then brown a minute after steaming.

*   *   *   *   *

CAKE.

CAKE-MAKING.

In all cake-making, see that every thing is ready to your hand,--pans buttered, or papered if necessary; flour sifted; all spices and other materials on your working-table; and the fire in good order.

No matter how plain the cake, there is a certain order in mixing, which, if followed, produces the best result from the materials used; and this order is easily reduced to rules.

First, always cream the butter; that is, stir it till light and creamy. If very cold, heat the bowl a little, but never enough to melt, only to soften the butter. Second, add the sugar to the butter, and mix thoroughly.

Third, if eggs are used, beat yolks and whites separately for a delicate cake; add yolks to sugar and butter, and beat together a minute. For a plain cake, beat yolks and whites together (a Dover egg-beater doing this better than any thing else can), and add to butter and sugar.

Fourth, if milk is used, add this.

Fifth, stir in the measure of flour little by little, and beat smooth.

Flavoring may be added at any time. If dry spices are used, mix them with the sugar. Always sift baking powder with the flour. If soda and cream of tartar are used, sift the cream of tartar with the flour, and dissolve the soda in a little milk or warm water. For very delicate cakes, powdered sugar is best. For gingerbreads and small cakes or cookies, light brown answers.

Where fruit cake is to be made, raisins should be stoned and chopped, and currants washed and dried, the day beforehand. A cup of currants being a nice and inexpensive addition to buns or any plain cake, it is well to prepare several pounds at once, drying thoroughly, and keeping in glass jars. Being the very dirtiest article known to the storeroom, currants require at least three washings in warm water, rubbing them well in the hands. Then spread them out on a towel, and proceed to pick out all the sticks, grit, small stones, and legs and wings to be found; then put the fruit into a slow oven, and dry it carefully, that none may scorch.

In baking, a moderate oven is one in which a teaspoonful of flour will brown while you count thirty; a quick one, where but twelve can be counted.

The "cup" used in all these receipts is the ordinary kitchen cup, holding half a pint. The measures of flour are, in all cases, of *sifted flour*, which can be sifted by the quantity, and kept in a wooden pail. "Prepared flour" is especially nice for dough-nuts and plain cakes. No great variety of receipts is given, as every family is sure to have one enthusiastic cake-maker who gleans from all sources; and this book aims to give fuller space to substantials than to sweets. Half the energy spent by many housekeepers upon cake would insure the perfect bread, which, nine times out of ten, is not found upon their tables, and success in which they count an impossibility. If cake is to be made, however, let it be done in the most perfect way; seeing only that bread is first irreproachable.

SPONGE CAKE.

One pound of the finest granulated, or of powdered, sugar; half a pound of sifted flour; ten eggs; grated rind of two lemons, and the juice of one; and a saltspoonful of salt.

Break the eggs, yolks and whites separately, and beat the yolks to a creamy froth. Beat the whites till they can be turned upside down without spilling. Put yolks and whites together, and beat till blended; then add the sugar slowly; then the lemon rind and juice and the salt, and last the flour. Whisk together as lightly and quickly as possible. Turn into either three buttered bread-pans of the size given on p. 201, or bake in a large loaf, as preferred. Fill the pans two-thirds full, and, when in the oven, do not open it for ten minutes. Bake about half an hour, and test by running a clean broom-straw into the loaf. If it comes out dry, they are done. Turn out, and cool on a sieve, or on the pans turned upside down.

ROLLED JELLY CAKE.

Three eggs, yolks and whites beaten separately; one heaped cup of sugar; one scant cup of flour in which a teaspoonful of baking powder and a pinch of salt have been sifted; quarter of a cup of boiling water.

Mix as in sponge cake; add the water last, and bake in a large roasting-pan, spreading the batter as thinly as possible. It will bake in ten minutes. When done, and while still hot, spread with any acid jelly, and roll carefully from one side. This cake is nice for lining Charlotte-Russe molds also. For that purpose the water may be omitted, its only use being to make the cake roll more easily.

CUP CAKE.

One cup of butter; two cups of sugar; four eggs, yolks and whites beaten separately; one cup of milk; three and a half cups of flour; a grated nutmeg, or a teaspoonful of vanilla or lemon; and a heaping teaspoonful of baking powder.

Cream the butter; add the sugar, and then the yolks; then the milk and the whites, and last the flour, in which the baking powder has been sifted. Bake half an hour, either in two brick loaves or one large one. It is nice, also, baked in little tins. Half may be flavored with essence, and the other half with a teaspoonful of mixed spice,--half cinnamon, and the rest mace and allspice. By using a heaping tablespoonful of yellow ginger, this becomes a delicious sugar gingerbread, or, with mixed spices and ginger, a spice gingerbread.

This cake with the variations upon it makes up page after page in the large cook-books. Use but half a cup of butter, and you have a plain *Cup Cake*. Add a cup of currants and one of chopped raisins, and it is plain *Fruit Cake*, needing to bake one hour. Bake on Washington-pie tins, and you have the foundation for *Cream and Jelly Cakes*. A little experience, and then invention, will show you how varied are the combinations, and how one page in your cook-book can do duty for twenty.

POUND CAKE.

One pound of sugar; one pound of flour; three-quarters of a pound of butter; nine eggs; one teaspoonful of baking powder, and one of lemon extract; one nutmeg grated.

Cream the butter, and add half the flour, sifting the baking powder with the other half. Beat the yolks to a creamy foam, and add; and then the sugar, beating hard. Have the whites a stiff froth, and stir in, adding flavoring and remainder of flour. Bake in one large loaf for one hour, letting the oven be moderate. Frost, if liked.

FRUIT CAKE.

One pound of butter; one pound of sugar; one pound and a quarter of sifted flour; ten eggs; two nutmegs grated; a tablespoonful each of ground cloves, cinnamon, and allspice; a teaspoonful of soda; a cup of brandy or wine, and one of dark molasses; one pound of citron; two pounds of stoned and chopped raisins, and two of currants washed and dried.

Dredge the prepared fruit with enough of the flour to coat it thoroughly. To have the cake very dark and rich looking, brown the flour a little, taking great care not to scorch it. Cream the butter, and add the sugar, in which the spices have been mixed; then the beaten yolks of eggs; then the whites beaten to a stiff froth, and the flour. Dissolve the soda in a very little warm water, and add. Now stir in the fruit. Have either one large, round pan, or two smaller ones. Put at least three thicknesses of buttered letter-paper on the sides and bottom; turn in the mixture, and bake for three hours in a moderate oven. Cover with thick paper if there is the least danger of scorching. This will keep, if well frosted, for two years.

DOVER CAKE.

One pound of flour; one pound of sugar; half a pound of butter; one teacup of milk; six eggs; one teaspoonful of baking powder; one grated nutmeg.

Cream the butter; add first sugar, then beaten yolks of eggs and milk, then whites of eggs beaten to a stiff froth, and last the flour. Bake forty-five minutes in a large dripping-pan, sifting fine sugar over the top, and cut in small squares; or it may be baked in one round loaf, and frosted on the bottom, or in small tins. Half a pound of citron cut fine is often added.

WHITE OR SILVER CAKE.

Half a cup of butter; a heaping cupful of powdered sugar; two cups of flour, with a teaspoonful of baking powder sifted in; half a cup of milk; whites of six eggs; one teaspoonful of almond extract.

Cream the butter, and add the flour, beating till it is a smooth paste. Beat the whites to a stiff froth, and add the sugar and essence. Now mix both quickly, and bake in a sheet about an inch and a half thick. About half an hour will be needed. Frost while hot, with one white of egg, beaten ten minutes with a small cup of sifted powdered sugar, and juice of half a lemon. This frosting hardens very quickly. Before it is quite hard, divide it into oblong or square pieces, scoring at intervals with the back of a large knife. The milk can be omitted if a richer cake is wanted. It may also be baked in jelly-cake tins; one small cocoanut grated, and mixed with one cup of sugar, and spread between, and the whole frosted. Or beat the white of an egg with one cup of sugar, and the juice of one large or two small oranges, and spread between. Either form is delicious.

GOLD CAKE.

One cup of sugar; half a cup of butter; two cups of flour; yolks of six eggs; grated rind and juice of a lemon or orange; half a teaspoonful of soda, mixed with the flour, and sifted twice.

Cream the butter; add the sugar, then the beaten yolks and the flour, beating hard for several minutes. Last, add the lemon or orange juice, and bake like silver cake; frosting, if liked. If frosting is made for either or both cakes, the extra yolks may be used in making this one, eight being still nicer than six.

BREAD CAKE.

Two cups or a pint-bowlful of raised dough ready for baking; one cup of butter; two cups of sugar; one teaspoonful of ground cinnamon, or half a nutmeg grated; three eggs; one teaspoonful of soda in quarter of a cup of warm water, and half a cup of flour.

Cream the butter, and add the sugar. Then put in the bread dough, and work together till well mixed. The hand is best for this, though it can be done with a wooden spoon. Add the eggs, then the flour, and last the soda. Let it stand in a warm place for one hour, and bake in a moderate oven forty-five minutes, testing with a broom-straw. A pound of stoned and chopped raisins is a nice addition. Omitting them, and adding flour enough to roll out, makes an excellent raised doughnut or bun. Let it rise two hours; then cut in shapes, and fry in boiling lard. Or, for buns, bake in a quick oven, and, a minute before taking out, brush the top with a spoonful of sugar and milk mixed together.

PLAIN BUNS.

One pint-bowlful of dough; one cup of sugar; butter the size of an egg; one teaspoonful of cinnamon.

Boll the dough thin. Spread the butter upon it. Mix sugar and cinnamon together, and sprinkle on it. Now turn over the edges of the dough carefully to keep the sugar in, and press and work gently for a few minutes, that it may not break through. Knead till thoroughly mixed. Roll out; cut like biscuit, and let them rise an hour, baking in a quick oven.

The same rule can be used for raised doughnuts.

DOUGHNUTS.

First put on the lard, and let it be heating gradually. To test it when hot, drop in a bit of bread; if it browns as you count twenty, it is right. Never let it boil furiously, or scorch. This is the rule for all frying, whether fritters, croquettes, or cakes.

One quart of flour into which has been sifted a teaspoonful of salt, and one of soda if sour milk is used, or two of baking powder if sweet milk. If cream can be had, use part cream, allowing one large cup of milk, or cream and milk. One heaping cup of fine brown sugar; one teaspoonful of ground cinnamon, and half a one of mace or nutmeg; use one spoonful of butter, if you have no cream, stirring it into the sugar. Add two or three beaten eggs; mixing all as in general directions for cake. They can be made without eggs. Roll out; cut in shapes, and fry brown, taking them out with a fork into a sieve set over a pan that all fat may drain off.

Cut thin, and baked brown in a quick oven, these make a good plain cooky.

GINGER SNAPS.

One cup of butter and lard or dripping mixed, or dripping alone can be used; one cup of molasses; one cup of brown sugar; two teaspoonfuls of ginger, and one each of clove, allspice, and mace; one teaspoonful of salt, and one of soda dissolved in half a cup of hot water; one egg.

Stir together the shortening, sugar, molasses, and spice. Add the soda, and then sifted flour enough to make a dough,--about three pints. Turn on to the board, and knead well. Take about quarter of it, and roll out thin as a knife-blade. Bake in a quick oven. They will bake in five minutes, and will keep for months. By using only four cups of flour, this can be baked in a loaf as spiced gingerbread; or it can be rolled half an inch thick, and baked as a cooky. In this, as in all cakes, experience will teach you many variations.

PLAIN GINGERBREAD.

Two cups of molasses; one of sour milk; half a cup of lard or drippings; four cups of flour; two teaspoonfuls of ginger, and one of cinnamon; half a teaspoonful of salt; one egg, and a teaspoonful of soda.

Mix molasses and shortening; add the spice and egg, then the milk, and last the flour, with soda sifted in it. Bake at once in a sheet about an inch thick for half an hour. Try with a broom-straw. Good hot for lunch with chocolate. A plain cooky is made by adding flour enough to roll out. The egg may be omitted.

JUMBLES.

The richest jumbles are made from either the rule for Pound or Dover Cake, with flour enough added to roll out. The Cup-Cake rule makes good but plainer ones. Make rings, either by cutting in long strips and joining the ends, or by using a large and small cutter. Sift sugar over the top, and bake a delicate brown. By adding a large spoonful of yellow ginger, any of these rules become hard sugar-gingerbread, and all will keep for a long time.

DROP CAKES.

Any of the rules last mentioned become drop cakes by buttering muffin-tins or tin sheets, and dropping a teaspoonful of these mixtures into them. If on sheets, let them be two inches apart. Sift sugar over the top, and bake in a quick oven. They are done as soon as brown.

CREAM CAKES.

One pint of boiling water in a saucepan. Melt in it a piece of butter the size of an egg. Add half a teaspoonful of salt. While still boiling, stir in one large cup of flour, and cook for three minutes. Take from the fire; cool ten minutes; then break in, one by one, six eggs, and beat till smooth. Have muffin-pans buttered, or large baking-sheets. Drop a spoonful of the mixture on them, allowing room to spread, and bake half an hour in a quick oven. Cool on a sieve, and, when cool, fill with a cream made as below.

FILLING FOR CREAM CAKES.

One pint of milk, one cup of sugar, two eggs, half a cup of flour, and a piece of butter the size of a walnut.

Mix the sugar and flour, add the beaten eggs, and beat all till smooth. Stir into the boiling milk with a teaspoonful of salt, and boil for fifteen minutes. When cold, add a teaspoonful of vanilla or lemon. Make a slit in each cake, and fill with the cream. Corn-starch may be used instead of flour. This makes a very nice filling for plain cup cake baked on jelly-cake tins.

MERINGUES, OR KISSES.

Whites of three eggs beaten to a stiff froth; quarter of a pound of sifted powdered sugar; a few drops of vanilla.

Add the sugar to the whites. Have ready a hard-wood board which fits the oven. Wet the top well with boiling water, and cover it with sheets of letter-paper. Drop the meringue mixture on this in large spoonfuls, and set in a *very slow* oven. The secret of a good meringue is to *dry*, not bake; and they should be in the oven at least half an hour. Take them out when dry. Slip a thin, sharp knife under each one, and put two together; or scoop out the soft part very carefully, and fill with a little jelly or with whipped cream.

PASTRY AND PIES.

In the first place, don't make either, except very semi-occasionally. Pastry, even when good, is so indigestible that children should never have it, and their elders but seldom. A nice short-cake made as on p. 209, and filled with stewed fruit, or with fresh berries mashed and sweetened, is quite as agreeable to eat, and far more wholesome. But, as people *will* both make and eat pie-crust, the best rules known are given.

Butter, being more wholesome than lard, should always be used if it can be afforded. A mixture of lard and butter is next best. Clarified dripping makes a good crust for meat pies, and cream can also be used. For dumplings nothing can be better than a light biscuit-crust, made as on p. 208. It is also good for meat pies.

PLAIN PIE-CRUST.

One quart of flour; one even teacup of lard, and one of butter; one teacup of ice-water or very cold water; and a teaspooonful of salt.

Rub the lard and salt into the flour till it is dry and crumbly. Add the ice-water, and work to a smooth dough. Wash the butter, and have it cold and firm as possible. Divide it in three parts. Roll out the paste, and dot it all over with bits from one part of the butter. Sprinkle with flour, and roll up. Roll out, and repeat till the butter is gone. If the crust can now stand on the ice for half an hour, it will be nicer and more flaky. This amount will make three good-sized pies. Enough for the bottom crusts can be taken off after one rolling in of butter, thus making the top crust richer. Lard alone will make a tender, but not a flaky, paste.

PUFF PASTE.

One pound of flour; three-quarters of a pound of butter; one teacupful of ice-water; one teaspoonful of salt, and one of sugar; yolk of one egg.

Wash the butter; divide into three parts, reserving a bit the size of an egg; and put it on the ice for an hour. Rub the bit of butter, the salt, and sugar, into the flour, and stir in the ice-water and egg beaten together. Make into a dough, and knead on the molding-board till glossy and firm: at least ten minutes will be required. Roll out into a sheet ten or twelve inches square. Cut a cake of the ice-cold butter in thin slices, or flatten it very thin with the rolling-pin. Lay it on the paste, sprinkle with flour, and fold over the edges. Press it in somewhat with the rolling-pin, and roll out again. Always roll *from* you. Do this again and again till the butter is all used, rolling up the paste after the last cake is in, and then putting it on the ice for an hour or more. Have filling all ready, and let the paste be as nearly ice-cold as possible when it goes into the oven. There are much more elaborate rules; but this insures handsome paste. Make a plainer one for the bottom crusts. Cover puff paste with a damp cloth, and it may be kept on the ice a day or two before baking.

PATTIES FROM PUFF PASTE.

Roll the paste about a third of an inch thick, and cut out with a round or oval cutter about two inches in diameter. Take a cutter half an inch smaller, and press it into the piece already cut out, so as to sink half-way through the crust: this to mark out the top piece. Lay on tins, and bake to a delicate brown. They should treble in thickness by rising, and require from twenty minutes to half an hour to bake. When done, the marked-out top can easily be removed. Take out the soft inside, and fill with sweetmeats for dessert, or with minced chicken or oysters prepared as on p. 140.

GRANDMOTHER'S APPLE PIE.

Line a deep pie-plate with plain paste. Pare sour apples,--greenings are best; quarter, and cut in thin slices. Allow one cup of sugar, and quarter of a grated nut-meg mixed with it. Fill the pie-plate heaping full of the sliced apple, sprinkling the sugar between the layers. It will require not less than six good-sized apples. Wet the edges of the pie with cold water; lay on the cover, and press down securely, that no juice may escape. Bake three-quarters of an hour, or a little less if the apples are very tender. No pie in which the apples are stewed beforehand can compare with this in flavor. If they are used, stew till tender, and strain. Sweeten and flavor to taste. Fill the pies, and bake half an hour.

DRIED-APPLE PIES.

Wash one pint of dried apples, and put in a porcelain kettle with two quarts of warm water. Let them stand all night. In the morning put on the fire, and stew slowly for an hour. Then add one pint of sugar, a teaspoonful of dried lemon or orange rind, or half a fresh lemon sliced, and half a teaspoonful of cinnamon. Stew half an hour longer, and then use for filling the pies. The apple can be strained if preferred, and a teaspoonful of butter added. This quantity will make two pies. Dried peaches are treated in the same way.

LEMON PIES.

Three lemons, juice of all and the grated rind of two; two cups of sugar; three cups of boiling water; three tablespoonfuls of corn-starch dissolved in a little cold water; three eggs; a piece of butter the size of an egg.

Pour the boiling water on the dissolved corn-starch, and boil for five minutes. Add the sugar and butter, the yolks of the eggs beaten to a froth, and last the lemon juice and rind. Line the plates with crust, putting a narrow rim of it around each one. Pour in the filling, and bake half an hour. Beat the whites to a stiff froth; add half a teacup of powdered sugar and ten drops of lemon extract, and, when the pie is baked, spread this on. The heat will cook it sufficiently, but it can be browned a moment in the oven. If to be kept a day, do not make the frosting till just before using. The whites will keep in a cold place. Orange pie can be made in the same way.

SWEET-POTATO PIE OR PUDDING.

One pound of hot, boiled sweet potato rubbed through a sieve; one cup of butter; one heaping cup of sugar; half a grated nutmeg; one glass of brandy; a pinch of salt; six eggs.

Add the sugar, spice, and butter to the hot potato. Beat whites and yolks separately, and add, and last the brandy. Line deep plates with nice paste, making a rim of puff paste. Fill with the mixture, and bake till the crust is done,--about half an hour. Wickedly rich, but very delicious. Irish potatoes can be treated in the same way, and are more delicate.

SQUASH OR PUMPKIN PIE.

Prepare and steam as in directions on p. 194. Strain through a sieve. To a quart of the strained squash add one quart of new milk, with a spoonful or two of cream if possible; one heaping cup of sugar into which has been stirred a teaspoonful of salt, a heaping one of ginger, and half a one of cinnamon. Mix this with the squash, and add from two to four well-beaten eggs. Bake in deep plates lined with plain pie-crust. They are done when a knife-blade on being run into the middle comes out clean. About forty minutes will be enough. For pumpkin pie half a cup of molasses may be added, and the eggs can be omitted, substituting half a cup of flour mixed with the sugar and spice before stirring in. A teaspoonful of butter can also be added.

CHERRY AND BERRY PIES.

Have a very deep plate, and either no under crust save a rim, or a very thin one. Allow a cup of sugar to a quart of fruit, but no spices. Stone cherries. Prick the upper crust half a dozen times with a fork to let out the steam.

For rhubarb or pie-plant pies, peel the stalks; cut them in little bits, and fill the pie. Bake with an upper crust.

CUSTARD PIE.

Line and rim deep plates with pastry, a thin custard pie being very poor. Beat together a teacupful of sugar, four eggs, and a pinch of salt, and mix slowly with one quart of milk. Fill the plate up to the pastry rim *after it is in the oven*, and bake till the custard is firm, trying, as for squash pies, with a knife-blade.

MINCE-MEAT FOR PIES.

Two pounds of cold roast or boiled beef, or a small beef-tongue, boiled the day beforehand, cooled and chopped; one pound of beef-suet, freed from all strings, and chopped fine as powder; two pounds of raisins stoned and chopped; one pound of currants washed and dried; six pounds of chopped apples; half a pound of citron cut in slips; two pounds of brown sugar; one pint of molasses; one quart of boiled cider; one pint of wine or brandy, or a pint of any nice sirup from sweet pickles may be substituted; two heaping tablespoonfuls of salt; one teaspoonful of pepper; three tablespoonfuls of ground cinnamon; two of allspice; one of clove; one of mace; three grated nutmegs; grated rind and juice of three lemons; a cupful of chopped, candied orange or lemon peel.

Mix spices and salt with sugar, and stir into the meat and suet. Add the apples, and then the cider and other wetting, stirring very thoroughly. Lastly, mix in the fruit. Fill and bake as in apple pies. This mince-meat will keep two months easily. If it ferments at all, put over the fire in a porcelain-lined kettle, and boil half an hour. Taste, and judge for yourselves whether more or less spice is needed. Butter can be used instead of suet, and proportions varied to taste.

RAMMEKINS, OR CHEESE STRAWS.

One pound of puff paste; one cup of good grated cheese. Roll the paste half an inch thick; sprinkle on half the cheese; press in lightly with the rolling-pin; roll up, and roll out again, using the other half of the cheese. Fold, and roll about a third of an inch thick. Cut in long, narrow strips, four or five inches long and half an inch wide, and bake in a quick oven to a delicate brown. Excellent with chocolate at lunch, or for dessert with fruit.

*   *   *   *   *

PUDDINGS BOILED AND BAKED.

For boiled puddings a regular pudding-boiler holding from three pints to two quarts is best, a tin pail with a very tight-fitting cover answering instead, though not as good. For large dumplings a thick pudding-cloth--the best being of Canton flannel, used with the nap-side out--should be dipped in hot water, and wrung out, dredged evenly and thickly with flour, and laid over a large bowl. From half to three-quarters of a yard square is a good size. In filling this, pile the fruit or berries on the rolled-out crust which has been laid in the middle of the cloth, and gather the edges of the paste evenly over it. Then gather the cloth up, leaving room for the dumpling to swell, and tying very tightly. In turning out, lift to a dish; press all the water from the ends of the cloth; untie and turn away from the pudding, and lay a hot dish upon it, turning over the pudding into it, and serving at once, as it darkens or falls by standing.

In using a boiler, butter well, and fill only two-thirds full that the mixture may have room to swell. Set it in boiling water, and see that it is kept at the same height, about an inch from the top. Cover the outer kettle that the steam may be kept in. Small dumplings, with a single apple or peach in each, can be cooked in a steamer. Puddings are not only much more wholesome, but less expensive than pies.

APPLE DUMPLING.

Make a crust, as for biscuit, or a potato-crust as follows: Three large potatoes, boiled and mashed while hot. Add to them two cups of sifted flour and one teaspoonful of salt, and mix thoroughly. Now chop or cut into it one small cup of butter, and mix into a paste with about a teacupful of cold water. Dredge the board thick with flour, and roll out,--thick in the middle, and thin at the edges. Fill, as directed, with apples pared and quartered, eight or ten good-sized ones being enough for this amount of crust. Boil for three hours. Turn out as directed, and eat with butter and sirup or with a made sauce. Peaches pared and halved, or canned ones drained from the sirup, can be used. In this case, prepare the sirup for sauce, as on p. 172. Blueberries are excellent in the same way.

ENGLISH PLUM PUDDING, OR CHRISTMAS PUDDING.

One pound of raisins stoned and cut in two; one pound of currants washed and dried; one pound of beef-suet chopped very fine; one pound of bread-crumbs; one pound of flour; half a pound of brown sugar; eight eggs; one pint of sweet milk; one teaspoonful of salt; a tablespoonful of cinnamon; two grated nutmegs; a glass each of wine and brandy.

Prepare the fruit, and dredge thickly with flour. Soak the bread in the milk; beat the eggs, and add. Stir in the rest of the flour, the suet, and last the fruit. Boil six hours either in a cloth or large mold. Half the amounts given makes a good-sized pudding; but, as it will keep three months, it might be boiled in two molds. Serve with a rich sauce.

ANY-DAY PLUM PUDDING.

One cup of sweet milk; one cup of molasses; one cup each of raisins and currants; one cup of suet chopped fine, or, instead, a small cup of butter; one teaspoonful of salt, and one of soda, sifted with three cups of flour; one teaspoonful each of cinnamon and allspice.

Mix milk, molasses, suet, and spice; add flour, and then the fruit. Put in a buttered mold, and boil three hours. Eat with hard or liquid sauce. A cupful each of prunes and dates or figs can be substituted for the fruit, and is very nice; and the same amount of dried apple, measured after soaking and chopping, is also good. Or the fruit can be omitted altogether, in which case it becomes "Troy Pudding."

BATTER PUDDING, BOILED OR BAKED.

Two cups of flour in which is sifted a heaping teaspoonful of baking powder, two cups of sweet milk, four eggs, one teaspoonful of salt. Stir the flour gradually into the milk, and beat hard for five minutes. Beat yolks and whites separately, and then add to batter. Have the pudding-boiler buttered. Pour in the batter, and boil steadily for two hours. It may also be baked an hour in a buttered pudding-dish. Serve at once, when done, with a liquid sauce.

SUNDERLAND PUDDINGS.

Are merely puffs or pop-overs eaten with sauce. See p. 209.

BREAD PUDDING.

One cup of dried and rolled bread-crumbs, or one pint of fresh ones; one quart of milk; two eggs; one cup of sugar; half a teaspoonful of cinnamon; a little grated nutmeg; a saltspoonful of salt.

Soak the crumbs in the milk for an hour or two; mix the spice and salt with the sugar, and beat the eggs with it, stirring them slowly into the milk. Butter a pudding-dish; pour in the mixture; and bake half an hour, or till done. Try with a knife-blade, as in general directions. The whites may be kept out for a meringue, allowing half a teacup of powdered sugar to them. By using fresh bread-crumbs and four eggs, this becomes what is known as "Queen of Puddings." As soon as done, spread the top with half a cup of any acid jelly, and cover with the whites which have been beaten stiff, with a teacupful of sugar. Brown slightly in the oven. Half a pound of raisins may be added.

BREAD-AND-BUTTER PUDDING.

Fill a pudding-dish two-thirds full with very thin slices of bread and butter. A cupful of currants or dried cherries may be sprinkled between the slices. Make a custard of two eggs beaten with a cup of sugar; add a quart of milk, and pour over the bread. Cover with a plate, and set on the back of the stove an hour; then bake from half to three-quarters of an hour. Serve very hot, as it falls when cool.

BREAD-AND-APPLE PUDDING.

Butter a deep pudding-dish, and put first a layer of crumbs, then one of any good acid apple, sliced rather thin, and so on till the dish is nearly full. Six or eight apples and a quart of fresh crumbs will fill a two-quart dish. Dissolve a cup of sugar and one teaspoonful of cinnamon in one pint of boiling water, and pour into the dish. Let the pudding stand half an hour to swell; then bake till brown,--about three-quarters of an hour,--and eat with liquid sauce. It can be made with slices of bread and butter, instead of crumbs.

BIRD'S-NEST PUDDING.

Wash one teacupful of tapioca, and put it in one quart of cold water to soak for several hours. Pare and core as many good apples as will fit in a two-quart buttered pudding-dish. When the tapioca is softened, add a cupful of sugar, a pinch of salt, and half a teaspoonful of cinnamon, and pour over the apples. Bake an hour, and eat with or without sauce.

TAPIOCA PUDDING.

One quart of milk; one teacupful of tapioca; three eggs; a cup of sugar; a teaspoonful of salt; a tablespoonful of butter; a teaspoonful of lemon extract.

Wash the tapioca, and soak in the milk for two hours, setting it on the back of the stove to swell. Beat eggs and sugar together, reserving whites for a meringue if liked; melt the butter, and add, and stir into the milk. Bake half an hour. Sago pudding is made in the same way.

TAPIOCA CREAM.

One teacupful of tapioca washed and soaked over-night in one pint of warm water. Next morning add a quart of milk and a teaspoonful of salt, and boil in a milk-boiler for two hours. Just before taking it from the fire, add a tablespoonful of butter, a teaspoonful of vanilla, and three eggs beaten with a cup of sugar. The whites may be made in a meringue. Pour into a glass dish which has had warm water standing in it, to prevent cracking, and eat cold. Rice or sago cream is made in the same way.

PLAIN RICE PUDDING.

One cup of rice; three pints of milk; one heaping cup of sugar; one teaspoonful of salt.

Wash the rice well. Butter a two-quart pudding-dish, and stir rice, sugar, and salt together. Pour on the milk. Grate nutmeg over it, and bake for three hours. Very good.

MINUTE PUDDING.

One quart of milk; one pint of flour; two eggs; one teaspoonful of salt.

Boil the milk in a double boiler. Beat the eggs, and add the flour slowly, with enough of the milk to make it smooth. Stir into the boiling milk, and cook it half an hour. Eat with liquid sauce or sirup. It is often made without eggs.

CORN-STARCH PUDDING.

One quart of milk; four tablespoonfuls of corn-starch; one cup of sugar; three eggs; a teaspoonful each of salt and vanilla.

Boil the milk; dissolve the corn-starch in a little cold milk, and add. Cook five minutes, and add the eggs and flavoring beaten with the sugar. Turn into a buttered dish, and bake fifteen minutes, covering then with a meringue made of the whites, or cool in molds, in this case using only the whites of the eggs. The yolks can be made in a custard to pour around them. A cup of grated cocoanut can be added, or two teaspoonfuls of chocolate stirred smooth in a little boiling water.

GELATINE PUDDING.

Four eggs; one pint of milk; one cup of sugar; a saltspoonful of salt; a teaspoonful of lemon or vanilla; a third of a box of gelatine.

Soak the gelatine a few minutes in a little cold water, and then dissolve it in three-quarters of a cup of boiling water. Have ready a custard made from the milk and yolks of the eggs. Beat the yolks and sugar together, and stir into the boiling milk. When cold, add the gelatine water and the whites of the eggs beaten very stiff. Pour into molds. It is both pretty and good.

CABINET PUDDING.

One quart of milk; half a package of gelatine; a teaspoonful each of salt and vanilla; a cup of sugar.

Boil the milk; soak the gelatine fifteen minutes in a little cold water; dissolve in the boiling milk, and add the sugar and salt. Now butter a Charlotte-Russe mold thickly. Cut slips of citron into leaves or pretty shapes, and stick on the mold. Fill it lightly with any light cake, either plain or rich. Strain on the gelatine and milk, and set in a cold place. Turn out before serving. Delicate crackers may be used instead of cake.

CORN-MEAL OR INDIAN PUDDING.

One quart of milk; one cup of sifted corn meal; one cup of molasses (not "sir-up"); one teaspoonful of salt.

Stir meal, salt, and molasses together. Boil the milk, and add slowly. Butter a pudding-dish, and pour in the mixture; adding, after it is set in the oven, one cup of cold milk poured over the top. Bake three hours in a moderate oven.

*   *   *   *   *

CUSTARDS, CREAMS, JELLIES, ETC.

BAKED CUSTARD.

One quart of milk; four eggs; one teacup of sugar; half a teaspoonful of salt; nutmeg.

Boil the milk. Beat the eggs very light, and add the sugar and salt. Pour on the milk very slowly, stirring constantly. Bake in a pudding-dish or in cups. If in cups, set them in a baking-pan, and half fill it with boiling water. Grate nutmeg over each. The secret of a good custard is in slow baking and the most careful watching. Test often with a knife-blade, and do not bake an instant after the blade comes out smooth and clean. To be eaten cold. Six eggs are generally used; but four are plenty.

BOILED CUSTARD.

One quart of milk; three or four eggs; one cup of sugar; one teaspoonful of vanilla; half a teaspoonful of salt; one teaspoonful of corn-starch.

Boil the milk. Dissolve the corn-starch in a little cold water, and boil in the milk five minutes. It prevents the custard from curdling, which otherwise it is very apt to do. Beat the eggs and sugar well together, stir into the milk, and add the salt and flavoring. Take at once from the fire, and, when cool, pour either into a large glass dish, covering with a meringue of the whites, or into small glasses with a little jelly or jam at the bottom of each. Or the whites can be used in making an apple-float, as below, and the yolks for the custard.

For *Cocoanut Custard* add a cup of grated cocoanut; for *Chocolate*, two tablespoonfuls of grated chocolate dissolved in half a cup of boiling water.

TIPSY PUDDING.

Make a boiled custard as directed. Half fill a deep dish with any light, stale cake. Add to a teacup of wine a teacup of boiling water, and pour over it. Add the custard just before serving.

APPLE FLOAT.

Six good, acid apples stewed and strained. When cold, add a teacupful of sugar, half a teaspoonful of vanilla, and the beaten whites of three or four eggs. Serve at once.

BLANCMANGE.

One quart of milk; one cup of sugar; half a package of gelatine; half a teaspoonful of salt; a teaspoonful of any essence liked.

Soak the gelatine ten minutes in half a cup of cold water. Boil the milk, and add gelatine and the other ingredients. Strain into molds, and let it stand in a cold place all night to harden. For chocolate blancmange add two tablespoonfuls of scraped chocolate dissolved in a little boiling water.

SPANISH CREAM.

Make a blancmange as on p. 238; but, just before taking from the fire, add the yolks of four eggs, and then strain. The whites can be used for meringues.

WHIPPED CREAM.

One pint of rich cream; one cup of sugar; one glass of sherry or Madeira.

Mix all, and put on the ice an hour, as cream whips much better when chilled.

Using a whip-churn enables it to be done in a few minutes; but a fork or egg-beater will answer. Skim off all the froth as it rises, and lay on a sieve to drain, returning the cream which drips away to be whipped over again. Set on the ice a short time before serving.

CHARLOTTE RUSSE.

Make a sponge cake as on p. 216, and line a Charlotte mold with it, cutting a piece the size of the bottom, and fitting the rest around the sides. Fill with cream whipped as above, and let it stand on the ice to set a little. This is the easiest form of Charlotte. It is improved by the beaten whites of three eggs stirred into the cream. Flavor with half a teaspoonful of vanilla if liked.

BAVARIAN CREAM.

Whip a pint of cream to a stiff froth. Boil a pint of rich milk with a teacupful of sugar, and add a teaspoonful of vanilla. Soak half a box of gelatine for an hour in half a cup of warm water, and add to the milk. Add the yolks of four eggs beaten smooth, and take from the fire instantly.

When cold and just beginning to thicken, stir in the whipped cream. Put in molds, and set in a cold place. This can be used also for filling Charlotte Russe. For chocolate add chocolate as directed in rule for boiled custard; for coffee, one teacup of clear, strong coffee.

STRAWBERRY CREAM.

Three pints of strawberries mashed fine. Strain the juice, and add a heaping cup of sugar, and then gelatine soaked as above, and dissolved in a teacup of boiling water. Add the pint of whipped cream, and pour into molds.

FRUIT CREAMS.

Half a pint of peach or pine-apple marmalade stirred smooth with a teacupful of sweet cream. Add gelatine dissolved as in rule for strawberry cream, and, when cold, the pint of whipped cream. These creams are very delicious, and not as expensive as rich pastry.

OMELETTE SOUFFLEE.

Six whites and three yolks of eggs; three tablespoonfuls of powdered sugar sifted; a few drops of lemon or vanilla. Beat the yolks, flavoring, and sugar to a light cream; beat the whites to the stiffest froth. Have the yolks in a deep bowl. Turn the whites on to them, and do not stir, but mix, by cutting down through the middle, and gradually mixing white and yellow. Turn on to a tin or earthen baking-dish with high sides, and bake in a moderate oven from ten to fifteen minutes. It will rise very high, and must be served the instant it is done, to avoid its falling.

FRIED CREAM.

One pint of milk; half a cup of sugar; yolks of three eggs; two tablespoonfuls of corn-starch and one of flour mixed; half a teaspoonful of vanilla, and two inches of stick-cinnamon; a teaspoonful of butter.

Boil the cinnamon in the milk. Stir the corn-starch and flour smooth in a little cold milk or water, and add to the milk. Beat the yolks light with the sugar, and add. Take from the fire; take out the cinnamon, and stir in the butter and vanilla, and pour out on a buttered tin or dish, letting it be about half an inch thick. When cold and stiff, cut into pieces about three inches long and two wide. Dip carefully in sifted cracker-crumbs; then in a beaten egg, and in crumbs again, and fry like croquettes. Dry in the oven four or five minutes, and serve at once. Very delicious.

PEACH FRITTERS.

Make a batter as on p. 208. Take the fruit from a small can of peaches, lay it on a plate, and sprinkle with a spoonful of sugar and a glass of wine. Let it lie an hour, turning it once. Dip each piece in batter, and drop in boiling lard, or chop and mix with batter. Prepare the juice for a sauce as on p. 172. Fresh peaches or slices of tender apple can be used in the same way. Drain on brown paper, and sift sugar over them, before they go to table.

FREEZING OF ICE CREAM AND ICES.

With a patent freezer ice cream and ices can be prepared with less trouble than puff paste. The essential points are the use of rock-salt, and pounding the ice into small bits. Set the freezer in the centre of the tub. Put a layer of ice three inches deep, then of salt, and so on till the tub is full, ending with ice. Put in the cream, and turn for ten minutes, or till you can not turn the beater. Then take off the cover, scrape down the sides, and beat like cake for at least five minutes. Pack the tub again, having let off all water; cover with a piece of old carpet. If molds are used, fill as soon as the cream is frozen; pack them full of it, and lay in ice and salt. When ready to turn out, dip in warm water a moment. Handle gently, and serve at once.

ICE CREAM OF CREAM.

To a gallon of sweet cream add two and a quarter pounds of sugar, and four tablespoonfuls of vanilla or other extract, as freezing destroys flavors. Freeze as directed.

ICE CREAM WITH EGGS.

Boil two quarts of rich milk, and add to it, when boiling, four tablespoonfuls of corn-starch wet with a cup of cold milk. Boil for ten minutes, stirring often. Beat twelve eggs to a creamy froth with a heaping quart of sugar, and stir in, taking from the fire as soon as it boils. When cold, add three tablespoonfuls of vanilla or lemon, and two quarts either of cream or very rich milk, and freeze. For strawberry or raspberry cream allow the juice of one quart of berries to a gallon of cream. For chocolate cream grate half a pound of chocolate; melt it with one pint of sugar and a little water, and add to above rule.

WATER ICES.

Are simply fruit juices and water made very sweet, with a few whites of eggs whipped stiff, and added. For lemon ice take two quarts of water, one quart of sugar, and the juice of seven lemons. Mix and add, after it has begun to freeze, the stiffly-beaten whites of four eggs. Orange ice is made in the same way.

WINE JELLY.

One box of gelatine; one cup of wine; three lemons, juice and rind; a small stick of cinnamon; one quart of boiling water; one pint of white sugar.

Soak the gelatine in one cup of cold water half an hour. Boil the cinnamon in the quart of water for five minutes, and then add the yellow rind of the lemons cut very thin, and boil a minute. Take out cinnamon and rinds, and add sugar, wine, and gelatine. Strain at once through a fine strainer into molds, and, when cold, set on the ice to harden. To turn out, dip for a moment in hot water. A pint of wine is used, if liked very strong.

LEMON JELLY.

Omit the wine, but make as above in other respects, using five lemons. Oranges are nice also. The juice may be used as in lemon jelly, or the little sections may be peeled as carefully as possible of all the white skin. Pour a little lemon jelly in a mold, and let it harden. Then fill with four oranges prepared in this way, and pour in liquid jelly to cover them. Candied fruit may be used instead. The jelly reserved to add to the mold can be kept in a warm place till the other has hardened. Fresh strawberries or raspberries, or cut-up peaches, can be used instead of oranges.

CANNING AND PRESERVING.

Canning is so simple an operation that it is unfortunate that most people consider it difficult. The directions generally given are so troublesome that one can not wonder it is not attempted oftener; but it need be hardly more care than the making of apple sauce, which, by the way, can always be made while apples are plenty, and canned for spring use. In an experience of years, not more than one can in a hundred has ever been lost, and fruit put up at home is far nicer than any from factories.

In canning, see first that the jars are clean, the rubbers whole and in perfect order, and the tops clean and ready to screw on. Fill the jars with hot (not boiling) water half an hour before using, and have them ready on a table sufficiently large to hold the preserving-kettle, a dish-pan quarter full of hot water, and the cans. Have ready, also, a deep plate, large enough to hold two cans; a silver spoon; an earthen cup with handle; and, if possible, a can-filler,--that is, a small tin in strainer-shape, but without the bottom, and fitting about the top. The utmost speed is needed in filling and screwing down tops, and for this reason every thing *must be* ready beforehand.

In filling the can let the fruit come to the top; then run the spoon-handle down on all sides to let out the air; pour in juice till it runs over freely, and screw the top down at once, using a towel to protect the hand. Set at once in a dish-pan of water, as this prevents the table being stained by juice, and also its hardening on the hot can. Proceed in this way till all are full; wipe them dry; and, when cold, give the tops an additional screw, as the glass contracts in cooling, and loosens them. Label them, and keep in a dark, cool closet. When the fruit is used, wash the jar, and dry carefully at the back of the stove. Wash the rubber also, and dry on a towel, putting it in the jar when dry, and screwing on the top. They are then ready for next year's use. Mason's cans are decidedly the best for general use.

GENERAL RULES FOR CANNING.

For all small fruits allow one-third of a pound of sugar to a pound of fruit. Make it into a sirup with a teacup of water to each pound, and skim carefully. Throw in the fruit, and boil ten minutes, canning as directed. Raspberries and blackberries are best; huckleberries are excellent for pies, and easily canned. Pie-plant can be stewed till tender. It requires half a pound of sugar to a pound of fruit.

For peaches, gages, &c, allow the same amount of sugar as for raspberries. Pare peaches, and can whole or in halves as preferred. Prick plums and gages with a large darning-needle to prevent their bursting. In canning pears, pare and drop at once, into cold water, as this prevents their turning dark.

Always use a porcelain-lined kettle, and stir either with a silver or a wooden spoon,--never an iron one. Currants are nice mixed with an equal weight of raspberries, and all fruit is more wholesome canned than in preserves.

TO CAN TOMATOES.

Unless very plenty, it is cheaper to buy these in the tins. Pour on boiling water to help in removing the skins; fill the preserving kettle, but add no water. Boil them five minutes, and then can. Do not season till ready to use them for the table. Okra and tomatoes may be scalded together in equal parts, and canned for soups.

PRESERVES.

Preserves are scarcely needed if canning is nicely done. They require much more trouble, and are too rich for ordinary use, a pound of sugar to one of fruit being required. If made at all, the fruit must be very fresh, and the sirup perfectly clear. For sirup allow one teacup of cold water to every pound of sugar, and, as it heats, add to every three or four pounds the white of an egg. Skim very carefully, boiling till no more rises, and it is ready for use. Peaches, pears, green gages, cherries, and crab-apples are all preserved alike. Peel, stone, and halve peaches, and boil only a few pieces at a time till clear. Peel, core, and halve pears. Prick plums and gages several times. Core crab-apples, and cut half the stem from cherries. Cook till tender. Put up *when cold* in small jars, and paste paper over them.

JAMS.

Make sirup as directed above. Use raspberries, strawberries, or any small fruit, and boil for half an hour. Put up in small jars or tumblers; lay papers dipped in brandy on the fruit, and paste on covers, or use patent jelly-glasses.

MARMALADE.

Quinces make the best; but crab-apples or any sour apple are also good. Poor quinces, unfit for other use, can be washed and cut in small pieces, coring, but not paring them. Allow three-quarters of a pound of sugar and a teacupful of water to a pound of fruit, and boil slowly two hours, stirring and mashing it fine. Strain through a colander, and put up in glasses or bowls. Peach marmalade is made in the same way.

CURRANT JELLY.

The fruit must be picked when just ripened, as when too old it will not form jelly. Look over, and then put stems and all in a porcelain-lined kettle. Crush a little of the fruit to form juice, but add no water. As it heats, jam with a potato-masher; and when hot through, strain through a jelly-bag. Let all run off that will, before squeezing the bag. It will be a little clearer than the squeezed juice. To every pint of this juice add one pound of best white sugar, taking care that it has not a blue tinge. Jelly from bluish-white sugars does not harden well. Boil the juice twenty-five minutes; add the sugar, and boil for five more. Put up in glasses.

ORANGE MARMALADE.

This recipe, taken from the "New York Evening Post," has been thoroughly tested by the author, and found delicious.

"A recipe for orange marmalade that I think will be entirely new to most housewives, and that I know is delicious, comes from an English housekeeper. It is a sweet that is choice and very healthful. If made now, when oranges and lemons are plentiful, it may be had at a cost of from five to six cents for a large glass. The recipe calls for one dozen oranges (sweet or part bitter), one half-dozen lemons, and ten pounds of granulated sugar. Wash the fruit in tepid water thoroughly, and scrub the skins with a soft brush to get rid of the possible microbes that it is said may lurk on the skins of fruit. Dry the fruit; take a very sharp knife, and on a hard-wood board slice it very thin. Throw away the thick pieces that come off from the ends. Save all the seeds, and put them in one bowl; the sliced fruit in another. Pour half a gallon of water over the contents of each bowl, and soak for thirty-six hours. Then put the fruit in your preserving-kettle, with the water that has been standing on it, and strain in (through a colander) the water put on the lemon-seeds. Cook gently two hours; then add the sugar, and cook another hour, or until the mixture jellies. Test by trying a little in a saucer. Put away in glasses or cans, as other jelly."

FRUIT JELLIES.

Crab-apple, quince, grapes, &c., are all made in the same way. Allow a teacup of water to a pound of fruit; boil till very tender; then strain through a cloth, and treat as currant jelly. Cherries will not jelly without gelatine, and grapes are sometimes troublesome. Where gelatine is needed, allow a package to two quarts of juice.

CANDIED FRUITS.

Make a sirup as for preserves, and boil any fruit, prepared as directed, until tender. Let them stand two days in the sirup. Take out; drain carefully; lay them on plates; sift sugar over them, and dry either in the sun or in a moderately warm oven.

PICKLES AND CATCHUPS.

Sour pickles are first prepared by soaking in a brine made of one pint of coarse salt to six quarts of water. Boil this, and pour it scalding hot over the pickle, cucumbers, green tomatoes, &c. Cucumbers may lie in this a week, or a month even, but must be soaked in cold water two days before using them. Other pickles lie only a month.

Sweet pickles are made from any fruit used in preserving, allowing three, or sometimes four, pounds of sugar to a quart of best cider vinegar, and boiling both together.

CUCUMBER PICKLES.

Half a bushel of cucumbers, small, and as nearly as possible the same size. Make a brine as directed, and pour over them. Next morning prepare a pickle as follows: Two gallons of cider vinegar; one quart of brown sugar. Boil, and skim carefully, and add to it half a pint of white mustard seed; one ounce of stick-cinnamon broken fine; one ounce of alum; half an ounce each of whole cloves and black pepper-corns. Boil five minutes, and pour over the cucumbers. They can be used in a week. In a month scald the vinegar once more, and pour over them.

TOMATO CHUTNEY.

One peck of green tomatoes; six large green peppers; six onions; one cup of salt. Chop onions and peppers fine, slice the tomatoes about quarter of an inch thick, and sprinkle the salt over all. In the morning drain off all the salt and water, and put the tomatoes in a porcelain-lined kettle. Mix together thoroughly two pounds of brown sugar; quarter of a pound of mustard-seed; one ounce each of powdered cloves, cinnamon, ginger, and black pepper; half an ounce of allspice; quarter of an ounce each of cayenne pepper and ground mustard. Stir all into the tomatoes; cover with cider vinegar,--about two quarts,--and boil slowly for two hours. Very nice, but very hot. If wanted less so, omit the cayenne and ground mustard.

RIPE CUCUMBER OR MELON-RIND PICKLES.

Pare, seed, and cut lengthwise into four pieces, or in thick slices. Boil an ounce of alum in one gallon of water, and pour over them, letting them stand at least half a day on the back of the stove. Take them out, and let them lie in cold water until cold. Have ready a quart of vinegar, three pounds of brown sugar, and an ounce of stick-cinnamon and half an ounce cloves. Boil the vinegar and sugar, and skim; add the spices and the melon rind or cucumber, and boil for half an hour.

SWEET-PICKLED PEACHES, PEARS, OR PLUMS.

Seven pounds of fruit; four pounds of brown sugar; one quart of vinegar; one ounce of cloves; two ounces of stick-cinnamon. Pare the peaches or not, as liked. If unpared, wash and wipe each one to rub off the wool. Boil vinegar and sugar, and skim well; add spices, sticking one or two cloves in each peach. Boil ten minutes, and take out into jars. Boil the sirup until reduced one-half, and pour over them. Pears are peeled and cored; apples peeled, cored, and quartered. They can all be put in stone jars; but Mason's cans are better.

TOMATO CATCHUP.

Boil one bushel of ripe tomatoes, skins and all, and, when soft, strain through a colander. Be sure that it is a colander, and *not* a sieve, for reasons to be given. Add to this pulp two quarts of best vinegar; one cup of salt; two pounds of brown sugar; half an ounce of cayenne pepper; three ounces each of powdered allspice and mace; two ounces of powdered cinnamon; three ounces of celery-seed. Mix spices and sugar well together, and stir into the tomato; add the vinegar, and stir thoroughly. Now strain the whole through a *sieve*. A good deal of rather thick pulp will not go through. Pour all that runs through into a large kettle, and let it boil slowly till reduced one-half. Put the thick pulp into a smaller kettle, and boil twenty minutes. Use as a pickle with cold meats or with boiled fish. A teacupful will flavor a soup. In the old family rule from which this is taken, a pint of brandy is added ten minutes before the catchup is done; but it is not necessary, though an improvement. Bottle, and keep in a cool, dark place. It keeps for years.

*   *   *   *   *

CANDIES.

CREAM CANDY.

One pound of granulated sugar; one teacupful of water; half a teacupful of vinegar. Boil--trying very often after the first ten minutes--till it will harden in cold water. Cool, and pull white.

CHOCOLATE CARAMELS.

One cup of sugar; one cup of milk; half a cup of molasses; two ounces of grated chocolate. Melt the chocolate in a very little water; add the sugar, milk, and molasses, and boil twenty minutes, or until very thick. Pour in buttered pans, and cut in small squares when cool.

MOLASSES CANDY.

Two cups of molasses, one of brown sugar, a teaspoonful of butter, and a tablespoonful of vinegar. Boil from twenty minutes to half an hour. Pour in a buttered dish, and pull when cool.

NUT CANDY.

Make molasses candy as above. Just before taking it from the fire, add a heaping pint of shelled peanuts or walnuts. Cut in strips before it is quite cold.

COCOANUT DROPS.

One cocoanut grated; half its weight in powdered sugar; whites of two eggs; one teaspoonful of corn-starch. Mix corn-starch and sugar; add cocoanut, and then whites of eggs beaten to a stiff froth. Make in little cones, and bake on buttered paper in a slow oven.

CHOCOLATE CREAMS.

One pound of granulated sugar; half a pound of chocolate; one teaspoonful of acetic acid; one tablespoonful of water; one teaspoonful of vanilla. Melt the sugar slowly, wetting a little with the water. Add the acid and vanilla, and boil till sugary, trying *very* often by stirring a little in a saucer. When sugary, take from the fire, and stir until almost hard; then roll in little balls, and put on a buttered plate. Melt the chocolate in two tablespoonfuls of water with a cup of sugar, and boil five minutes. When just warm, dip in the little balls till well coated, and lay on plates to dry. Very nice.

*　　*　　*　　*　　*

SICK-ROOM COOKERY.

GENERAL HINTS.

As recovery from any illness depends in large part upon proper food, and as the appetite of the sick is always capricious and often requires tempting, the greatest pains should be taken in the preparation of their meals. If only dry toast and tea, let each be perfect, remembering instructions for making each, and serving on the freshest of napkins and in dainty china. A *tete-a-tete* service is very nice for use in a sick-room; and in any case a very small teapot can be had, that the tea may always be made fresh. Prepare only a small amount of any thing, and never discuss it beforehand. A surprise will often rouse a flagging appetite. Be ready, too, to have your best attempts rejected. The article disliked one day may be just what is wanted the next. Never let food stand in a sick-room,--for it becomes hateful to a sensitive patient,--and have every thing as daintily clean as possible. Remember, too, that gelatine is not nourishing, and do not be satisfied to feed a patient on jellies. Bread from any brown flour will be more nourishing than wheat. Corn meal is especially valuable for thin, chilly invalids, as it contains so much heat. In severe sickness a glass tube is very useful for feeding gruels and drinks, and little white china boats with spouts are also good. A wooden tray with legs six or seven inches high, to stand on the bed, is very convenient for serving meals. Let ventilation, sunshine, and absolute cleanliness rule in the sick-room. Never raise a dust, but wipe the carpet with a damp cloth, and pick up bits as needed. Never let lamp or sun light shine directly in the eyes, and, when the patient shows desire to sleep, darken the room a little. Never whisper, nor wear rustling dresses, nor become irritated at exactions, but keep a cheerful countenance, which helps often far more than drugs. Experience must teach the rest.

BEEF TEA, OR ESSENCE OF BEEF.

Cut a pound of perfectly lean beef into small bits. Do not allow any particle of fat to remain. Put in a wide-mouthed bottle, cork tightly, and set in a kettle of cold water. Boil for three hours; pour off the juice, which is now completely extracted from the meat. There will be probably a small cupful. Season with a saltspoonful of salt. This is given in extreme sickness, feeding a teaspoonful at a time.

BEEF TEA FOR CONVALESCENTS.

One pound of lean beef prepared as above. Add a pint of cold water,--rain-water is best,--and soak for an hour. Cover closely, and boil for ten minutes; or put in the oven, and let it remain an hour. Pour off the juice, season with half a teaspoonful of salt, and use. A little celery salt makes a change.

CHICKEN BROTH.

The bones and a pound of meat from a chicken put in three pints of cold water. Skim thoroughly when it comes to a boil, add a teaspoonful of salt, and simmer for three hours. Strain and serve. A tablespoonful of soaked rice or tapioca may be added after the broth is strained. Return it in this case to the fire, and boil half an hour longer.

CHICKEN JELLY.

Boil chicken as for broth, but reduce the liquid to half a pint. Strain into a cup or little mold, and turn out when cold.

CHICKEN PANADA.

Take the breast of the chicken boiled as above; cut in bits, and pound smooth in a mortar. Take a teacupful of bread-crumbs; soak them soft in warm milk, or, if liked better, in a little broth. Mix them with the chicken; add a saltspoonful of salt, and, if allowed, a pinch of mace; and serve in a cup with a spoon.

BEEF, TAPIOCA, AND EGG BROTH.

One pound of lean beef, prepared as for beef tea, and soaked one hour in a quart of cold water. Boil slowly for two hours. Strain it. Add a half teaspoonful of salt, and half a cupful of tapioca which has been washed and soaked an hour in warm water. Boil slowly half an hour. Serve in a shallow bowl, in which a poached egg is put at the last, or stir a beaten egg into one cup of the boiling soup, and serve at once with wafers or crackers.

MUTTON BROTH.

Made as chicken broth. Any strong stock, from which the fat has been taken, answers for broths.

OATMEAL GRUEL.

Have ready, in a double boiler, one quart of boiling water with a teaspoonful of salt, and sprinkle in two tablespoonfuls of fine oatmeal. Boil an hour; then strain, and serve with cream or milk and sugar if ordered. Farina gruel is made in the same way.

INDIAN OR CORN MEAL GRUEL.

One quart of boiling water; one teaspoonful of salt. Mix three tablespoonfuls of corn meal with a little cold water, and stir in slowly. Boil one hour; strain and serve, a cupful at once.

MILK PORRIDGE.

One quart of boiling milk; two tablespoonfuls of flour mixed with a little cold milk and half a teaspoonful of salt. Stir into the milk, and boil half an hour.

Strain and serve. If allowed, a handful of raisins and a little grated nutmeg may be boiled with it.

WINE WHEY.

Boil one cup of new milk, and add half a wine-glass of good sherry or Madeira wine. Boil a minute; strain, and use with or without sugar as liked.

EGG-NOG.

One egg; one tablespoonful of sugar; half a cup of milk; one tablespoonful of wine.

Beat the sugar and yolk to a cream; add the wine, and then the milk. Beat the white to a stiff froth, and stir in very lightly.

Omit the milk where more condensed nourishment is desired.

ARROW-ROOT OR RICE JELLY.

Two heaping teaspoonfuls of either arrow-root or rice flour; a pinch of salt; a heaping tablespoonful of sugar; one cup of boiling water.

Mix the flour with a little cold water, and add to the boiling water. Boil until transparent, and pour into cups or small molds. For a patient with summer complaint, flavor by boiling a stick of cinnamon in it. For a fever patient add the juice of quarter of a lemon.

DR. GAUNT'S RICE JELLY.

Take four tablespoonfuls of rice, and boil it hard in three pints of water for twenty minutes. Let simmer for two hours. Then force through fine hair strainer, and allow it to cool. Place in an ice chest over night.

DIRECTIONS FOR USE.

Dissolve two tablespoonfuls of the rice jelly in each one-half pint of milk.

RICE WATER FOR DRINK.

One quart of boiling water; a pinch of salt; one tablespoonful of rice or rice flour. Boil half an hour, and strain.

TOAST WATER.

Toast two slices of bread very brown, but do not scorch. Put in a pitcher, and while hot pour on one quart of cold water. Let it stand half an hour, and it is ready for use.

CRUST COFFEE.

Two thick slices of graham or Boston brown bread toasted as brown as possible. Pour on one pint of boiling water, and steep ten minutes. Serve with milk and sugar, like coffee.

BEEF JUICE.

Broil a thick piece of beef steak three minutes. Squeeze all the juice with a lemon-squeezer into a cup; salt very lightly, and give like beef tea.

JELLY AND ICE.

Break ice in bits no bigger than a pea. A large pin will break off bits from a lump very easily. To a tablespoonful add one of wine jelly broken up. It is very refreshing in fever.

PANADA.

Lay in a bowl two Boston or graham crackers split; sprinkle on a pinch of salt, and cover with boiling water. Set the bowl in a saucepan of boiling water, and let it stand half an hour, till the crackers look clear. Slide into a hot saucer without breaking, and eat with cream and sugar. As they are only good hot, do just enough for the patient's appetite at one time.

MILK TOAST.

Toast one or two thin slices of bread; dip quickly in a little salted boiling water, and spread on a little butter. Boil a teacupful of milk; thicken with a teaspoonful of flour mixed in a little cold water with a pinch of salt; lay the toast in a small, hot, deep plate, and pour over the milk. Cream toast is made in the same way.

BEEF SANDWICH.

Two or three tablespoonfuls of raw, very tender beef, scraped fine, and spread between two slices of slightly buttered bread. Sprinkle on pepper and salt.

PREPARED FLOUR.

Tie a pint of flour tightly in a cloth, and boil for four hours. Scrape off the outer crust, and the inside will be found to be a dry ball. Grate this as required, allowing one tablespoonful wet in cold milk to a pint of boiling milk, and boiling till smooth. Add a saltspoonful of salt. This is excellent for summer complaint, whether in adults or children. The beaten white of an egg can also be stirred in if ordered. If this porridge is used from the beginning of the complaint, little or no medicine will be required.

PARCHED RICE.

Roast to a deep brown as you would coffee, and then cook as in rule for boiled rice, p. 199, and eat with cream and sugar.

RICE COFFEE.

Parch as above, and grind. Allow half a cup to a quart of boiling water, and let it steep fifteen minutes. Strain, and drink plain, or with milk and sugar.

HERB TEAS.

For the dried herbs allow one teaspoonful to a cup of boiling water. Pour the water on them; cover, and steep ten minutes or so. Camomile tea is good for sleeplessness; calamus and catnip for babies' colic; and cinnamon for hemorrhages and summer complaint. Slippery-elm and flax-seed are also good for the latter.

BEEF STEAK OR CHOPS, ETC.

With beef steak, cut a small thick piece of a nice shape; broil carefully, and serve on a very hot plate, salting a little, but using no butter unless allowed by the physician.

Chops should be trimmed very neatly, and cooked in the same way. A nice way of serving a chop is to broil, and cut in small bits. Have ready a baked potato. Cut a slice from the top; take out the inside, and season as for eating; add the chop, and return all to the skin, covering it, and serving as hot as possible.

When appetite has returned, poached eggs on toast, a little salt cod with cream, or many of the dishes given under the head of Breakfast Dishes, are relished. Prepare small quantities, preserving the right proportions of seasoning.

TAPIOCA JELLY.

Two ounces of tapioca,--about two tablespoonfuls,--soaked over-night in one cup of cold water. In the morning add a second cup of cold water, and boil till very clear. Add quarter of a cup of sugar; two teaspoonfuls of brandy or four of wine; or the thin rind and juice of a lemon may be used instead. Very good hot, but better poured into small molds wet with cold water, and turned out when firm.

TAPIOCA GRUEL.

Half a cup of tapioca soaked over-night in a cup of cold water. In the morning add a quart of milk and half a teaspoonful of salt, and boil three hours. It can be eaten plain, or with sugar and wine. Most of the blancmanges and creams given can be prepared in smaller quantities, if allowed. Baked custards can be made with the whites of the eggs, if a very delicate one is desired.

APPLE WATER.

Two roasted sour apples, or one pint of washed dried apples. Pour on one quart of boiling water; cover, and let it stand half an hour, when it is ready for use.

HOUSEHOLD HINTS.

SOFT SOAP.

All mutton and ham fat should be melted and strained into a large stone pot. The practice of throwing lumps of fat into a pot, and waiting till there are several pounds before trying them out, is a disgusting one, as often such a receptacle is alive with maggots. Try out the fat, and strain as carefully as you would lard or beef drippings, and it is then always ready for use. If concentrated lye or potash, which comes in little tins, is used, directions will be found on the tins. Otherwise allow a pound of stone potash to every pound of grease. Twelve pounds of each will make a barrel of soft soap.

Crack the potash in small pieces. Put in a large kettle with two gallons of water, and boil till dissolved. Then add the grease, and, when melted, pour all into a tight barrel. Fill it up with boiling water, and for a week, stir daily for five or ten minutes. It will gradually become like jelly.

TO PURIFY SINKS AND DRAINS.

To one pound of common copperas add one gallon of boiling water, and use when dissolved. The copperas is poison, and must never be left unmarked.

FURNITURE POLISH.

Mix two tablespoonfuls of sweet or linseed oil with a tablespoonful of turpentine, and rub on with a piece of flannel, polishing with a dry piece.

TO KEEP EGGS.

Be sure that the eggs are fresh. Place them points down in a stone jar or tight firkin, and pour over them the following brine, which is enough for a hundred and fifty:--

One pint of slacked lime, one pint of salt, two ounces of cream of tartar, and four gallons of water. Boil all together for ten minutes; skim, and, when cold, pour it over the eggs. They can also be kept in salt tightly packed, but not as well.

TO MAKE HARD WATER SOFT.

Dissolve in one gallon of boiling water a pound and a quarter of washing soda, and a quarter of a pound of borax. In washing clothes allow quarter of a cup of this to every gallon of water.

TO TAKE OUT FRUIT-STAINS.

Stretch the stained part tightly over a bowl, and pour on boiling water till it is free from spot.

TO TAKE OUT INK-SPOTS.

Ink spilled upon carpets or on woolen table-covers can be taken out, if washed at once in cold water. Change the water often, and continue till the stain is gone.

MIXED SPICES.

Three heaping tablespoonfuls of ground cinnamon, one heaping one each of clove and mace, and one even one of allspice. Mix thoroughly, and use for dark cakes and for puddings.

SPICE SALT.

Four ounces of salt; one of black pepper; one each of thyme, sweet marjoram, and summer savory; half an ounce each of clove, allspice, and mace; quarter of an ounce of cayenne pepper; one ounce of celery salt. Mix all together; sift three times, and keep closely covered. Half an ounce will flavor a stuffing for roast meat; and a tablespoonful is nice in many soups and stews.

TO WASH GREASY TIN AND IRON.

Pour a few drops of ammonia into every greasy roasting-pan, first half-filling with warm water. A bottle of ammonia should always stand near the sink for such uses. Never allow dirty pots or pans to stand and dry; for it doubles the labor of washing. Pour in water, and use ammonia, and the work is half done.

TO CLEAN BRASS AND COPPER.

Scrape a little rotten-stone fine, and make into a paste with sweet oil. Rub on with a piece of flannel; let it dry, and polish with a chamois-skin. Copper is cleaned either with vinegar and salt mixed in equal parts, or with oxalic acid. The latter is a deadly poison, and must be treated accordingly.

WEIGHTS AND MEASURES.

As many families have no scales for weighing, a table of measures is given which can be used instead. Weighing is always best, but not always convenient. The cup used is the ordinary coffee or kitchen cup, holding half a pint. A set of tin measures, from a gill up to a quart, is very useful in all cooking operations.

One quart of sifted flour is one pound.

One pint of granulated sugar is one pound.

Two cups of butter packed are one pound.

Ten eggs are one pound.

Five cupfuls of sifted flour are one pound.

A wine-glassful is half a gill.

Eight even tablespoonfuls are a gill.

Four even saltspoonfuls make a teaspoonful.

A saltspoonful is a good measure of salt for all custards, puddings, blancmanges, &c.

One teaspoonful of soda to a quart of flour.

Two teaspoonfuls of soda to one of cream of tartar.

The teaspoonful given in all these receipts is just rounded full, not heaped.

Two heaping teaspoonfuls of baking powder to one quart of flour.

One cup of sweet or sour milk as wetting for one quart of flour.

TIME TABLE FOR ROASTED MEATS.

Beef, from six to eight pounds, one hour and a half, or twelve minutes to the pound.

Mutton, ten minutes to the pound for rare; fifteen for well-done.

Lamb, a very little less according to age and size of roast.

Veal, twenty minutes to a pound.

Pork, half an hour to a pound.

Turkey of eight or ten pounds weight, not less than three hours.

Goose of seven or eight pounds, two hours.

Chickens, from an hour to an hour and a half.

Tame ducks, one hour.

Game duck, from thirty to forty minutes.

Partridges, grouse, &c., half an hour.

Pigeons, half an hour.

Small birds, twenty minutes.

TIME TABLE FOR BOILED MEATS.

Beef *a la mode*, eight pounds, four hours.

Corned beef, eight pounds, four hours.

Corned or smoked tongue, eight pounds, four hours.

Ham, eight or ten pounds, five hours.

Mutton, twenty minutes to a pound.

Veal, half an hour to a pound.

Turkey, ten pounds, three hours.

Chickens, one hour and a half.

Old fowls, two or three hours.

TIME TABLE FOR FISH.

Halibut and salmon, fifteen minutes to a pound.

Blue-fish, bass, &c., ten minutes to a pound.

Fresh cod, six minutes to a pound.

Baked halibut, twelve minutes to a pound.

Baked blue-fish, &c., ten minutes to a pound.

Trout, pickerel, &c., eight minutes to a pound.

TIME TABLE FOR VEGETABLES.

Half an hour,--Pease, potatoes, asparagus, rice, corn, summer squash, canned tomatoes, macaroni.

Three-quarters of an hour,--Young beets, young turnips, young carrots and parsnips, baked potatoes (sweet and Irish), boiled sweet potatoes, onions, canned corn, tomatoes.

One hour,--New cabbage, shelled and string beans, spinach and greens, cauliflower, oyster-plant, and winter squash.

Two hours,--Winter carrots, parsnips, turnips, cabbage, and onions.

Three to eight hours,--Old beets.

TIME TABLE FOR BREAD, CAKES, ETC.

Bread,--large loaves, an hour; small loaves, from half to three-quarters of an hour.

Biscuits and rolls, in from fifteen to twenty minutes.

Brown bread, steamed, three hours.

Loaves of sponge cake, forty-five minutes; if thin, about thirty.

Loaves of richer cake, from forty-five minutes to an hour.

Fruit cake, about two hours, if in two or three pound loaves.

Small thin cakes and cookies, from ten to fifteen minutes. Watch carefully.

Baked puddings, rice, &c., one hour.

Boiled puddings, three hours.

Custards to be watched and tested after the first fifteen minutes.

Batter puddings baked, forty-five minutes.

Pie-crust, about half an hour.

DEVILED HAM.

For this purpose, use either the knuckle or any odds and ends remaining. Cut off all dark or hard bits, and see that at least a quarter of the amount is fat. Chop as finely as possible, reducing it almost to a paste. For a pint-bowl of this, make a dressing as follows:--

One even tablespoonful of sugar; one even teaspoonful of ground mustard; one saltspoonful of Cayenne pepper; one teacupful of good vinegar. Mix the sugar, mustard, and pepper thoroughly, and add the vinegar little by little. Stir it into the chopped ham, and pack it in small molds, if it is to be served as a lunch or supper relish, turning out upon a small platter and garnishing with parsley.

For sandwiches, cut the bread very thin; butter lightly, and spread with about a teaspoonful of the deviled ham. The root of a boiled tongue can be prepared in the same way. If it is to be kept some time, pack in little jars, and pour melted butter over the top.

This receipt should have had place under "Meats," but was overlooked.

LIST OF UTENSILS REQUIRED FOR SUCCESSFUL WORKING.

TIN WARE.

One boiler for clothes, holding eight or ten gallons.--Two dish-pans,--one large, one medium-sized.--One two-quart covered tin pail.--One four-quart covered tin pail.--Two thick tin four-quart saucepans.--Two two-quart saucepans.--Four measures, from one gill to a quart, and broad and low, rather than high.--Three tin scoops of different sizes for flour, sugar, &c.--Two pint and two half-pint molds for jellies.--Two quart molds.--One skimmer with long handle.--One large and one small dipper.--Four bread-pans, 10x4x4.--Three jelly-cake tins.--Six pie-plates.--Two long biscuit-tins.--One coffee-pot.--One colander.--One large grater.--One nutmeg-grater.--Two wire sieves; one ten inches across, the other four, and with tin sides.--One flour-sifter.--One fine jelly-strainer.--One frying-basket.--One Dover egg-beater.--One wire egg-beater.--One apple-corer.--One pancake-turner.--One set of spice-boxes, or a spice-caster.--One pepper-box.--One flour-dredger.--One sugar-dredger.--One biscuit-cutter.--One potato-cutter.--A dozen muffin-rings.--Small tins for little cakes.--One muffin-pan.--One double milk-boiler, the inside boiler holding two quarts.--One fish-boiler, which can also be used for hams.--One deep bread-pan; a dish-pan is good, but must be kept for this.--One steamer.--One pudding-boiler.--One cake-box.--Six teaspoons.

WOODEN WARE.

One bread-board.--One rolling-pin.--One meat-board.--One wash-board.--One lemon-squeezer.--One potato-masher.--Two large spoons.--One small one.--Nest of wooden boxes for rice, tapioca, &c.--Wooden pails for graham and corn meal.--Chopping-tray.--Water-pail.--Scrubbing-pail.--Wooden cover for flour-barrel.--One board for cutting bread.--One partitioned knife-box.

IRON WARE.

One pair of scales.--One two-gallon pot with steamer to fit.--One three-gallon soup-pot with close-fitting cover.--One three-gallon porcelain-lined kettle, to be kept only for preserving.--One four or six quart one, for apple sauce, &c.--One tea-kettle.--One large and one small frying-pan.--Two Russia or sheet iron dripping-pans; one large enough for a large turkey.--Two gem-pans with deep cups.--Two long-handled spoons.--Two spoons with shorter handles.--One large meat-fork.--One meat-saw.--One cleaver.--One griddle.--One wire broiler.--One toaster.--One waffle-iron.--One can-opener.--Three pairs of common knives and forks.--One small Scotch or frying kettle.--One chopping-knife.--One meat-knife.--One bread-knife.--One set of skewers.--Trussing-needles.

EARTHEN AND STONE WARE.

Two large mixing-bowls, holding eight or ten quarts each.--One eight-quart lip-bowl for cake.--Half a dozen quart bowls.--Half a dozen pint bowls.--Three or four deep plates for putting away cold food.--Six baking-dishes of different sizes, round or oval.--Two quart blancmange-molds.--Two or three pitchers.--Two stone crocks, holding a gallon each.--Two, holding two quarts each.--One bean-pot for baked beans.--One dozen Mason's jars for holding yeast, and many things used in a store closet.--Stone jugs for vinegar and molasses.--Two or three large covered stone jars for pickles.--One deep one for bread.--One earthen teapot.--One dozen pop-over cups.--One dozen custard-cups.--Measuring-cup.

MISCELLANEOUS.

Scrubbing and blacking brushes.--Soap-dish.--Knife-board.-- Vegetable-cutters.--Pastry-brush.--Egg-basket.--Market-basket.--   Broom.--Brush.--Dust-pan.--Floor and sink cloths.--Whisk-broom.-- Four roller-towels.--Twelve dish-towels.--Dishes enough for setting servants' table, heavy stone-china being best.

HINTS TO TEACHERS.

In beginning with a class of school-girls from fourteen to eighteen, it is best to let the first two or three lessons be demonstration lessons; that is, to have all operations performed by the teacher. An assistant may be chosen from the class, who can help in any required way. The receipts for the day should first be read, and copied plainly by all the pupils. Each process must be fully explained, and be as daintily and deftly performed as possible. Not more than six dishes at the most can be prepared in one lesson, and four will be the usual number. Two lessons a week, from two to three hours each, are all for which the regular school-course gives time; and there should be not more than one day between, as many dishes can not be completed in one lesson.

After yeast and bread have been once made by the teacher, bread should be the first item in every lesson thereafter, and the class made a practice-class. Each pupil should make bread twice,--once under the teacher's supervision, and at least once entirely alone. In a large class this may occupy the entire time in the school-year. Let the most important operations be thoroughly learned, even if there is little variety. To make and bake all forms of bread, to broil a steak, boil a potato, and make good tea and coffee, may not seem sufficient result for a year's work; but the girl who can do this has mastered the principles of cooking, and is abundantly able to go on alone.

The fire should be made and cared for by each in turn, and the best modes of washing dishes, and keeping the room and stores in the best order, be part of each lesson.

Once a week let a topic be given out, on which all are to write, any ingredient in cooking being chosen, and the papers read and marked in order of merit.

Once a month examine on these topics, and on what has been learned. Let digestion and forms of food be well understood, and spare no pains to make the lesson attractive and stimulating to interest.

In classes for ladies the work is usually done entirely by the teacher, and at least five dishes are prepared. A large class can thus be taught; but the results will never be as satisfactory as in a practice-class, though the latter is of course much more troublesome to the teacher, as it requires far more patience and tact to watch and direct the imperfect doing of a thing than to do it one's self.

A class lunch or supper is a pleasant way of demonstrating what progress has been made; and, in such entertainment, do not aim at great variety, but insist upon the perfect preparation of a few things. To lay and decorate a table prettily is an accomplishment, and each classroom should have enough china and glass to admit of this.

To indicate the method which the writer has found practicable and useful, a course of twelve lessons is given, embracing the essential operations; and beyond this the teacher can construct her own bills of fare. When the making of bread begins, it will be found that not more than two or three other things can be made at one lesson. Let one of these be a simple cake or pudding for the benefit of the class, whose interest is wonderfully stimulated by something good to eat.

Large white aprons and small half-sleeves to draw on over the dress-sleeves are essential, and must be insisted upon. A little cap of Swiss muslin is pretty, and finishes the uniform well, but is not a necessity.

For the rest each teacher must judge for herself, only remembering to *demand the most absolute neatness* in all work done, and to *give the most perfect patience* no matter how stupid the pupil may seem.

TWELVE LESSONS.

LESSON FIRST.

To make stock. Beef rolls. Apple float. Boiled custard.

LESSON SECOND.

To clarify fat or drippings. Clear soup. Beef soup with vegetables. To make caramel. Cream cakes.

LESSON THIRD.

Beef *a la mode*. To boil potatoes. Mashed potatoes. Potato snow. Potato croquettes. Yeast. Wine jelly.

LESSON FOURTH.

Bread. Plain rolls. Beef hash with potatoes. Beef croquettes. Coddled apples.

LESSON FIFTH.

Graham bread. Rye bread. To broil beef steak. To boil macaroni. Macaroni baked with cheese. To make a *roux*. Baked custard.

LESSON SIXTH.

Parker-House rolls. Steamed brown bread. Puree of salmon. Croquettes of salmon. Corn-starch pudding.

LESSON SEVENTH.

Baked fish. To devil ham. Stuffed eggs. Plain omelet. Saratoga potatoes. To use stale bread. Bread pudding and plain sauce.

LESSON EIGHTH.

Irish stew. Boiled cabbage. Baked cabbage. Lyonnaise potatoes. Whipped cream. Sponge cake. Charlotte Russe.

LESSON NINTH.

Bean soup. To dress and truss a chicken. Chicken fricassee,--brown. Chicken pie. Meringues, plain and with jelly.

LESSON TENTH.

Oyster soup. Oyster scallop. Fried oysters. Pie-crust. Oyster patties. Lemon and apple pie.

LESSON ELEVENTH.

To bone a turkey or chicken. Force-meat. Boiled parsnips. To boil rice. Parsnip fritters.

LESSON TWELFTH.

To decorate boned turkey. To roast beef. To bake potatoes with beef. Gravy. Rice croquettes. Chicken or turkey croquettes.

LIST OF TOPICS FOR TWENTY LESSONS.

Wheat and corn. Making of flour and meal. Tea. Coffee. Chocolate and cocoa.

Tapioca and sago. Rice. Salt. Pepper. Cloves and allspice. Cinnamon, nutmegs, and mace. Ginger and mustard. Olive-oil. Raisins and currants. Macaroni and vermicelli. Potatoes. Sweet potatoes. Yeast and bread. Butter. Fats.

LIST OF AUTHORITIES TO WHICH THE TEACHER MAY REFER.

Draper's Physiology. Dalton's Physiology. Carpenter's Physiology. Foster's Physiology. Youman's Chemistry. Johnston's Chemistry of Common Life. Lewes's Physiology of Common Life. Gray's How Plants Grow. Rand's Vegetable Kingdom. Brillat Savarin's Art of Dining. Brillat Savarin's Physiologie du Gout. The Cook's Oracle, Dr. Kitchener. Food and Dietetics, by Dr. Chambers. Food and Dietetics, by Dr. Pary. Food and Digestion, by Dr. Brinton. Food, by Dr. Letheby. Cook-books at discretion.

QUESTIONS FOR FINAL EXAMINATION AT END OF YEAR.

1. How is soup-stock made?
2. How is white soup made?
3. What are purees?
4. How is clear soup made?
5. How is caramel made, and what are its uses?
6. How is meat jelly made and colored?
7. How is meat boiled, roasted, and broiled?
8. How can cold meat be used?
9. How is poultry roasted and broiled?
10. How are potatoes cooked?
11. How are dried leguminous vegetables cooked?
12. How is rice boiled dry?
13. How is macaroni boiled?
14. How are white and brown sauces made?
15. Give plain salad-dressing and mayonnaise.
16. How are beef tea and chicken broth made?
17. Give receipts for plain omelet and omelette soufflee.
18. How are bread, biscuit, and rolls made?
19. How is pie-crust made?
20. Rule for puff paste?
21. How should you furnish a kitchen?

22. What are the best kinds of cooking utensils?

END.

BIBLIOGRAPHY.

THE CHEMISTRY OF COOKERY. By W. Mattieu Williams.

THE PERFECT WAY IN DIET. By Dr. Anna Kingsford.

FOODS. By Edward Smith.

FRUITS, AND HOW TO USE THEM. By Hester M. Poole.

EATING FOR STRENGTH. Dr. M.L. Holbrook.

FRUIT AND BREAD. By Gustav Schlickeyesen. Translated by Dr. M.L. Holbrook.

FOOD AND FEEDING. By Sir Henry Thompson.

MRS. LINCOLN'S BOSTON COOK BOOK. What to Do and What not to Do in Cooking.

JUST HOW. By Mrs. A.D.T. Whitney.

MRS. RORER'S PHILADELPHIA COOK BOOK.

PRACTICAL COOKING AND DINNER-GIVING. Mrs. Henderson.

IN THE KITCHEN. By Mrs. E.S. Miller.

GOOD LIVING. A Practical Cook Book for Town and Country. By Sara Van Buren Brugiere.

FRENCH DISHES FOR AMERICAN TABLES. By Pierre Caron.

CUISINE CLASSIQUE. Urbain-Dubois.

CAREME.

GOUFFE.

SOYER.

DIET FOR THE SICK. A Treatise on the Values of Foods, their Application to Special Conditions of Health and Disease, and on the Best Methods of their Preparation. By Mrs. Mary E. Henderson.

Cookery-Books at discretion.

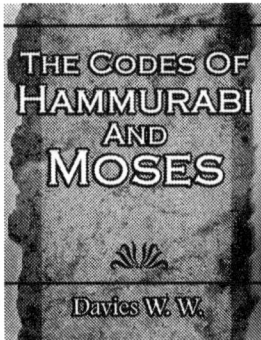

The Codes Of Hammurabi And Moses
W. W. Davies

QTY

The discovery of the Hammurabi Code is one of the greatest achievements of archaeology, and is of paramount interest, not only to the student of the Bible, but also to all those interested in ancient history...

Religion   **ISBN:** *1-59462-338-4*   **Pages:132**
MSRP $12.95

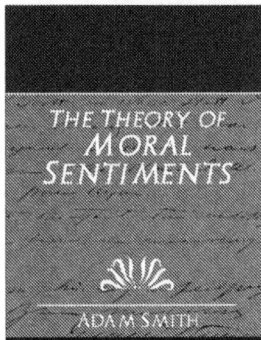

The Theory of Moral Sentiments
Adam Smith

QTY

This work from 1749. contains original theories of conscience amd moral judgment and it is the foundation for systemof morals.

Philosophy **ISBN:** *1-59462-777-0*   **Pages:536**
MSRP $19.95

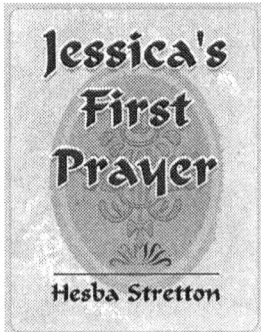

Jessica's First Prayer
Hesba Stretton

QTY

In a screened and secluded corner of one of the many railway-bridges which span the streets of London there could be seen a few years ago, from five o'clock every morning until half past eight, a tidily set-out coffee-stall, consisting of a trestle and board, upon which stood two large tin cans, with a small fire of charcoal burning under each so as to keep the coffee boiling during the early hours of the morning when the work-people were thronging into the city on their way to their daily toil...

Childrens   **ISBN:** *1-59462-373-2*   **Pages:84**
MSRP $9.95

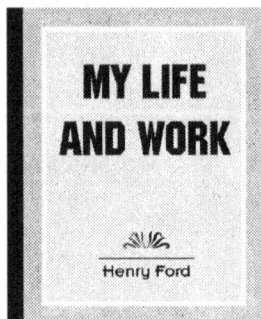

My Life and Work
Henry Ford

QTY

Henry Ford revolutionized the world with his implementation of mass production for the Model T automobile. Gain valuable business insight into his life and work with his own auto-biography... "We have only started on our development of our country we have not as yet, with all our talk of wonderful progress, done more than scratch the surface. The progress has been wonderful enough but..."

Biographies/   **ISBN:** *1-59462-198-5*   **Pages:300**
MSRP $21.95

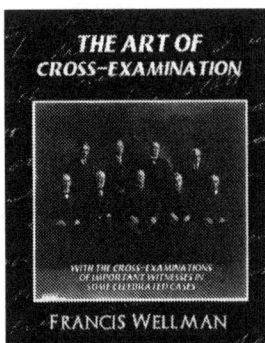

The Art of Cross-Examination
Francis Wellman

QTY

I presume it is the experience of every author, after his first book is published upon an important subject, to be almost overwhelmed with a wealth of ideas and illustrations which could readily have been included in his book, and which to his own mind, at least, seem to make a second edition inevitable. Such certainly was the case with me; and when the first edition had reached its sixth impression in five months, I rejoiced to learn that it seemed to my publishers that the book had met with a sufficiently favorable reception to justify a second and considerably enlarged edition. ..

Pages:412

Reference   ISBN: *1-59462-647-2*   *MSRP $19.95*

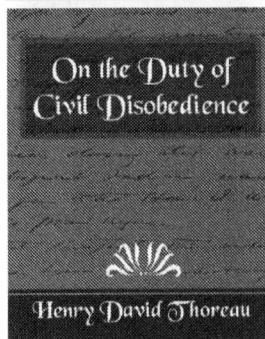

On the Duty of Civil Disobedience
Henry David Thoreau

QTY

Thoreau wrote his famous essay, On the Duty of Civil Disobedience, as a protest against an unjust but popular war and the immoral but popular institution of slave-owning. He did more than write—he declined to pay his taxes,   and was hauled off to gaol in consequence. Who can say how much this refusal of his hastened the end of the war and of slavery ?

Law   ISBN: *1-59462-747-9*   **Pages:48**
MSRP $7.45

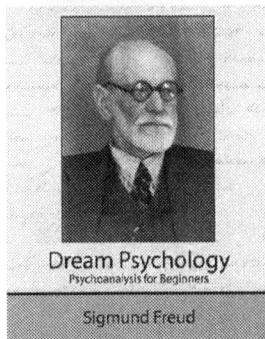

Dream Psychology Psychoanalysis for Beginners
Sigmund Freud

QTY

Sigmund Freud, born Sigismund Schlomo Freud (May 6, 1856 - September 23, 1939), was a Jewish-Austrian neurologist and psychiatrist who co-founded the psychoanalytic school of psychology. Freud is best known for his theories of the unconscious mind, especially involving the mechanism of repression; his redefinition of sexual desire as mobile and directed towards a wide variety of objects; and his therapeutic techniques, especially his understanding of transference in the therapeutic relationship and the presumed value of dreams as sources of insight into unconscious desires.

Pages:196

Psychology   ISBN: *1-59462-905-6*   *MSRP $15.45*

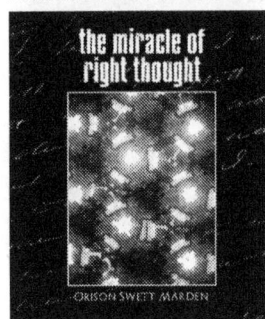

The Miracle of Right Thought
Orison Swett Marden

QTY

Believe with all of your heart that you will do what you were made to do. When the mind has once formed the habit of holding cheerful, happy, prosperous pictures, it will not be easy to form the opposite habit. It does not matter how improbable or how far away this realization may see, or how dark the prospects may be, if we visualize them as best we can, as vividly as possible, hold tenaciously to them and vigorously struggle to attain them, they will gradually become actualized, realized in the life. But a desire, a longing without endeavor, a yearning abandoned or held indifferently will vanish without realization.

Pages:360

Self Help   ISBN: *1-59462-644-8*   *MSRP $25.45*

QTY

The Rosicrucian Cosmo-Conception Mystic Christianity *by Max Heindel* ISBN: *1-59462-188-8* **$38.95**
The Rosicrucian Cosmo-conception is not dogmatic, neither does it appeal to any other authority than the reason of the student. It is: not controversial, but is: sent forth in the, hope that it may help to clear.. New Age/Religion Pages 646

Abandonment To Divine Providence *by Jean-Pierre de Caussade* ISBN: *1-59462-228-0* **$25.95**
"The Rev. Jean Pierre De Caussade was one of the most remarkable spiritual writers of the Society of Jesus in France in the 18th Century. His death took place at Toulouse in 1751. His works have gone through many editions and have been republished... Inspirational/Religion Pages 400

Mental Chemistry *by Charles Haanel* ISBN: *1-59462-192-6* **$23.95**
Mental Chemistry allows the change of material conditions by combining and appropriately utilizing the power of the mind. Much like applied chemistry creates something new and unique out of careful combinations of chemicals the mastery of mental chemistry... New Age Pages 354

The Letters of Robert Browning and Elizabeth Barret Barrett 1845-1846 vol II ISBN: *1-59462-193-4* **$35.95**
by Robert Browning and Elizabeth Barrett Biographies Pages 596

Gleanings In Genesis (volume I) *by Arthur W. Pink* ISBN: *1-59462-130-6* **$27.45**
Appropriately has Genesis been termed "the seed plot of the Bible" for in it we have, in germ form, almost all of the great doctrines which are afterwards fully developed in the books of Scripture which follow.. Religion/Inspirational Pages 420

The Master Key *by L. W. de Laurence* ISBN: *1-59462-001-6* **$30.95**
In no branch of human knowledge has there been a more lively increase of the spirit of research during the past few years than in the study of Psychology, Concentration and Mental Discipline. The requests for authentic lessons in Thought Control, Mental Discipline and... New Age/Business Pages 422

The Lesser Key Of Solomon Goetia *by L. W. de Laurence* ISBN: *1-59462-092-X* **$9.95**
This translation of the first book of the "Lernegton" which is now for the first time made accessible to students of Talismanic Magic was done, after careful collation and edition, from numerous Ancient Manuscripts in Hebrew, Latin, and French.. New Age/Occult Pages 92

Rubaiyat Of Omar Khayyam *by Edward Fitzgerald* ISBN: *1-59462-332-5* **$13.95**
Edward Fitzgerald, whom the world has already learned, in spite of his own efforts to remain within the shadow of anonymity, to look upon as one of the rarest poets of the century, was born at Bredfield, in Suffolk, on the 31st of March, 1809. He was the third son of John Purcell... Music Pages 172

Ancient Law *by Henry Maine* ISBN: *1-59462-128-4* **$29.95**
The chief object of the following pages is to indicate some of the earliest ideas of mankind, as they are reflected in Ancient Law, and to point out the relation of those ideas to modern thought. Religion/History Pages 452

Far-Away Stories *by William J. Locke* ISBN: *1-59462-129-2* **$19.45**
"Good wine needs no bush, but a collection of mixed vintages does. And this book is just such a collection. Some of the stories I do not want to remain buried for ever in the museum files of dead magazine-numbers an author's not unpardonable vanity..." Fiction Pages 272

Life of David Crockett *by David Crockett* ISBN: *1-59462-250-7* **$27.45**
"Colonel David Crockett was one of the most remarkable men of the times in which he lived. Born in humble life, but gifted with a strong will, an indomitable courage, and unremitting perseverance... Biographies/New Age Pages 424

Lip-Reading *by Edward Nitchie* ISBN: *1-59462-206-X* **$25.95**
Edward B. Nitchie, founder of the New York School for the Hard of Hearing, now the Nitchie School of Lip-Reading, Inc, wrote "LIP-READING Principles and Practice". The development and perfecting of this meritorious work on lip-reading was an undertaking... How-to Pages 400

A Handbook of Suggestive Therapeutics, Applied Hypnotism, Psychic Science ISBN: *1-59462-214-0* **$24.95**
by Henry Munro Health/New Age/Health/Self-help Pages 376

A Doll's House: and Two Other Plays *by Henrik Ibsen* ISBN: *1-59462-112-8* **$19.95**
Henrik Ibsen created this classic when in revolutionary 1848 Rome. Introducing some striking concepts in playwriting for the realist genre, this play has been studied the world over. Fiction/Classics/Plays 308

The Light of Asia *by sir Edwin Arnold* ISBN: *1-59462-204-3* **$13.95**
In this poetic masterpiece, Edwin Arnold describes the life and teachings of Buddha. The man who was to become known as Buddha to the world was born as Prince Gautama of India but he rejected the worldly riches and abandoned the reigns of power when... Religion/History/Biographies Pages 170

The Complete Works of Guy de Maupassant *by Guy de Maupassant* ISBN: *1-59462-157-8* **$16.95**
"For days and days, nights and nights, I had dreamed of that first kiss which was to consecrate our engagement, and I knew not on what spot I should put my lips..." Fiction/Classics Pages 240

The Art of Cross-Examination *by Francis L. Wellman* ISBN: *1-59462-309-0* **$26.95**
Written by a renowned trial lawyer, Wellman imparts his experience and uses case studies to explain how to use psychology to extract desired information through questioning. How-to/Science/Reference Pages 408

Answered or Unanswered? *by Louisa Vaughan* ISBN: *1-59462-248-5* **$10.95**
Miracles of Faith in China Religion Pages 112

The Edinburgh Lectures on Mental Science (1909) *by Thomas* ISBN: *1-59462-008-3* **$11.95**
This book contains the substance of a course of lectures recently given by the writer in the Queen Street Hall, Edinburgh. Its purpose is to indicate the Natural Principles governing the relation between Mental Action and Material Conditions.. New Age/Psychology Pages 148

Ayesha *by H. Rider Haggard* ISBN: *1-59462-301-5* **$24.95**
Verily and indeed it is the unexpected that happens! Probably if there was one person upon the earth from whom the Editor of this, and of a certain previous history, did not expect to hear again... Classics Pages 380

Ayala's Angel *by Anthony Trollope* ISBN: *1-59462-352-X* **$29.95**
The two girls were both pretty; but Lucy who was twenty-one who supposed to be simple and comparatively unattractive, whereas Ayala was credited, as her Bombwhat romantic name might show, with poetic charm and a taste for romance. Ayala when her father died was nineteen... Fiction Pages 484

The American Commonwealth *by James Bryce* ISBN: *1-59462-286-8* **$34.45**
An interpretation of American democratic political theory. It examines political mechanics and society from the perspective of Scotsman James Bryce Politics Pages 572

Stories of the Pilgrims *by Margaret P. Pumphrey* ISBN: *1-59462-116-0* **$17.95**
This book explores pilgrims religious oppression in England as well as their escape to Holland and eventual crossing to America on the Mayflower, and their early days in New England... History Pages 268

www.bookjungle.com *email: sales@bookjungle.com fax: 630-214-0564 mail: Book Jungle PO Box 2226 Champaign, IL 61825*

QTY

The Fasting Cure *by Sinclair Upton*　　　　　　　　　　ISBN: *1-59462-222-1*　**$13.95**
In the Cosmopolitan Magazine for May, 1910, and in the Contemporary Review (London) for April, 1910, I published an article dealing with my experiences in fasting. I have written a great many magazine articles, but never one which attracted so much attention... New Age/Self Help/Health Pages 164

Hebrew Astrology *by Sepharial*　　　　　　　　　　ISBN: *1-59462-308-2*　**$13.45**
In these days of advanced thinking it is a matter of common observation that we have left many of the old landmarks behind and that we are now pressing forward to greater heights and to a wider horizon than that which represented the mind-content of our progenitors... Astrology Pages 144

Thought Vibration or The Law of Attraction in the Thought World　　ISBN: *1-59462-127-6*　**$12.95**
by William Walker Atkinson　　　　　　　　　　　　Psychology/Religion Pages 144

Optimism *by Helen Keller*　　　　　　　　　　ISBN: *1-59462-108-X*　**$15.95**
Helen Keller was blind, deaf, and mute since 19 months old, yet famously learned how to overcome these handicaps, communicate with the world, and spread her lectures promoting optimism. An inspiring read for everyone... Biographies/Inspirational Pages 84

Sara Crewe *by Frances Burnett*　　　　　　　　　　ISBN: *1-59462-360-0*　**$9.45**
In the first place, Miss Minchin lived in London. Her home was a large, dull, tall one, in a large, dull square, where all the houses were alike, and all the sparrows were alike, and where all the door-knockers made the same heavy sound... Childrens/Classic Pages 88

The Autobiography of Benjamin Franklin *by Benjamin Franklin*　　ISBN: *1-59462-135-7*　**$24.95**
The Autobiography of Benjamin Franklin has probably been more extensively read than any other American historical work, and no other book of its kind has had such ups and downs of fortune. Franklin lived for many years in England, where he was agent... Biographies/History Pages 332

Name	
Email	
Telephone	
Address	
City, State ZIP	

☐ **Credit Card**　　　　☐ **Check / Money Order**

Credit Card Number	
Expiration Date	
Signature	

Please Mail to:　Book Jungle
PO Box 2226
Champaign, IL 61825
or Fax to:　　　630-214-0564

ORDERING INFORMATION

web: *www.bookjungle.com*
email: *sales@bookjungle.com*
fax: *630-214-0564*
mail: *Book Jungle PO Box 2226 Champaign, IL 61825*
or PayPal *to sales@bookjungle.com*

Please contact us for bulk discounts

DIRECT-ORDER TERMS

**20% Discount if You Order
Two or More Books**
Free Domestic Shipping!
Accepted: Master Card, Visa,
Discover, American Express

www.ingramcontent.com/pod-product-compliance
Lightning Source LLC
Chambersburg PA
CBHW081150270326

41930CB00014B/3098